Second

Homes

American Design

Second

Homes

TEXT BY CHIPPY IRVINE
PHOTOGRAPHS BY BILLY CUNNINGHAM
FOREWORD BY MARK HAMPTON
INTRODUCTION BY VIRGINIA AND LEE MCALESTER
DESIGN BY B. W. HONEYCUTT
PRODUCED BY THE MILLER PRESS, INC.

BANTAM BOOKS • NEW YORK • TORONTO • LONDON • SYDNEY • AUCKLAND

SECOND HOMES

————

A Bantam Book
October 1990

Library of Congress Cataloging-in-Publication Data

Irvine, Chippy.
Second homes / text by Chippy Irvine; photographs by Billy
Cunningham; foreword by Mark Hampton; introduction by Virginia and
Lee McAlester; produced by The Miller Press, Inc.
    p.   cm.—(American design)
Includes bibliographical references.
    ISBN 0-553-05798-7
1. Second homes—United States.   2. Architecture, Domestic—United
States.   I. Cunningham, Billy.   II. Title.   III. Series.
    NA7575.I7   1990
728′.37′0973—dc20   90-30830
                                                                            CIP

ISBN 0-553-05798-7

Published simultaneously in the United States and Canada

Printed in Italy by New InterLitho S.p.A.-Milan
0 9 8 7 6 5 4 3 2 1

For my sister, Elisabeth Ann Bowden

—Chippy Irvine

For Hugh Cunningham,
who suggested I become a photographer,
and
Tad Yamashiro,
who gave me a job when everybody else said no,
and
John Loring and Paige Rense,
who have continued to say yes,
I am truly grateful.

—Billy Cunningham

A change, the cliché goes, is as good as a rest. More than ever, Americans are contriving to escape from their cooped-up city dwellings to alternate homes, houses that offer contrasts to workaday lives. Formerly called summer places, some of these getaways are now year-round retreats, complete with phone and fax. This book sets out to show a variety of such second homes in many different American locations.

A big thank-you is due to all of the families who generously allowed us to photograph their second homes, including: Mr. and Mrs. Kenneth Bates; Mr. and Mrs. Stephane Groueff; Mr. and Mrs. Robert Cooke Howison, Jr.; Hilary and John Heminway; David Jackson; Mr. and Mrs. Richard Kughn; Joseph Pell Lombardi; Dr. and Mrs. Gene McCallum; Mr. and Mrs. Robert McMillan; James Merrill; Joshua Odell; Mrs. Anne French Thorington; Mr. and Mrs. Cornelius Vanderbilt Whitney; and those who wish to remain unnamed.

It would have been impossible to have found the houses without help from people who generously steered me in the right directions or volunteered valuable information, including: Tina Barney, Elaine Benson, Gracelyn Blackmer, Sam and Charlene Blount, Bunny Browning, Nora Burba, William F., Mary and Ben Burr; David Cassidy, Robin Crofts,

Leamond Dean, Louise Hall Dietz, Frank Driscoff, David Gibbons, Lou and Howard Erskine, Gregory Evans, Georgina Fairholme, Ann Ferebee, Tom Fleming, Susan Friedman, Carla Glasser, Lester and Ruth Glen, Peter Glen, Betsy Gold, Martin Greene, Jack Hagstrom, David Hamilton, Jim Hathaway, Liz Hilton, Myric Howard, Richard Keith Langham, Caroline Lassoe, Harry and Dorothy Lawenda, Ginger Lawrence, Liz Lear, Rosemary Lincoln, Max Kent, Gabriele Knecht, Mark Magowan, Jean and Jerry Marchildon, Governor William Milliken, Raenell Haring Murray, Anthony Muto, Martha Lee Owen, Priscilla Rea, Isobel Reeves, Rose Ross, Allan M. Schneider, Judith Seip, John Shane, Betty Sherrill, O'Nile Stalnaker, Madeleine Stoner, Mrs. Etta Whitesell, and Jean Winslow.

For help in research I'd like to thank Marilyn Schlansky and Virginia Sweeney of Reed Memorial Library in Carmel, New York; Donna McMorrow and Patricia Di Beradino of Patterson Library, New York: the staff of the New York Public Library; Jerold Pepper of the Adirondacks Museum; and Thomas L. Hambright of the Monroe County Public Library in Key West. For helping me to join the world of word processing I'd like to thank Dr. John Shershow and William J. Sawyer. For generous hospitality, grateful thanks to Arnold Dobrin and Linda Humphrey.

None of this book would have been possible without the skill and encouragement of Angela Miller of Miller Press and IMG. All of her staff, especially Sharon Squibb and Suzanne Dooley, have been wonderful. I'm grateful to Bantam, and especially to Coleen O'Shea, my editor. To those who formed the book, my appreciation goes to designer B. W. Honeycutt. To my comrade throughout all our adventures, photographer Billy Cunningham, gratitude and affection. I'm also grateful to Mark Hampton for his foreword. Last but never least, thanks to my family: to my husband Keith, and daughters Emma and Jassy, for allowing me the time to travel and write.

CHIPPY IRVINE

Acknowledgments

I would like to thank the following people who have contributed to my life and my profession: Patricia and John Ahern, Yone Akiyama, Tony Apilado, Joann Barwick, Sara Beaudry, Marck Black, Dan Bloom, Marty Boghosian, Douglas Boltson, Betty Boote, Bob Bray, Kitty and Michael Bush, Mario Butta, François Cailliarec, Tricia Callas, Dara Caponigro, Dawn Cieplensky, Barbara Collecillo, Sybil Connolly, David Cooperberg, Jose Corrales, Anne Cunningham, Bill Cunningham, James Cunningham, James and Nora Cunningham, Mary Cunningham, Patrick and Lena Cunningham, Barry Cuttler, Joseph Daley, Frank DeGregorie, Michael DeSantis, Susan Devon, Angelo Donghia, Gary Dougan, Robert Edmunds, Stewart Emmery, Carolyn Englefield, Werner Erhart, Don Erickson, John Evans, Nelsea Farrar, Moshe Feldenkrais, Feliciano, Ricky Fingerhut, Bernice Fisher, Tom Fleming, Peter and Lilly Flood, John Funt, James Gandina, Elizabeth Gaynor, Patrick and Noel Gilmartin, Lewis and Michael Greenley, Diane Marie Hamilton, Peter and Gail Hamory, Mark Hampton, John Handy, Zack Hanle, Thomas Hanna, Steve Harper, Jerry Hillman, Elizabeth Hough, Larry Hough, James G. Huntington, Keith Irvine, Eli Jaxon-Bear, Lawrence A. Karol, Margaret Kennedy, Hugh Keptes, Alan Klein, Ellen Klein, Sara Klein, Margery Kreitman, Jim Kustas, Dub Leigh, Stephen Levine, Robert K. Lewis, John Loengard, Warren Lyons, Rue Mahoney, George Mamo, Sheila Marbain, Alita Martin, Pat McInnery, Elizabeth McMillian, Meryl Meisler, Duane Michals, Karen Miller, Juan Montoya, Derry Moore, Peggy Mullholand, John Musco, Audrey Nakamura, Bruce Nozick, Suzanne O'Neill, Tom O'Toole, John Ostrow, Anna Pannero, Allison Percival, Beverly J. Perkins, Mary Peters, Stephanie Peters, Kathleen Pirkl, George Quevedo, Catherine A. Richardson, Katie Ridder, Gail Moss Rosenberg, Charles Ross, Bernard Rotondo, Cyprian Rowe, Ilana Rubenfeld, Alan Rudolf, Barbara Runnette, Charles Ryskamp, Regina Sappah, Mike Schaible, Evan Senreich, Scot Simon, Ira Sitomer, Stephen Sondheim, Jay Spectre, Barbara Spiegel, Tom Starace, Sheila Sullivan, Tom Sullivan, Nancy Tribush, Peter Vitale, Ross Wisdom, Michael Wollaeger, Danita Wright, Via Wynroth, Pat Yamashiro, Cal Yeomans, Susan Zises.

A special thanks to: Martin Friedman and Michael J. Peters for their assistance on this book and many, many other projects. Chippy Irvine for putting up with me and Angela Miller for asking me to work on this project.

BILLY CUNNINGHAM

Contents

Second homes, weekend places, summer cottages—call them what you will, these are dwelling places that allow their owners to indulge in an outlook that they frequently deny themselves in their more serious residences. There is usually a relaxed informality symbolic of the carefree life one is supposed to lead in these easy, cheerful houses. Oftentimes, there is a deeply nostalgic tone as well, and this is perhaps the most delightful aspect of second homes. Since many of them date from the turn of the century and before, their architectural qualities possess the old-fashioned charm of the past. Frequently, along with this enchanting glance backward, there are also childhood reminders from long ago. How often, turning the pages of this romantic book, the reader will come on a house in the woods, a cabin on the beach, or an old farmhouse under ancient maple trees and feel the appeal of time standing still.

A slower pace, the need for which explains the existence of all these houses in the first place, usually bestows a reflective atmosphere, and everywhere in these second homes, one sees a fond lingering over charming details—the arrangement of a still life or a collection of found objects gathered from the beach or the roadside. There is a distinct leaning toward easy, homey elements that lack the serious qualities of rarity and great value that make grander dwellings so daunting. These houses are from a world of gentle charm.

There is also—and this is perhaps the most precious quality that all these second homes share—a deep love of nature that flows in and out of the windows and doors, across the porches and verandas, and into the gardens, the woods, and the beaches that lie outside. The stress of twentieth century urban life makes the thought of a peaceful weekend deep in some natural setting one of the most appealing ideas imaginable. There might even be space for a few hours of solitude. Whatever seems to be lacking in life, these beckoning houses promise the peace and quiet and the visual charm with which we can put the frantic, everyday world out of our minds. These are houses for real activities—cooking, gardening, painting, reading—or just daydreams of activities. In either case, once you've made the escape, you are in control. The possible delights in store are limitless.

MARK HAMPTON

Second

Homes

The urge to have more than one home is older than man himself. Long before *Homo sapiens* appeared on the scene the forces of annual climatic change led many animals to develop patterns of migration between cooler and warmer regions over the course of each year. Birds, mammals, insects, and fish include many species whose multiple "homes" allow them to seek seasonal food supplies or to return to particularly favorable sites during the breeding season. Perhaps our most familiar reminder of these animal migrants are the great V's of honking geese seen high in fall and spring skies—moving south for the winter and then returning north the next summer.

Early man also developed many versions of such migratory or nomadic behavior. Today, we tend to use the word "nomad" to describe those who wander irregularly from place to place, but most nomadic peoples had fixed patterns of movement that closely followed seasonal food supplies. This usually involved several relatively permanent home or campsites where families or entire tribes returned each year.

With the rise of civilized societies and the growth of urban centers, city dwellers began to seek part-time escape to the leisurely countryside, while country squires enjoyed temporary sojourns in the bustling cities. Thus, periodic pilgrimages to second, or even third and fourth, homes became the preferred lifestyle of leisured wealth almost everywhere. Many of the grand French chateaux of the Loire River Valley were built as noblemen's country homes. English aristocrats have long maintained both large country estates and London town houses, while numerous Italian country villas were built for the wealthy merchants of Venice or Florence. In the United States this ideal persisted and gained popularity as the new country grew more prosperous. Once the industrial age created a large middle class, the ranks of those able to afford second homes increased and is still growing today.

Second home living also has practical justifications beyond the mere desire for a stimulating change of setting. Among the most important of these is health. Southern planters in the coastal United States, for example, found that their lowland farms were subject to periodic and devastating summer epidemics of yellow fever and malaria. Those that could afford it thus sought out higher, cooler locations for summer homes in order to avoid these dread diseases. Other health-related movements involved long visits to "spa" towns where mineral-laden springs or muds were reputed to have healing powers for various diseases, particularly arthritis and digestive disorders. Ancient Romans and nineteenth-century Europeans and Americans were particularly fond of spending regular seasons at such locations.

Still another important reason to build a second home has been to provide for periodic social interaction with friends or family. By the late eighteenth century many wealthy southern planters also built houses in nearby cities such as Annapolis, Charleston, or Savannah. Here they could escape the isolation of plantation life and enjoy a busy season of parties and entertainment. A related pattern is sometimes seen in rural communities such as Fredericksburg, Texas. Here nineteenth-century German farmers built tiny "Sunday houses" used each weekend for a social Saturday night and a day of church before returning to the isolation of distant farms. The many turn-of-the-century summer "Chautauqua" communities had a related origin. These featured a series of lectures, concerts, classes, and other cultural events and thus became favored destinations for families wanting to combine self-improvement with socialization.

A similar second home phenomenon provides for the periodic reunion of scattered families. Interrelated groups of nomadic tribesmen commonly lived together at a single base camp for several months of the year, usually during the season with the most plentiful food supply, and then scattered more widely to find food throughout the rest of the year, maintaining only minimal contact. This same pattern survives today both in family "compounds" and in small towns where members of the same family maintain separate summer homes. As with early man, this is a convenient way for large and extended families, whose members may have far-flung permanent dwellings, to spend some time together each year. It is interesting to note that six of the delightful homes featured in this book were originally part of such a group of second homes built for members of the same family.

Perhaps the single most important motivation for second home living has always been simple physical comfort—the escape from bitter winter cold or oppressive summer heat. It is hard for us to recall in these days of universal air-conditioning that escape from summer heat was traditionally the more difficult problem. Winter warmth—from hearths, fireplaces, stoves, or furnaces—is almost as old as man himself, as is warm winter clothing and bedding. On the other hand, oppressively long and hot summers, such as those that plague much of the United States outside of New England and the Pacific Coast, were largely inescapable before the spread of air-conditioning in the 1950s. Thus arose the long tradition of the "summer home," typically either in hills or mountains and thus cooled by altitude, or located near the cooling breezes of the ocean or a large lake. Note that most of the second homes included here were built in such settings principally for summer use. Islands, completely surrounded by cooling waters, were particularly favored locations for summer homes. Almost half of the houses in this book have island settings: "Painted Galleon" on Maine's North Haven Island; "High-Style Cottage" on New York's Long Island; "Fishing Shack" on North Carolina's Nag's Head Island; "Seventies Style" on Florida's Santa Rosa Island; "Conch House" on Florida's Key West; "Summer-Style Queen Anne" on Michigan's Mackinac Island; and "Converted Coast Guard" on Washington's Lopez Island.

The desire to maximize cooling summer breezes is also shown by the many wonderful porches featured throughout the book. Most are furnished for use as full-scale outdoor living rooms. This once almost universal tradition of summer porch living has steadily died in cities because of air-conditioning but remains alive and well in summer homes.

The fifteen charming dwellings featured on the following pages give a fascinating glimpse into the second home lifestyles of a diverse group of modern American families. A de-emphasis on showy decor and a concern with informal interiors and outdoor activities is a unifying theme. No fewer than three of the fifteen houses were purchased fully furnished from their previous owners, an unusual approach to possessions that suggests a healthy desire not to let mere "things" get in the way of serious relaxation. The same informality is evidenced by the fact that in their exterior design, about a third of the featured homes are simple folk houses that eschew citified architectural "style." Here is a book that is almost as relaxing to read and enjoy as spending a long and restful weekend in one of its delightful homes.

VIRGINIA AND LEE McALESTER

When the colonists first arrived in New England, all their efforts went into sheer survival. Only after the Civil War did the idea of a second home—usually called a "summer place"—become a possibility for affluent New Englanders. By then, towns in the northeastern regions of America were becoming industrial centers. The harsh grit of commerce and manufacturing, the influx of the poor from the South or from abroad seeking better-paying jobs packed tenements and boarding houses, making towns strident and disagreeable. The affluent got away during the hot summers.

American children have always been allowed long summer vacations from school. The pattern was set when America was primarily an agricultural country, and all hands, including children, were needed to work the fields during harvest. Though this system is now an anachronism, no one seems to be able to break it. From Memorial Day—or in the more northern areas like Maine, from the Fourth of July—to Labor Day, families who could afford it moved to their summer "cottage." These ran the gamut from simple rustic dwellings to elaborate mansions of the kind found in Newport, Rhode Island, but no matter how grand they were, their owners, with reverse snobbery, dubbed them "cottages."

As Americans became more prosperous in the twentieth century, many began to consider taking time off during winter months. Some went south to find sunshine, while others took up the European sport of skiing, for which the mountains of New Hampshire and Vermont were ideal. Ski lodges became a popular building concept—some Tyrolean in flavor, some in steep-roofed Vermont style, some casual bunkhouses that sleep twenty or more, or some converted from charming old New England houses. As roads improved, automobiles proliferated, and air flights became affordable, families, couples, or singles took quick weekend getaways . . . to the sun or to the snow. Whether for summer, winter, or all-year use, the Second Home was born.

9

FROM THE HARBOR, THE WHARF HOUSE (SOMETIMES CALLED THE SHIP HOUSE OR THE FISH HOUSE BY
LOCALS) LOOKS LIKE A GALLEON HEADING OUT TO SEA, THOUGH ORIGINALLY IT WAS A FISHERY. THE
NAUTICAL ARCHITECTURAL DETAILS WERE ALL ADDED AROUND 1917, INCLUDING THE HANDSOME WOODEN
EAGLE THAT SITS ON THE CREST OF THE ROOF. THE DECK SURROUNDING THE HOUSE LEADS TO A BOAT
DOCK, AND AT ONE TIME, A FIGUREHEAD OF A WOMAN LEANED OUT INTO THE HARBOR.

———

Painted Galleon

A HARBOR HOUSE IN MAINE

North Haven is an island off the coast of Maine, irregularly shaped but roughly eight miles long and three miles wide. To reach it, some twelve miles from the mainland, most people take a ferry. Cars line up on the dock, one queue for the prudent who have reserved a place on the smallish boat, and another for those taking a chance. The ferry makes few crossings each day, and the ferryman doesn't exactly encourage strangers. He's been known to tell them there is nothing much to do or see at North Haven; consequently tourists often go to the larger sister island of Vinalhaven instead, ensuring North Haven's status as one of the best kept secrets of the Maine coast.

The ferry enters a peaceful harbor, passing by banks with well-established houses. The architecture is varied, for many are summer homes. Some of them are quirky, as if the owners, in the privacy of the island, are finally able to indulge in their own eccentricities.

As the ferry pulls in to a simple dock consisting of a gangway, an office, and a minute parking lot, one house close by is arresting. It appears to be a galleon jutting out into the harbor. This is the Wharf House. The building sums up the spirit of the robust summer home, built on the water; a bit of a hassle to reach, and harder to

leave, but, for those who are used to the excesses of city life, probably not luxurious enough to live in year round.

Maine is a rugged state. Its coastline is rocky with more inlets and islands than any other location in North America. According to geologists, the Gulf of Maine, about halfway along the State's coast, was once a lush coastal plain watered by the Penobscot River. Ranges of hills sprang up, caused by early volcanic tumult. As the abundant river valley subsided under layers of glaciers and the sea swelled in, these hills formed islands, which were later named the Fox Islands. One of them is North Haven.

In a book, *The North Island*, compiled by Norwood P. Beveridge for the bicentennial, we learn that ancient cultures lived on these islands as many as 5,300 years ago.

According to Beveridge, "the earliest written reference to the Fox Islands (not yet called by that name) is found in *Cosmographie*, the work of a Frenchman named Thevet, who, returning from a Huguenot colony in Brazil, sailed north along the entire American coast. Near the end of that voyage, in the year 1556, he spent several days at nearby Islesboro as the somewhat nervous guest of Indians there."

Englishman Martin Pring, arriving at the Maine coast in 1603 on his ships *Speedwell* and *Recovery* named the Fox Islands because of the large number of silver-gray foxes he found there.

North Haven is the northern island in a group of two major islands accompanied by a number of smaller ones. The southern island is known as Vinalhaven.

Historians have found it difficult to get accurate information about the early days of North Haven. This is partly because of the confusion of names given to the two islands. Both North Island (North Haven) and the South Island were

WATER, AT HIGH TIDE, REACHES ALMOST TO THE WOOD SUPPORTS ABOVE THE GRANITE PILINGS (LEFT). THE GRANITE BLOCKS WERE PROBABLY ORIGINALLY MINED AT ONE OF THE NEARBY ISLANDS, SUCH AS VINALHAVEN OR HURRICANE ISLAND, BUT THESE BLOCKS WERE MOST LIKELY TO HAVE BEEN USED ON ANOTHER STRUCTURE IN NORTH HAVEN BEFORE BEING SET IN PLACE BELOW THE WHARF HOUSE.

VIEWED FROM THE SIDE, THE SIMPLE SHAPE OF THE ORIGINAL, MID-NINETEENTH-CENTURY FISHERY IS OBVIOUS. THE HOUSE WAS CONVERTED INTO A RESIDENCE AT THE END OF THE NINETEENTH CENTURY.

Two large living rooms, one above the other, provide plenty of space for a large family to relax, especially if there are rainy, shut-in days. Furniture here, much of it inherited from the Reynolds, the original residents, has been given new slipcovers time after time. Ben Burr, a direct descendant of the Reynolds family, remembers the novelty of playing on the sofa, which had a swivel back like those in railway carriages. The blinds, on a pulley system, are made from ship's canvas.

14

known as Vinalhaven for their first fifty-seven years. Between the two islands runs the narrow waterway known as the Thoroughfare. Once the domain of sailboats, it is used by ferries, rowboats, and motor-driven boats as well. Charles Lindbergh anchored his Lockheed Sirius in the Thoroughfare in 1933 when he was visiting his mother-in-law's home on North Haven.

Maine has never been a luxurious place to live. Most colonists headed first for the climes blessed by the rich vegetation and more easily worked terrain farther south. Maine was the last of the New England states to be settled. However, the original colonists, of mostly Scottish, Irish, and English stock—though beset by continual setbacks, hostile Indians, the closing of Boston Harbor during the Revolutionary War, encounters with the British during the War of 1812, and everyday dealings with harsh nature, rocky terrain, and bitterly cold winters—hung on.

Maine found an unexpected influx of people at the end of the nineteenth century when those who could afford it tried to escape the growing industrialization of the big cities, and, at least for the summer months, find a rustic haven in the cooler climate farther north. Here, in Maine, they found fairly unspoiled territory where land was still inexpensive, and civilization had not encroached too far.

Though many changes have taken place in this century, and the old-timers remember with fondness a simpler life, North Haven is still such a place. Nowadays there are cars and telephones, yet North Haven still reminds one of the past.

Despite conscientious work by the active North Haven Historical Society, the date when the Wharf House was first built is not clear. The original building supposedly was a fishery built on what was once a part of Oliver and Rachel (Crabtree) Lewis' farm. Some put the date around the middle of the nineteenth century but it might be later, probably around 1870, for this is when Rachel Lewis became the sole owner of the property, and, as she was in need of money, she sold off some lots. Others say that the entire shore area may have been under the control of Captain Lewis McDonald, who was in the coal and fish business.

James M. Lewis, an owner of the remaining part of the Lewis estate, recalls that the house was used to store fishing goods for outfitting vessels, but he can't be sure the place was ever used to process or store fish. However, along the Thoroughfare, many buildings were used for fish processing. Cod was the major fish, so common it was merely referred to as "fish." All other varieties were referred to by their specific names. Preserving fish by salt-drying was known to the islanders as "making fish." The fish were cleaned, split and pickled in brine, drained briefly, then spread to dry on open-latticed tables called "flakes." Though most of the islanders made their own fish this way, commercial enterprises, starting in the early nineteenth century, shipped salt-dried codfish to the West Indies and Europe. These activities could have taken place at the Wharf House. At any rate, the structure was conveniently placed right next to Brown's shipyard, and the close-by ferry dock. A tool shed and another wharf to the right of the house were used to unload the fish.

In the late 1800s John Phillips Reynolds, Jr. (1863–1920) the son and grandson of Boston physicians, was sailing with friends around the Maine coast looking, as was fashionable, for a summer haven. These "rusticators," as they were often termed, tended to cluster in colonies. For the most part they were viewed by the natives with amused tolerance, though the summer and winter groups never mixed socially.

John Reynolds, one of eight siblings, had married Lucretia Revere Munroe in 1884. He bought the Wharf House for his growing family and during the 1890s renovated the building and turned the once-commercial structure into a domestic residence. His family used it during the summer months. In 1917, the house underwent another series of alterations, and it was then that it acquired the distinctive look it has today. Two decks were constructed facing the harbor; and the galleon-styled windows were installed. During the 1917 renovations, a kitchen was added on at the back of the house, a room used for the same purpose today.

John Reynolds died in 1920. He had been a gregarious man, and eventually he and his children owned six houses on the island. Though summer vacations were rustic, certain formalities prevailed. Afternoon tea was served on the upper poop deck or the sitting room; rituals such as sailboat racing and organized games took place; and on Sunday nights, there was hymn singing. The old guard were still very much in evidence in the twenties and thirties.

The house was purchased in 1948 from the Reynolds family by the Davidsons, the parents of the present owner. The Davidsons' primary home was a farm in Maryland. The present family, now based in Pennsylvania, has six children, but the house makes easy accommodations for the many friends that large families invariably attract.

The back of the house, which faces the nearest road, looks unassuming. Though the building sports a handsome front door flanked by carved wooden eagles, the most frequently used entrance is the back door going through the kitchen, for this is a shelter for casual, summer living, not a house of the formal, Southampton variety. A cannon with five, twelve-gauge shotgun shells once stood as a doorstop. There is an air of nonchalant, sporty grandeur about the place, a raffishness that eases along with deliberately worn sneakers and old but good clothes.

THE PANTRY (TOP LEFT) WITH ITS WOODEN SINK SURROUND IS LINED WITH SHELVES OF ASSORTED CHINA ACCUMULATED BY THE FAMILY FOR OVER FORTY YEARS.

A LARGE STOVE IN THE DINING ROOM (TOP RIGHT) IS USED WHEN MAINE, AS OFTEN HAPPENS, TURNS CHILLY. A SHELF OF COLORFUL BAVARIAN FIGURES IS HELD IN PLACE BY A CARVED WOODEN CARYATID.

THE DINING ROOM HAS SPACE FOR TWO GOOD-SIZED TABLES, AND CAN THUS ACCOMMODATE YOUNG AND OLD ALIKE (BOTTOM LEFT). A PAINTING OF THE HARBOR HANGS OVER THE SIDEBOARD. A MIXTURE OF BLUE AND WHITE CHINA, INTERSPERSED WITH CANDLES IN HURRICANE LAMPS, ON A SIMPLE WHITE PINE TABLE THAT WAS THE REYNOLDS' PRIDE AND JOY, IS AS FORMAL AS DINNER AT THE WHARF HOUSE GETS.

AN IDIOSYNCRASY OF SUCH A LARGE HOUSEHOLD IS TO USE CLOTHESPINS, INDIVIDUALLY NAMED, AS NAPKIN RINGS (BOTTOM RIGHT). UNDER THE PLATES ARE ROPE MATS, FOSTERING THE NAUTICAL TONE.

A SHIP-SHAPED WINDOW IN THIS SECOND FLOOR BEDROOM GIVES ARCHITECTURAL INTEREST TO AN OTHERWISE SIMPLE VACATION ROOM. THE INSIDE SHUTTERS ARE PRECISELY SHAPED TO THE CURVE OF THE WINDOWS, AS ARE THE SCREEN WINDOWS, WHICH WHEN NOT IN USE, ARE AFFIXED TO THE WALL. CANDLES ARE A PREREQUISITE IN CASE OF ELECTRICITY FAILURES.

A passage from the kitchen, with its huge oven, reveals pantries (one used to be an ice chest) where shelves are loaded with crockery accumulated over many years. It leads to a large dining room that holds two good-sized tables. Beyond the dining room is the hall, where the front door entrance leads into the downstairs living room. Sustaining the nautical motif of the house, the hall coat closet masquerades as a purser's office, always referred to as "the brig," complete with turned wooden bars on the door. The living room beyond functions as an entertainment center, with record and tape players. A deck outside surrounds three sides of the room, and extends to a long boardwalk that juts out into the

harbor and serves as a dock. A ship's rope is used as a stair rail, and a life preserver decorates the upstairs landing. Another living room with a poop deck outside provides a perfect place to sit and watch the harbor and the changing light, and to sip a drink. For festive occasions, colorful bunting is hung along the deck.

Galleon-styled windows decorate the main bedrooms on this floor. Even the screen windows are cut to the same shape and fixed by holders on the walls, ready to be easily inserted for the summer.

There are more bathrooms and bedrooms on the second floor but these have their own staircase at the back of the

A WRITING DESK, COMPLETE WITH THE NOSTALGIA OF REAL BLOTTING PAPER, FRONTS RUDIMENTARY BOOKSHELVES THAT HOLD STATIONERY AND FAVORITE SUMMER READING MATTER. LOCAL LILACS ADD A WELCOME TO THIS SECOND FLOOR BEDROOM.

house over the "new" kitchen. And, via a ladderlike stairway in the upstairs hall, an attic floor can be reached, filled with more accommodations. This attic is known as the sail loft, for that is where sails were supposedly dried. The house, without any strain, can sleep about twenty-two people in various degrees of comfort.

Throughout the house, the decor is relaxed. Because the Davidsons bought the house furnished, many of the furnishings are leftovers from the Reynolds family. New pieces have been added as needed, but the furnishing is mostly of a simple, unpretentious style. As neighboring housekeeper Frances Smith remarks, "Some of the linen still has the R monogram.

I always make sure that ends up in Richard's (the son of the present owner) bedroom."

Judged by 1980s standards, both the kitchen and bathrooms appear primitive, but the stove and the showers all function, and the family, who go there to relax and rough it, are perfectly satisfied despite the peeling paint. In bedrooms, bathrooms, and reception rooms, decorative objects tend to be glass jars filled with gleanings from the rocky inlets, pieces of glass smoothed by the sea, shells, driftwood, and boat pulleys, rather than the *objets de vertu* to be found in the family's primary home. Pictures are often those that were painted by the children when they were young, framed and

19

THIS IS ONE OF SEVERAL ATTIC BEDROOMS, REACHED BY A STEPLADDER OFF THE SECOND FLOOR (RIGHT). TUCKED UNDER THE EAVES THAT FEATURE CURVED EYEBROW WINDOWS, THE MANY CHILDREN OF BOTH THE REYNOLDS AND DAVIDSON FAMILIES HAVE WILED AWAY THE SUMMERTIME PLAYING GAMES.

AT THE FRONT DOOR, FLANKED BY CARVED WOODEN EAGLES' HEADS, IS A SHIP'S BELL TO SIGNAL THE ARRIVAL OF A VISITOR (FAR RIGHT). FAMILY MEMBERS, AS IN MOST SUMMER HOUSES, TEND TO ENTER AT THE BACK KITCHEN DOOR.

still prized. Sun-bleached magazines left over from previous years may have curled pages. Shelves are filled with faded novels saved from earlier summer seasons. Chairs and sofas have been covered and recovered. Cushions might be slightly faded, and could perhaps use a little more stuffing. Family photographs on the side tables may be dimming despite being carefully turned face down for the winter. An assortment of games, from preplastic dominoes to Trivial Pursuit, are all

well thumbed. Iced tea might be served in unmatched glasses, accumulated over the past forty years, ranging in style from a grandmother's legacy to garage giveaways. Traditions in this house, in contrast to the family's way of life during the rest of the year, have nothing to do with formality, but everything to do with family activities: boating, sport, collecting shells, conversations with visiting friends, and the active life of summertime.

20

THE PARSONAGE WAS BUILT IN 1850 BY J. J. HAPGOOD FOR THE PERU FIRST CONGREGATIONAL CHURCH. ITS GREEK REVIVAL STYLE REACHED THIS REMOTE PART OF VERMONT RATHER LATER THAN IT DID THE REST OF THE COUNTRY.

Village PArSonage

A VERMONT SKI RETREAT

A subtle change in scenery takes place as one crosses the state line into Vermont, whether from Quebec, New Hampshire, Massachusetts, or New York. Roofs become more pointed, road signs smaller, garish billboards nonexistent, and woodpiles more neatly stacked. Around the mountain resorts in winter, every other car, it seems, is crested with ski racks. Vermont is dubbed the Green Mountain State, or *"vert mont,"* and the name reminds us that the state's first European explorers were the French led by Samuel de Champlain in 1609. By mid-eighteenth century, the English had the upper hand, and some of their legacy remains today in Vermonters' attitudes—their concern for privacy and a played-down pride-of-place.

Since the 1950s, skiing has become a major part of Vermont's economy. Set in the middle of several flourishing ski centers—Stratton, Bromley, Magic, and Killington—is an almost storybook Vermont hamlet called Peru. It is the kind of village that a child might design from a box of wood blocks. Centered on a slightly meandering main street, Peru proper consists of a post office, a general store, a church, ten houses, and fifty inhabitants including three selectmen, a town clerk, and a constable. The village is so authentic it was chosen as the retreat to which Diane Keaton escaped from New York City in the movie *Baby Boom*. Peru's inhabitants

23

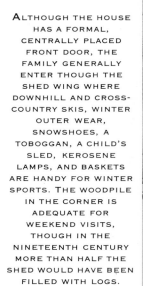

ALTHOUGH THE HOUSE HAS A FORMAL, CENTRALLY PLACED FRONT DOOR, THE FAMILY GENERALLY ENTER THOUGH THE SHED WING WHERE DOWNHILL AND CROSS-COUNTRY SKIS, WINTER OUTER WEAR, SNOWSHOES, A TOBOGGAN, A CHILD'S SLED, KEROSENE LAMPS, AND BASKETS ARE HANDY FOR WINTER SPORTS. THE WOODPILE IN THE CORNER IS ADEQUATE FOR WEEKEND VISITS, THOUGH IN THE NINETEENTH CENTURY MORE THAN HALF THE SHED WOULD HAVE BEEN FILLED WITH LOGS.

THE PARSONAGE (RIGHT) CAN BE SEEN NEXT TO THE PERU FIRST CONGREGATIONAL CHURCH. BEHIND THE HOUSE IS A RESTORED WOOD BARN THAT ONCE WOULD HAVE HOUSED THE PARSON'S LIVESTOCK AND CARRIAGE.

still tell of the general casting call when many of them were given roles; scenes took place in the local general store, J.J. Hapgood, and the house we show here can also be identified in the film.

Peru was originally called Bromley, but in 1804 was re-named after the fabled gold-rich state in South America. According to Evelyn H. Beattie in Peru's *Bicentennial Historical Album*, the reason for the change was the townspeople's attempt to attract to the hitherto rugged, mostly sheep-farming area a similar lucky strike of gold. The village slowly grew and work was hard; local industry at times included agriculture, logging, sawmills, and charcoal and brickmaking. Today these activities have disappeared; only one dairy farm still operates. The village, bypassed by the highway, has remained unspoiled, and even more miraculously, it maintains its simplicity and integrity despite its appeal to tourists.

For Joseph Pell Lombardi the Old Parsonage in Peru is a second home, situated right next to the town's First Con-

gregational Church. According to the bicentennial album, it was the second parsonage to be constructed in the village, built in 1850 by J. J. Hapgood, a member of an early Peru family. The family name is perpetuated not only in the general store but also by Hapgood Pond, donated by the family to the national park preserves in the area. For building the second parsonage, Mr. Hapgood—who also built the church —received the Old Parsonage and $400.

The second parsonage became the home for a succession of twenty parsons and their families. In 1950, Peru ceased to have a resident cleric and the parsonage was rented out annually. While skiing in Vermont with friends, restoration ar-

chitect Joseph Pell Lombardi heard about the house, and in the 1970s, he bought the parsonage from the church, together with its original parcel of land. He has spent many years restoring the exterior and interior of the house, paying respect to its parsonage flavor by returning it as closely as possible to its origins as an unpretentious, comfortable house. Lombardi's restoration practice takes him throughout the world, but the purity and simplicity of the old parsonage in Peru is always a welcome retreat.

Surrounded by sugar maples, the property includes a barn—which would have housed the parson's horse and conveyance, and probably a cow or a pig at times. A wing at-

tached to the side of the house was used to keep firewood and as a cold-storage area for preserves. Now it also houses equipment for winter sports. The roof of the wing forms a low attic over the kitchen.

In the parson's day, visitors would have used the formal front door. This door is centered on the main house's symmetrical facade and leads into a central hall with a parlor on one side and a dining room on the other. Nowadays, the most-used entrance is through the woodshed into the kitchen, where family and friends tend to gather and casual meals are served on a long table surrounded with painted Vermont chairs. In the kitchen and throughout the house there are no masonry fireplaces, for in the 1850s when the house was built, cast-iron stoves were more up-to-date; however, though the house can still be heated entirely by wood-burning stoves, an alternate central heating system has been installed. A large 1870s nickel-trimmed Oakland E wood-burning stove, restored by the Barnstable Stove Shop of Barnstable, Massachusetts, sits against one wall of the kitchen. It can be used both to warm the room and for family cooking. An iron kettle simmers on the stove and works as a humidifier. Heavy cast-iron pans—Griswald are considered the best—have to be used on the iron stove, as other metals would melt. Hanging on the wall with these pans is one that's

27

A NINETEENTH-CENTURY CAST-IRON STOVE CAN WARM THE ENTIRE PARLOR (LEFT), AND HEAT IS CARRIED UP BY DUCTS TO THE BEDROOM ABOVE. THE ROCKING CHAIR IN THE FOREGROUND IS BELIEVED TO HAVE BEEN CUT DOWN FROM A REGULAR CHAIR. IT STILL BEARS REMNANTS OF ITS ORIGINAL PAINTED EMBELLISHMENTS.

SIMPLE PERIOD REPRODUCTION, CAMELBACK COUNTRY SOFAS (ABOVE LEFT) ARE FROM ANGEL HOUSE. THE PATCHWORK CUSHIONS WERE MADE LOCALLY, AS WERE THE ANTIQUE HOOKED RUGS THAT DOT THE FLOOR.

A WINTER LANDSCAPE CAN BE SEEN OUTSIDE THE PARLOR WINDOW (ABOVE RIGHT). THE BRAID-EDGED MUSLIN CURTAINS ARE READY-MADE FROM COUNTRY CURTAINS.

used for making corn bread and has indentations in the form of ears of corn. On the top of the stove is a perfectly functioning 1900 toaster, which operates using the stove's heat. A sink is on one side of the room and the stove on the other, with a worktable between. Wall cupboards of authentic proportion have been reinstalled and painted the toffee-brown color that was discovered when the room was scraped down to its original paint. Similar paint analyses took place in all the rooms. The counters are covered, also authentically, with Vermont marble. If only one or two people are staying, an alternative electric stove can be used. Though all the lighting fixtures have been electrified, a simple exchange of each burner can revert it back to kerosene use.

Beyond the kitchen is the dining room used for formal meals. Painstakingly peeled from the walls in this and other rooms were as many as ten layers of wallpaper, testament to the decorating fervor of various parsons' wives. Each fragment has been preserved. The bottom layer found in the dining room showed sprigs of green sage leaves on a warm, light-brown ground. Scalamandré, a firm that makes elegant decorative papers and fabrics, was commissioned to reproduce it, and the resulting wallpaper is now part of the firm's current documentary collection. A green-painted Hitchcock chair found in the house was used as a prototype for the dining room chairs. A matching set was reproduced by the Hitchcock Company in Connecticut. The sideboard, formed

from a variety of woods, is of a particular style made in Vermont between 1830 and 1850 called locally "high-country Sheraton." A corner cupboard installed by Joseph Lombardi disguises necessary pipes, but is in keeping with the spirit of the period. Cockerel-patterned plates, milk-glass chicken dishes, and local pottery showing the Peru First Congregational Church are displayed in it. Maple and mahogany ogee-framed mirrors, necessary in the 1850s to bring light into the rooms, reflect across the room. On one wall are David Robert's prints of mid-Victorian discoveries in Egypt that caused a sensation at the time—the half-buried temple at Edfu and the dramatic, colossi-flanked temple at Abu Simbel in its pre-Aswan Dam location. Other pictures include nineteenth-century Vermont landscapes in period frames. Perhaps the most unusual object in the room is an airtight, cast-iron wood-burning stove of the period in the form of a Gothic church with a steeple. Found by Lombardi, and forged either in Vermont or Albany, it is perfectly suited to a parsonage.

To one side of the dining room is a small sitting room. The front-hall stairs, lit by a diagonally fluted, red mid-nineteenth-century overhead lamp, are authentically painted with light-colored rises and dark treads. The hall wallpaper, in a style quite similar to the original paper, was found at Bradbury & Bradbury.

THE DINING ROOM TABLE (LEFT) IS LAID FOR DINNER WITH BLUE-SPECKLED POTTERY MADE IN BENNINGTON, VERMONT. ON THE PLATES ARE LOCAL BREADS AND A HOMEMADE FRUITCAKE. THE TABLE IS SURROUNDED BY PAINTED HITCHCOCK CHAIRS MADE LIKE ONE THAT WAS FOUND IN THE HOUSE. SIMPLE CURTAINS ARE READY-MADE FROM COUNTRY CURTAINS. THE CORNER CUPBOARD WAS INSTALLED BY THE OWNER AND CONTAINS LOCAL POTTERY. MAHOGANY AND MAPLE OGEE-FRAMED MIRRORS AND NINETEENTH-CENTURY VERMONT LANDSCAPES IN PERIOD FRAMES DECORATE THE WALLS.

THE DINING ROOM SIDEBOARD (ABOVE) IS IN A STYLE KNOWN AS HIGH-COUNTRY SHERATON, AND IS MADE OF BIRD'S-EYE MAPLE, MAPLE, AND MAHOGANY VENEER. MIRRORS, SUCH AS THIS ONE FRAMED IN MAPLE AND MAHOGANY, WERE NEEDED IN THE 1850S TO BRING AS MUCH LIGHT AS POSSIBLE INTO ROOMS.

In the nineteenth century, the parlor would have displayed the most elaborate furnishings of the house. Of course, most parsons in this rural part of Vermont would have owned much simpler furniture than city folks, but prime wood with its natural grain showing is used here rather than the faux-painted pine used at the time for the less-important rooms. The parlor walls are light-painted plaster with a Greek key-paper ceiling border from Bradbury & Bradbury. An 1850 cast-iron stove embellished with two polished brass balls was installed where the original Franklin stove once stood. Vermont landscapes in mahogany frames hang from the picture rail on plain-gold silk cords. A corner cupboard provides shelves for a variety of leather-bound books and hymnals associated with a parsonage. Vermont-made hooked rugs adorn the painted-wood floor. Joseph Lombardi bought two reproduction sofas from Angel House, a company that specializes in period-style sofas. By the windows is a set of dashingly painted chairs, a cut above the ordinary kitchen variety, taken from a Vermont house. Two painted-wood rocking chairs, one large and one small—the latter probably converted from a regular chair to a rocker—complete the seating arrangement.

A CAST-IRON AIRTIGHT HEATING STOVE, CIRCA 1850, WAS FOUND LOCALLY (LEFT). ITS SHAPE, THAT OF A CHURCH AND STEEPLE, IS ESPECIALLY SUITABLE FOR A PARSONAGE.

A GOOD WAY TO START THE DAY IN MID-WINTER IS WITH A HEARTY BREAKFAST. THE RESTORED 1870S OAKLAND E WOOD-BURNING STOVE (RIGHT) IS EFFICIENT AND WARMS THE WHOLE ROOM, AS WELL AS PROVIDING HOT WATER FOR COFFEE AND HEAT FOR THE FRYING PAN AND TOASTER. BREAD, BACON, SPECKLED BROWN EGGS, JAMS, AND MAPLE SYRUP ARE ALL LOCAL PRODUCTS.

Next to the parlor is the parson's small study, which Joseph Lombardi has converted into his own office. He installed an old-fashioned telephone, partly because it *doesn't* always work efficiently, thus excusing him from business calls on a relaxing weekend! One wall is given over to bookshelves. Another displays maps of the neighborhood. In a corner is an 1850 parson's traveling desk that ingeniously folds flat for carrying. Though it was once a place where sermons were written, it is now more likely to hold architectural blueprints.

Upstairs are three simply furnished bedrooms, each able to accommodate two people. Plain muslin curtains hang at the

windows. Locally made quilts cover the beds, and the furniture is mainly of a painted, or *faux bois* variety. In the master bedroom, a mid-nineteenth-century chest of drawers, painted with wood graining to imitate rosewood, is decorated with brass rosettes on its drawer knobs. An 1812 child's sampler hangs on the wall. Heating ducts, leading from the wood-burning stove below, bring heat into the room. On the floor are reproductions of authentic fancy cast-iron gratings, made by Reggio Ironworks, which bring hot air up from the central heating system. Next to the master bedroom is a bathroom in what was once a servant's room. As there were no

IN THE MASTER BEDROOM (RIGHT), THE CHEST OF DRAWERS WITH ITS ORIGINAL BRASS-TRIMMED KNOBS IS PAINTED TO LOOK LIKE MAHOGANY. IT AND THE ANTIQUE MIRROR ABOVE ARE BOTH VERMONT PIECES. THE BATHROOM BEYOND WOULD HAVE ONCE BEEN A SERVANT'S ROOM. ITS PAINTED WAINSCOTING, PUT IN BY JOSEPH LOMBARDI, ECHOES THE ORIGINAL WAINSCOTING OF THE KITCHEN. HE ALSO INSTALLED THE WOOD OVERHEAD TANK AND TOILET SEAT.

bathrooms in the original house (outhouses would have been used) the decor here is not fastidiously authentic. The room has been given simple, white seersucker curtains, wainscoting similar to that in the kitchen, and an overhead tank, chain pull, and toilet seat made of grained wood. A second upstairs bathroom was fitted into space that once accommodated a back staircase that was used by servants.

Though the Old Parsonage and its setting in Peru reflect the past, such restoration may well embrace Vermont's look into the future. The house can be made totally independent of fossil fuels and electricity, giving the residence great flexibility and mirroring Vermont's independent, environmentally conscious style. The state's people are prepared to undergo inconvenience in order to maintain their stringent clean-environment policies, and time may well prove them right. As other getaway places become unbearably polluted, this Green Mountain State with its crisp air and clear streams may be the most luxurious of all.

A BED OF CHERRY WOOD WITH MAPLE-TRIMMED FINIALS AND ROSETTES IN THE MASTER BEDROOM WOULD ONCE HAVE HAD A REMOVABLE, CURTAINED CANOPY USED FOR WARMTH. THE RUG BY THE BED IS EGYPTIAN; THE ANTIQUE OVAL-MOTIF HOOKED RUG WAS MADE IN VERMONT. THE HALL BEYOND HAS A HOOKED RUG DEPICTING A COVERED BRIDGE. A DOUBLE BEDROOM CAN BE SEEN ON THE OTHER SIDE OF THE HALL.

The Mid-Atlantic States

At the end of the nineteenth century, affluent industrialists often felt a need to throw off their business worries and escape to a rural setting. The wildness of the Adirondacks in Upstate New York attracted these rusticators, who built "camps"—some of which were elaborate enclaves run by dozens of household servants.

Many New Yorkers, living at the heart of America's busiest and most rewarding city, search for a second home as soon as they can afford it. The rich often have more than one. Average New Yorkers, who work unusually hard under trying circumstances in an overcrowded and increasingly tough city, endeavor to get out of town as often as possible. Their second homes tend to be easy-to-run weekend retreats within train or driving distance. For them, the beaches of the Hamptons, or Fire Island are summer lures. Others go north to Upstate New York. Philadelphians tend to choose the Jersey Coast or the bucolic, rolling hills of Bucks County, Pennsylvania.

Along with the pleasures of a second home go responsibilities. To "put down roots," some homeowners delve into local history and find an old house to restore, while others build their dream house from scratch. Creating a second home takes time, money, care, and a great deal of organization—especially if one is raising a family (the sneakers . . . or the sun-dried tomatoes . . . are always in the other house). But the pleasure and the physical and mental lift gained by being able to leave a cramped city apartment and live a vastly different kind of life even for a few days is worth the effort.

MOSS-COVERED, WOODED WALKWAYS LEAD FROM THE MAIN HOUSE TO SIX OTHER HOUSES OWNED BY
MEMBERS OF THE FAMILY, INCLUDING THE ORIGINAL HOUSE THAT WAS BUILT BY DR. MOONEY, FROM
WHOM THE INVENTOR PURCHASED THE PROPERTY AT THE TURN OF THE NINETEENTH CENTURY.

———

Lakeside Rustic

AN ADIRONDACKS CAMP

Branching off from New York's scenic Northway above Saratoga Springs, secondary roads lined with evergreens exude fresh pine scents; purple mountains decorate the horizon with stage-set drama; discrete road signs become colored brown with gold lettering so as not to jar the serenity; houses are painted forest green, to blend with nature. This is the Adirondack Park, which at 5,927,600 acres is the largest state park in the country, far bigger than Yellowstone or Mount McKinley. Nowadays, and especially since the area became host to the Winter Olympics, the great Adirondacks region is a resort both summer and winter. In summer, cars take to the roads with canoes on their roofs; these will be replaced in winter by racks of skis. On a hot July day, a lone, cross-country skier might be sighted, dressed only in shorts, working his way along the roadside on a skateboard, using poles to build his strength for the coming competitive winter sports. Hopeful young girls in busy Lake Placid, wearing shiny tights and skating skirts, spend many hours practicing in the frigid air of the Olympic Arena, then mingle on the sun-warmed streets with halter-topped tourists.

This was not so true in the nineteenth century when the "Great Northern Wilderness" was first discovered as a sportsman's haven by wealthy outsiders lured by the romance—at least for the short span of summer—of the rustic life. These rusticators started by building hunters' retreats—simple lean-tos or tent platforms—that, by the end of the century when wives and families were included, had often developed into elaborate compounds. Though these were still referred to as "camps," some were more like castles. As with Marie Antoinette's rustic retreat *Le Hameau*, eye-catching simplicity was achieved at ruinous expense. In *The Adirondack Park*, Frank Graham, Jr. says:

> ". . . buildings were enclosed by walls made of unpeeled logs. Insects tended to crawl in under the bark, however, and as time went by the builders peeled and varnished the logs. The interiors were decorated with all sorts of rustic and ingenious bric-a-brac—the mounted heads of deer, unique mobiles of mounted ducks hung from rafters by bits of wire, lamps made from obsolete guns, coat racks whose 'hooks' were the bent hooves of deer."

Separate buildings were provided for the teams of servants needed to maintain this elaborately simple way of life. This was the era of the Great Camps of the Adirondacks when William West Durant designed fantasy havens for heavyweight capitalists like Whitney, Vanderbilt, and Morgan.

Long before these captains of industry appropriated the region, forest-living Algonquin Indians hunted in the mountainous and lake-scattered wilderness. They were named Adirondacks by rival Iroquois. The name has been translated as "Those who eat bark," and also "They of the Great Rocks," and opinions vary as to which is most accurate. The first white settlers were trackers and trappers, then came loggers, and after them, miners after iron.

The Adirondacks remained relatively unspoiled until the middle of the nineteenth century. To its south, however, development of Saratoga Springs as a flourishing resort persuaded vacationers to look northward. The land was still inexpensive enough to be bought in large tracts, and inaccessible enough to remain inexpensive for some time.

Adding to the area's popularity was its reputation as a beneficent spa. Tuberculosis was the era's most dreaded dis-

THE FIFTY- BY FIFTY-FOOT LIVING ROOM IS FURNISHED WITH NATURAL WICKER AND COMFORTABLE CHINTZ-UPHOLSTERED SOFAS AND ARMCHAIRS. THE GREEN-STAINED WALLS AND CEILING, WALL-MOUNTED ANIMAL HEADS, TWIG CHANDELIERS AND RUSTIC LOG BANISTERS ARE TYPICAL OF ADIRONDACK HOUSE DECORATION. A CENTRAL TABLE HOLDING TWO LAMPS IS ONE OF THE INVENTOR'S FAUX MAHOGANY METAL PIECES AND CAME FROM A U.S. WORLD WAR I BATTLESHIP.

THOUGH THE CHINTZ SLIPCOVERS HAVE BEEN REPLACED, THE ARMCHAIRS, WICKER TABLE, AND TABLE LAMP ARE ALL PART OF THE ORIGINAL FURNISHINGS IN THIS CORNER OF THE LIVING ROOM (TOP LEFT). THE DOOR LEADS TO AN OUTSIDE PORCH OVERLOOKING THE LAKE.

INSTALLED WHEN THE HOUSE WAS FIRST BUILT, THIS PLAYER PIANO, COMPLETE WITH PIANO ROLLS, IS CROWDED WITH FRAMED FAMILY PHOTOGRAPHS INCLUDING THOSE OF THE ORIGINAL INVENTOR-BUILDER, HIS WIFE, AND THEIR CHILDREN (MIDDLE LEFT).

A LARGE FIELDSTONE FIREPLACE IS FLANKED BY CUSHIONED SEATS (BOTTOM LEFT). IN FRONT OF A RUGGED LEATHER-COVERED SOFA, A TOBOGGAN IS USED AS A COFFEE TABLE. ON THE TABLE IN THE FOREGROUND IS A BOOK OF POETRY PUBLISHED BY THE ORIGINAL BUILDER, TOGETHER WITH MAGAZINES OF THE PERIOD.

FOR FANCY OCCASIONS, OR SIMPLY TO DRESS UP AN ORDINARY HAMBURGER, THE FAMILY OFTEN GETS OUT THE CHINA MADE ESPECIALLY FOR THE CAMP (RIGHT). HOWEVER, THE FLORAL ARRANGEMENTS MIGHT BE HUMBLE SEPTEMBER WEED, AS FEW WILDFLOWERS GROW NEAR THE HEAVILY SHADED CAMP. THROUGHOUT THE HOUSE FAUX MAHOGANY METAL FURNITURE CAN BE FOUND. THE CABINET HOLDING GLASSES IS ONE SUCH PIECE.

ease, and the clear mountain air was deemed corrective. Teddy Roosevelt was a spa visitor. He learned of President McKinley's assassination while on a hunting trip in the Adirondacks, and took the oath of office as president the same day.

Many lakes, large and small, dot the area. Around the turn of the century, on the shore of one lake, lived a doctor whose offices could only be reached by boat. Though by then the era of the Great Camps was just past—most were built in the 1880s—an inventor who was the scion of a merchant in upstate New York heard that Dr. Mooney's house was for sale and, envisioning it as an idyllic summer home for his growing family, bought the doctor's property.

The inventor, having discovered that the life of a merchant was not for him, had opened his own company. A visionary with the dreamy mind of a poet and a music composer—he published several books of his own poetry and established a music publishing company to hold his copyrights—he worked in metal, and made significant contributions to the then flourishing railroad business. He designed the trap door and folding steps that let down allowing passengers to alight from trains. In the family's folklore it is said he designed the Yale lock, but sold the patent, thinking the lock would never sell. The company he owned made all kinds of metal office furniture—filing cabinets, desks, tables, and chairs, and catalogues of these wares still exist.

A house was built on his newly acquired Adirondack property. This was known as "the Cottage," built in 1909, but no sooner had it been finished when it became clear a larger house would be necessary. Within the year, the Syracuse architectural firm of Gaggin & Gaggin drew up plans for another house near the Cottage but closer to the water. Immediately dubbed the "Boat House" as it is built over six boat slips, it has since become known as the "Main House." Eventually the camp grew to be a compound, with seven houses for the various branches of the family. All the houses of the camp are still owned by descendants of the original family, and there is now a fifth generation of children toddling about each summer.

ORIGINALLY AN OPEN PORCH, THIS NOW SCREENED-IN DECK IS USED AS A PLEASANT PLACE TO ENJOY BREAKFAST, LUNCH, OR DRINKS IN THE EVENING. THE SUN, MOON, AND STARS CHINTZ IS A FRENCH EMPIRE DESIGN, FROM BRUNSCHWIG & FILS. THE OLD HICKORY WICKER, NOW MUCH COLLECTED, HAS BEEN USED IN THE HOUSE SINCE ITS INCEPTION.

48

It wasn't until the mid-1920s that the camp could be reached by automobile as the roads as yet were unsuitable. The family would get there in long-snouted boats with mahogany decks chuffing down ten miles of lakes and canals. The camp was managed by a guide, and his wife cooked, often for twenty to thirty guests. Servants were brought from Syracuse, along with all the necessary supplies.

The camp's entrance is flanked by two stone pillars bearing the compound's official name. A sloping drive leads through tall evergreens to a tennis court, and nearby are several outbuildings. One of these is known as the Mail House, and earlier in the century, when people wrote copious letters, it was necessary. Mail was still delivered daily until the early 1960s. Another building houses machinery; a third is what was once an ice house—ice cut from the lake was dragged up a long chute which became legendary as the perfect toboggan slide. A fourth provides shelter for cars. Nameplates for each of the inventor's five children still hang from the garage roof over the car slots. In the inventor's day, a tiny separate building nearby housed Himmy, the Himalayan ape that was his beloved personal pet.

Steps lead down past the Cottage to the Main House, where, it is said, the inventor kept birds of paradise in open roosts hanging from the ceiling. In this house, the most impressive room is the fifty-by fifty-foot living room where there is still space for the now greatly expanded family to gather. The room gives the impression of a step back in time. Almost everything is preserved from 1910 when the house was built and furnished. Time—and because of it, the market for furniture—has given the furnishings a very special flavor. For precious little money, the inventor bought from a catalogue produced by a Fayetteville artisan by the name of Stickley (both Gustav and his brothers, Leopold and John George who were partners) Old Hickory, and various Arts and Crafts furniture—nowadays much sought after by collectors. Unpainted wicker chairs and chaises longues have aged and gathered character even though their chintz cushions and wool throws might have been added recently. Comfortably upholstered sofas and armchairs, though freshly slipcovered,

have long settled in their logical places, dividing the room into smaller, more manageable units.

A special corner of the room is meant for children. A thirty-year-old doll's house mingles happily with vintage toy cars and seasoned toy animals on wheels. Another area is set up for table games. A third holds a solid, executive-sized desk, which the paterfamilias used in his factory and is now perfect for writing long, leisurely letters to those unfortunate enough not to be enjoying the camp. A player piano, laden with family photographs, displays the song hits of World War I and a book of hymns. Even magazines scattered on tables are pre-1920, such as a *National Geographic* dated 1917.

Two stairways whose banisters were originally draped in deerskins, flank the fieldstone fireplace—a great, roaring fire becomes a necessity in this often cool terrain. A chunky, leather-covered sofa of the period, its surface worn to a pleasing decay, faces the open hearth while a six-foot toboggan doubles as a coffee table.

To one side of the fireplace alcove is the kitchen area. Well stocked with a pantry, eating space, and a mud room, this kitchen is used for casual breakfasts or lunches with the children. On the other side of the fireplace is the dining room. The Main House takes turns with the neighboring Cottage in entertaining family members for the main meal of the day. China commissioned for the original owner and decorated with the camp's insignia is used. Some of the founder's inventions can be found in the dining room. The sideboard and glass-fronted cabinets which look like dark mahogany came from his metal workshops. Originally designed for the U.S. Navy, items such as these were ideal for boats and steamers that sought some formality but had to be, first and foremost, practical. This furniture is ideal in the Adirondacks where, left alone during winter, rodents tend to eat wooden pieces. (For the same reason, many houses in the region have huge walk-in pantries, and even upstairs closets lined with tin.) Next to the dining room is a hidden door leading to a secret passageway, designed by the architects to satisfy a romantic whim of the inventor.

A fifty-foot-long porch opens off the vast living room

A GLIMPSE OF THIS SIMPLE BATHROOM (ABOVE LEFT) SHOWS THE TYPICAL ACCOMMODATIONS OF THE HOUSE. THOUGH MUCH OF THE PLUMBING HAS BEEN RECENTLY REWORKED, THE WHITE PORCELAIN BASINS HAVE REMAINED IN PLACE. MOST OF THE LIGHT FIXTURES ARE ORIGINAL. THE PERIOD POSTER DATES FROM WORLD WAR I.

AN UPSTAIRS SITTING ROOM LEADS OFF THE MASTER BEDROOM ON THE SECOND FLOOR (ABOVE RIGHT). A FIELDSTONE FIREPLACE WITH A MASSIVE LOG MANTEL, ORIGINAL WICKER FURNITURE, OCCASIONAL RUGS ON BARE WOOD FLOORS, BOOKS, AND WELL-USED TOYS COMBINE TO GIVE SIMPLE, LOW-MAINTENANCE COMFORT TO THE ROOM.

through French doors and faces the lake. Glassed in since the founder's day and generously supplied with wicker lounging settees and cushioned sofas, it's a perfect place to sit and gaze at the view no matter what the weather. Occasionally one is startled to see a body fall past the window. This is an ongoing ritual. Everyone in the family and their guests jump off the roof of the porch into the lake. Many go much further and jump off the roof of the observation room at the very top of the house. If one asks, a bit worriedly, how deep the water is, the answer is, "Deep enough."

The complete set of blueprints from Gaggin & Gaggin are framed and hung on the wall next to one of the staircases leading to the second floor. Amid various bedrooms that include sleeping porches, on this floor are two sitting rooms

with ample fireplaces. Throughout these rooms are more examples of the distinctive faux mahogany metal furniture from the founder's workshops. A hall area contains large closets. Behind a narrow door in this hall is a steep stairway that leads up to the observation room. This is now converted into two romantic bedrooms with a small hall passage between them.

When the house was originally built, a furnace in the basement supplied central heat and a generator was installed to supply electricity for lighting. Now, having passed its eightieth birthday, the house has been entirely rewired, and all the early plumbing overhauled. However, the original greentoned, rubbed-down stain used on the walls and ceiling, giving a typical Adirondacks effect, is as good as the first day it was put on.

50

ORIGINALLY BUILT AS AN OBSERVATION ROOM AND A PLACE FOR THE FOUNDER TO SIP A POSTPRANDIAL LIQUEUR, THIS TOP FLOOR REACHED BY A NARROW HIDDEN STAIRWAY HAS NOW BEEN CONVERTED INTO TWO BEDROOMS. THIS ONE SPORTS WICKER FURNITURE AND A TYPICALLY RUSTICATED ADIRONDACK TWIG BED BUILT BY KEN HEITZ, A CRAFTSMAN IN INDIAN LAKE.

THE COTTAGE, THE FIRST HOUSE BUILT FOR THE INVENTOR'S FAMILY, CAN BE SEEN FROM A DECK OUTSIDE THE MAIN HOUSE. A MOTIF RUNNING THROUGHOUT THE COTTAGE DÉCOR IS A BROAD RED STRIPE ON DARK GREEN, SEEN ON CHAIRS, STEPS, CUSHIONS, AND EVEN ASHTRAYS. THIS WAS INSTIGATED BY A GREAT-GRANDCHILD OF THE INVENTOR, THE PRESENT CO-OWNER OF THE COTTAGE.

───

Up-to-date equipment for water sports is stored next door to the boathouse (**ABOVE LEFT**). Racks of life jackets arranged by size, and a larger variety of wetsuits than found in many dive shops, are available to family members and their guests.

The large boathouse (**ABOVE RIGHT**) still houses vintage wooden boats that are over seventy years old. In the foreground, equipped with wicker chairs, is the *Josephine*, named after the inventor's wife.

Though this house might be considered elaborate for a second home, its whole reason for being rests beneath the Main House. Here is the launch room. Because the house sits on the side of a lake, all summer activities revolve around boats, lake, and water sports. The large launch room still harbors vintage boats with wooden hulls dating from its inception. One of the handsomest, the *Josephine*, named after the first matriarch of the house, has a distinctive long prow, and is equipped with free-standing wicker chairs. It was made by Fay & Bowen, the classic launch boat makers of the time. Many of the other original boats are, alas, no longer around. The larger ones were used to bring visitors from the nearest railway depot, or to carry heavy freight and stores. Their huge size can be seen by their slips, which have now been filled in, though the outlines of their shapes remain on the floor of the room. On one side of the room is a row of individual changing rooms.

All the family—from each of the compound's houses— use the boathouse, which is run with admirable efficiency by the family member who now co-owns the Cottage. An adjoining boat room is stocked with every size of life jacket and wetsuit imaginable. Water skis, windsurfers, and dinghies lean against the walls. The children learn to swim at an early age, and boats whiz by with alarming frequency towing daring skiers on everything from bare feet to kitchen chairs perched precariously on an aquaplane. As an alternative diversion for the tiny ones, a sandbox and diminutive playground can be found near the Main House. For those wanting to camp out, an authentic "open camp" that was a required napping place for several generations of children,

and later a great place for teenage romance, is within walking distance of the Main House.

Until the late sixties, the camp was supported by the original founder's company. In 1971, it was partitioned among his descendants, with each responsible for the upkeep of his or her own house. To maintain common space such as the trails, a company was formed in which each family member owns stock. An annual meeting is held at the camp over Labor Day.

This then is a house where family members, now scattered all over America, gather to spend time away from the routine and bustle of their lives. It is, as its original owner wrote,

"Located in a country where life is worth living.
Where cares fold their tents
like the Arabs, and as
silently, steal away."

THE STARS AND STRIPES SHARES THE FLAGPOLE WITH THE CAMP'S OWN FLAG (ABOVE). DOCK AND DECKS, A VIEW OF THE LAKE, AND THE WOODED TERRAIN OF THE ADIRONDACKS CAN BE SEEN FROM THE HOUSE (RIGHT).

54

CADY HILL HOUSE STARTED AS A FARM HOUSE AND LATER BECAME A STAGE COACH INN. NOW IT IS ONE OF THE CORNELIUS VANDERBILT WHITNEY'S HOUSES. ITS SECOND STORY PORCH IS FITTED WITH TRANSPARENT PLASTIC SHEETS THAT CAN BE LET DOWN WITH PULLEYS TO GUARD AGAINST INCLEMENT WEATHER.

Racing Colors

A SARATOGA SPRINGS ESTATE

The very name of the town possesses captivating overtones. To some people, Saratoga Springs is remembered as the therapeutic spa that made it famous in the early part of the nineteenth century. To others, from big spender Diamond Jim Brady and "Bet-a-Million" Gates to Damon Runyan's guys and their dolls, Saratoga means the lure of gambling; everlovin' Adelaide lamented her lost hopes for a real honeymoon at Niagara Falls when she sang to inveterate gambler Nathan Detroit, "then we get off at Saratoga for the fourteenth time."

Nowadays it is the glamour of thoroughbred racing that brings the big crowds to Saratoga Springs. Wealthy families, many that are household names, breed and run their horses here and during the frenzied month of August—The Saratoga Season—attend spectacular parties and entertain lavishly. Cady Hill House belongs to one such family, the Cornelius Vanderbilt Whitneys. An approach to their Saratoga house can be made by passing the Performing Arts Center (another of Saratoga's lures with one of the world's largest theaters, and the Whitneys as major beneficiaries and fund raisers), and driving through the impressive Avenue of the Pines to aptly named Geyser Road, for Saratoga's origins are rooted in its health-giving springs and geysers. Cady Hill's entrance is through stone pillars, past a sentinel

COVERED WALKWAYS (**ABOVE LEFT**), BUILT IN 1980, HAVE BEEN CONSTRUCTED WITH PLYWOOD FRAMES THAT HOLD LARGE, REMOVABLE PLEXIGLASS WINDOWS SO THAT THE CORRIDORS CAN BE ENCLOSED IN THE WINTER, MAKING WARM AND COZY ACCESS TO THE HEATED SWIMMING POOL.

A SEPARATE ENTRANCE LEADS TO THE SWIMMING POOL OFF THE MAIN DRIVE (**ABOVE RIGHT**).

SUN POURS IN THROUGH THE ROOF OF THE INDOOR SWIMMING POOL (**RIGHT**). ITS ELEMENTS INCLUDE COTTON-COVERED FLOOR PILLOWS, PATIO-STYLE TABLES AND CHAIRS, A WELL-STOCKED BAR, MEN'S AND WOMEN'S CHANGING ROOMS, TENNIS RACKETS, MULTICOLORED UNBREAKABLE GLASSES, AND A PICTURE GALLERY OF FAMILY AND FRIENDS. CHRISTMAS IS OFTEN SPENT IN CADY HILL HOUSE, AND A LARGE CHRISTMAS PARTY IS HELD IN THIS SPACE, COMPLETE WITH A CHRISTMAS TREE AT THE END OF THE POOL.

gatehouse, and along a road which winds past various buildings to the residence itself surrounded by some sixty acres of well-maintained grounds.

At the approach of the Saratoga Season, the place becomes a hive of activity. Extra helping hands are brought in to bed out borders around the paths, sprinkle velvety lawns, set varieties of flowers in the geometrically laid out cutting garden, roll and chalk the tennis court, and prepare the hanging baskets of geraniums and impatiens that punctuate arbors and covered walkways.

Cady Hill is one of seven houses belonging to Mr. and Mrs. Whitney—distinguished from other well-known Whitneys by their nicknames Sonny and Marylou. Their other residences are to be found·in New York City, Kentucky, Florida, the

Adirondacks, and Majorca. Cady Hill House has increasingly become one of the Whitneys' favorites, and the Saratoga Season would not be as amusing or sparkling without them.

In a book called *Saratoga: Saga of an Impious Era*, George Waller writes: "In the beginning were the springs, welling from underground streams formed deep within the earth during the prehistoric glacial era and absorbing the earth's minerals until natural gases thrust the waters upward through the earth's surface and released them in geysers near the southern foothills of the towering mountains which would be called Adirondack." Waller goes on to describe how more than a century before the time of Columbus, the Iroquois found and called these beneficial waters "the Medicine Springs of the Great Spirit." The area surrounding the min-

A PERFECT PLACE TO CATCH THE SUN FOR MORNING COFFEE OR RELAXED LUNCHEONS, THIS SOUTH PORCH WAS GLASSED IN BY MARYLOU WHITNEY IN 1987. SHE DECORATED IT USING WHITE PAINTED WICKER, PASTEL DHURRIE RUGS ON PINK PAINTED FLOORBOARDS, AND PLENTY OF WELL-STUFFED PRETTY COLORED CUSHIONS.

eral springs belonged to the Mohawk Indians, one of the Iroquois nations. According to historians, a Jesuit priest named Father Isaac Jogues was the first white man to stay in the region, but he was eventually killed by Mohawks, and later canonized as the first saint in North America.

Another non-native hero of the area was Englishman William Johnson, who in 1738 arrived in the Mohawk Valley to establish a trading post. He lived as one of the Indians, learning the Mohawk language and marrying Molly Brant, a sister of the chief. Later, as Superintendent of Indian Affairs, Johnson was instrumental in establishing English supremacy in the region. When he fell sick, he was taken to the till-then

secret springs, and the medicinal waters effected his cure. As Waller points out, this took place in August, the month when the Season in Saratoga is traditionally celebrated.

The name Saratoga developed from the Mohawk language, though it was originally spelled in many different ways, each with slightly different meaning. *Sarachtogoe*, "hillside country of a great river," or "place of the swift water," became officially Saratoga in 1791, after the two Battles of Saratoga during the Revolutionary War. During this time, the area was brought to the attention of George Washington, who was so impressed with the benefits of one of the geysers, High Rock Spring, that he considered building a

summer home nearby. It is Mr. Whitney's belief that Washington stayed in the guest house of the present Cady Hill House complex (then called the Tavern). The center part of the main house, where the original Cady family lived, is from an even earlier date, marked on pre-Revolutionary maps.

After hostilities ceased, Saratoga gradually developed as a resort spa. More springs were discovered such as Congress Spring, which became famous throughout the country, but each spouting gush of mineral water was reached only by uncomfortable, strenuous travel. An entrepreneur, Gideon Putnam realized the potential of these natural geysers. He bought land surrounding Congress Spring, cleared it and

built accommodations for visitors. His plans included other springs, and he built roads to make them accessible, surrounding the springs with wooden enclosures to protect them. He began to lay out a proper village but died after an injury he received falling from the scaffold on his most ambitious construction, a grand hotel (by 1812 standards) called Congress Hall.

Though the nearby town of Ballston, also blessed by natural springs, threatened to outdo Saratoga as a spa in the early days of the nineteenth century, Saratoga eventually won out by offering visitors more varied distractions and amusements. The resort, which started off as a strait-laced, bible-reading,

61

THE LIBRARY IS ONE OF THE PLACES WHERE FAMILY OR GUESTS GATHER FOR DRINKS OR AFTERNOON TEA (LEFT). THOUGH THE ROOM WAS BADLY BURNED IN A 1985 FIRE THAT STARTED DUE TO FAULTY WIRING, IT HAS BEEN COMPLETELY RESTORED. THE BOOKCASES WERE CONSTRUCTED IN THE WORKSHOP AT CADY HILL AND MAPLE WAS CUT THERE FOR THE FLOORING. ARTIST'S CANVAS COVERS A SIDE DOOR AND WALL ON WHICH COLUMNS AND BORDERS ARE PAINTED BY DECORATIVE ARTISTS, ED STILES AND GORDON HOSFORD; M'LOU LLEWELLYN, MRS. WHITNEY'S DAUGHTER; AND MARYLOU WHITNEY, HERSELF.

hymn-singing community, soon became known for its fashionable licentiousness. Casinos for gambling sprang up. A racetrack for thoroughbred horses was built in 1863, and rebuilt with improvements the following year, inaugurating the Travers Stakes, and establishing Saratoga as a racy town in every sense of the word. Huge hotels provided splendid accommodations, luxurious banquets, and dancing—including the polka, which Queen Victoria had banned in her presence as being too risqué. These amenities attracted rich or adventurous men who brought stylish wives or pretty young mistresses. The more proper families tended to patronize Newport on the coast of Rhode Island, where they stayed in private "cottages" rather than mingle with the more classless society of the Springs. Women brought to Saratoga such elaborate wardrobes that the Saratoga trunk became as well known as the Wellington Boot or the Cardigan jacket. It was a roomy hogshead, dreaded by porters because of its weight, for it could hold a whole summer's supply of whalebone corsets and crinolines.

COMFORTABLE AND UNAFFECTED, SONNY WHITNEY'S ROOM HAS A MASCULINE, ALMOST SPARTAN QUALITY COMPARED TO THE REST OF THE DÉCOR AT CADY HILL HOUSE. COZY ARMCHAIRS, A HITCHCOCK CHAIR, A FIREPLACE, AND PLENTY OF BOOKS MAKE UP THE ATMOSPHERE.

LACE PILLOWS ADORN MARYLOU WHITNEY'S BED ON WHICH A DRESS IS LAID OUT IN READINESS. A TINY BED BESIDE IT IS FOR EIDELWIESS, HER WHITE MINIATURE POODLE (TOP LEFT).

THIS CORNER OF MARYLOU WHITNEY'S DRESSING ROOM SHOWS SOME OF THE ELEMENTS OF HER WELL-KNOWN FANCY DRESS STYLE (MIDDLE LEFT). HAIR RIBBONS ARE ARRANGED ON A RACK IN COLORS OF THE RAINBOW, WHILE PARASOLS, NECKLACES, AND SCARVES ARE ALL CLOSE TO HAND.

SOMEWHAT LARGER THAN THE FABLED SARATOGA TRUNK, MARYLOU WHITNEY'S DRESSING ROOM (BOTTOM LEFT) COULD MAKE ANY WOMAN ENVIOUS. REFLECTING HER LOVE OF PARTIES AND GUSSYING UP, THESE CLOSETS HOLD HER SIGNATURE DRESSES, WITH THEIR FULL SKIRTS HELD OUT BY CRINOLINE PETTICOATS THAT ARE IN THE TRUE SARATOGA SPRINGS TRADITION.

Cady Hill House existed through all these events whirling around the town of Saratoga Springs. Originally the house consisted only of the part that is now the dining room, butler's pantry, and the eating section of the kitchen. The rest of the kitchen, which is now used for cooking, was first used as a cattle barn. This kitchen area has been enlarged and completely redesigned to incorporate both sections by Marylou Whitney. She also revamped the basement below to make a playroom for all the visiting children in the family.

A variety of other owners lived in the house after the Cadys. It began to be used as a stagecoach inn stop as well as a tavern. By 1851, it belonged to a Mr. Townsend, who added a new front to the original building. New bedrooms were added to accommodate travelers, which is the reason there are now many bedrooms in the house—useful nowadays to house the flood of guests during August. Townsend also built the carriage house that was used for stagecoach horses. This building now accommodates offices and a painting studio for Mrs. Whitney.

In 1901, Sonny Whitney's father, Harry Payne Whitney, bought Cady Hill. He was known for his interest in racing (he headed the syndicate of wealthy sportsmen who owned the Saratoga racetrack, and had the most illustrious stable in the country) as well as for being the builder of New York City's streetcar system. He added the north and south porches, which were originally screened. With a view to making the house more comfortable in winter as well as during the Season, Marylou Whitney glassed them in in 1987.

Sonny Whitney has continued and extended his family's legacy. A sportsman, he has also served on many boards, written books, been involved with environmental issues, and produced movies, including *Gone With the Wind.*

Most of the renovations have borne comfort in mind. Since Mr. and Mrs. Whitney married in 1957, she has tried to make life both more serene and more fun for her husband, who, as the son of Harry Payne and Gertrude Vanderbilt Whitney, had lived in a fast-moving, sophisticated and, in many ways, far from homey world. For decorating advice, she turned to Stephen Stempler of the New York designing firm Cronin-

WHITE-PAINTED CHAIRS FOR SPECTATORS WAIT BESIDE A WELL-MAINTAINED GRASS TENNIS COURT (FAR TOP LEFT).

IN A FLOWER BED OUTSIDE THE FARMHOUSE, A FOUNTAIN SCULPTED IN THE FORM OF TWO CHILDREN UNDER AN UMBRELLA IS SURROUNDED BY BEGONIAS (TOP LEFT).

THE GAZEBO IS A PERFECT SPOT FOR A COOL SUMMER DRINK (FAR BOTTOM LEFT).

BRICKWORK, A STONE BENCH, AND A CUTE FIGURINE OF A BABY ARE FOUND IN THE CUTTING GARDEN (BOTTOM LEFT).

FORMAL FLOWER BEDS ARE IN KEEPING WITH SARATOGA SPRINGS' NEAT VICTORIAN STYLE (LEFT).

Stempler, though, he admits, she has a will, style, and opinion all her own.

Typical of the remodeling are the constructed walkways leading from the house to the glassed-in swimming pool, making them accessible in winter as well as summer. These alleys are hung with baskets of flowers in the summer, but during the winter months they are fenced in with Plexiglass panels and heated. Central heating, which had not been necessary when the Whitneys first owned the house, has been added throughout. The masculine-looking sporting club décor from the forties was changed to a lighter, more feminine atmosphere in all but Sonny Whitney's bedroom and the of-

fices in the stage coach barn. Though formal reception rooms are grand—with luxuriously draped curtains, lacquered furniture and Chinese porcelains—the light touch appears in pastel-colored silks and touches like the white painted piano in the library for informal sing-alongs. A room that combines both a sporting and a light touch is the Saratoga room, where the walls are covered with paintings of horses from the Whitney stables.

The house is welcoming, yet it retains an opulent style that echoes Saratoga of the nineteenth century. The bedrooms are luxuriously cosy even when small. Practicality is stressed over the scholarly burden of antiques. This is apparent in Marylou

Whitney's dressing room, which is conveniently near a maid's suite complete with sewing and ironing facilities. In her own fashion, Marylou Whitney has embraced the lavish style of nineteenth century Saratoga right down to the crinolines, and her dressing room is in the tradition of the Saratoga trunk.

All this might appear frivolous, but it is a necessary part of her function as a fund-raiser and one of the town's most hard-working hostesses. This activity takes energy and super-human organization. Her famous theme parties are planned months in advance, and her hectic schedule involves having the right clothes in the right trunks with their color-keyed identifying tags packed and ready to go. This can only be achieved with loyal support from family and help. In return the Whitneys give Saratoga Springs plenty of excitement.

IN THE DINING ROOM A BOWL HOLDING A FUCHSIA PLANT RESTS ON A BAMBOO TABLE THAT SITS IN FRONT OF A PAINTED SCREEN. THIS SCREEN WAS USED IN LIL GROUEFF'S PARISIAN APARTMENT ON THE RUE DE BAC, ONCE LIVED IN BY MME. DE STAEL AND OWNED BY PIERRE DE MONACO (PRINCE RAINIER'S FATHER). THERE WAS A LITTLE *BIBLIOTEQUE* THAT HAD BROWN TAFFETA CURTAINS AND THE SCREEN WAS ON THE WALL TO GIVE THE APPEARANCE OF A MATCHING WINDOW. THE APARTMENT HAD BEEN DECORATED BY JACQUES FRANK. THE EMBROIDERED STOOL IS ENGLISH. THE PINE DOOR LEADS INTO THE KITCHEN.

———

High Style Cottage

A GETAWAY IN THE HAMPTONS

t the end of June, resort areas in eastern Long Island reach a point of perfection never quite recaptured the rest of the summer. Grand houses and simple cottages are opened up, cleaned, and aired, sofas are dressed in laundered slipcovers, basic stores are in place on kitchen shelves, patchwork quilts are on beds, and invitations have begun to collect on mantels and mirror frames. Those who can take the summer off will stay until Labor Day. They will be joined by the breadwinners, exhausted from New York's grueling bustle, on weekends. Bikes have been oiled, rubber rafts have not yet sprung leaks, nor have floors yet gathered their irritating dusting of sand. In the super-social towns or villages, boutiques are stocked with chic, all-cotton clothes for the summer folk, and antique shops are ready with charmingly rustic merchandise.

This is when the roses put forth their first bloom in a profusion of blossom and fragrance, celebrated by a glorious rose competition. Flowers in general, but roses in particular, set the tone of the Hamptons cottage belonging to Lil and Stephane Groueff. Hidden behind an allée of high, clipped privet, the cottage is shielded by Lil's "Irish wall," made of sod, and heavy with honeysuckle and wild roses, giving off a heady scent accompanied by the hum of bees. More hedges of blushing white

IN THE LIVING ROOM (LEFT) A
FEDERAL MANTELPIECE, BOUGHT
FROM DANNY ALESSANDRO, WAS
STRIPPED TO THE NATURAL WOOD.
THE TILES ARE FROM COUNTRY
FLOORS. THE WOOD CARVING ABOVE
WAS FOUND IN A LOCAL ANTIQUE
SHOP. TWO SAINT FIGURES ON THE
MANTEL AND MOTHER-OF-PEARL
NAPOLEONIC SILHOUETTES ARE
FROM SWITZERLAND. HORNS, A
MEMORIAL, MINIATURE BLUE AND
WHITE CHINA, A FEATHER FAN, AND A
GRANDDAUGHTER'S GIFT OF WIND
CHIMES MINGLE OVER THE MANTEL.
TWO 1840S THEOREM PAINTINGS ON
VELVET FLANK THE MANTELPIECE.
SCHUMACHER CHINTZ COVERS THE
FURNITURE. THE ROUND DINING
ROOM TABLE TO THE RIGHT WAS
FOUND IN LORD & TAYLOR'S
ANTIQUES DEPARTMENT, AND THE
CHAIRS ARE FROM ETCETERA IN
SOUTHAMPTON.

New Dawn roses scatter petals on the well-mowed grass and gravel drive. An espaliered peach tree forms a pattern on the side of the house. Dazzled by these details, one bypasses the everyday architecture of the house itself.

Designed by Lil Groueff and built in 1969 by contractor Archie Colledge, this is a house of interior details. Decorator Lil Groueff shows capricious wit in the way she assembles an agglomeration of furniture and objects. She is mad for tiny chairs, old suitcases, interesting fabrics, and odd but arrestingly framed prints and pictures that, massed together, reveal an artfully developed, sophisticated taste.

The Hamptons, in particular Southold on the North Fork and Southampton on the South Fork of Long Island, have the distinction of being the earliest English settlements in New York State. It is believed by some historians that a group of

Two tan-painted antique wicker chairs flank a 1930s wicker sofa, the seat draped in a rag rug and an assortment of cushions covered in batik sarongs found in Bangkok. The tiny cushions are French and stiff with dried lavender—flowers, stalks, and all. Above are Lil Groueff's versions of Renoir, Manet, and Seurat paintings surrounding shelves of Japanese blue and white china. The American tin trunk used as a coffee table was found in Virginia. On it is Stephane Groueff's book about the King, Boris of Bulgaria, and a book by family friend Aline Romanones. The lamp is covered in a batik shade made by Lil Groueff. The wallpaper is from Schumacher.

———

AN ANTIQUE QUILT-COVERED TABLE SITS BY FRENCH WINDOWS THAT FACE THE OCEAN. HAND-PAINTED PLATES DESIGNED BY LYN EVANS WERE FOUND AT GORDON FOSTER ANTIQUES IN NEW YORK CITY. THE DRIED FLOWER ARRANGEMENT IS BY FLORETTE FLOWERS, IN SOUTHAMPTON (ABOVE LEFT).

THE SUN-ROOM LEADS OUT TO A POOL AND ROSE GARDEN. A SUN-BLEACHED 1950S CHAIR THAT ONCE BELONGED TO LIL GROUEFF'S MOTHER IS BACKED BY SHELVES OF PICTURES, MEMENTOS, AND CERAMICS, MANY OF THEM FOUND LOCALLY. THE GROUPING INCLUDES A PICTURE OF DAUGHTER TINA, SOME MOVABLE TIN CALENDARS CIRCA 1910, AND A PAINTING BY LOCAL BRIDGEHAMPTON ARTIST STUBBINGS (ABOVE RIGHT).

British citizens came from Antigua to Southold as early as 1637. East Hampton (then called "Maidstone") followed in 1648, and Shelter Island in 1652.

After the middle of the nineteenth century, Americans began to put some of their time aside for leisure. Long Island was already a popular playground. Horse racing here had been an early sport dating back almost to the first colonists. Hunting, fishing, and sailing now became sports instead of means of livelihood. The Long Island Railroad, built originally as a link between Manhattan and Boston, brought New Yorkers to eastern Long Island to play. Ocean bathing became fashionable. As affluence grew, rich sportsmen espoused the smart European pursuits of polo, golf, and tennis. Cycling was taken up for exercise and transport, then car and

airplane racing followed. The Roaring Twenties brought rum-running to the South Shore that faced the Atlantic and the North Shore facing the bay. Millionaires built grand houses shielded by high, wall-smooth hedges in East Hampton and Southampton. Generations of privileged children vacationed at their "summer place," and later as young adults enjoying the romance of Great Gatsbyesque parties on manicured lawns lit with Chinese lanterns.

Decorator Lil and writer Stephane Groueff are not new to the ritzy side of the Hamptons. For many summers they lived and entertained in a larger house, not far away from their present cottage. Now the children have grown and left home. Both Lil Groueff's daughters and her sons have married and have their own homes. Jill Blanchard lives nearby in an 1812

A HATCH AND COUNTER, WITH SIMPLE UNFINISHED WOOD BAR STOOLS, SEPARATES THE LIVING ROOM AND THE KITCHEN. BLEACHED PINE SHUTTERS CAN CLOSE IT OFF WHEN NEEDED.

farmhouse. Photographer Tina Barney, whose work is shown in galleries and on magazine covers, lives in Watch Hill, Rhode Island. Paul, the youngest and a musician, lives with his family in Bozeman, Montana. With the children gone, the house proved much too cumbersome for the odd winter weekend with just two people. In 1969 the Groueffs decided to build a weekend cottage for use all year round—a way to escape the grind of New York City. Lil Groueff drew up the designs herself, working with a contractor on the blueprints. As their big house had had a twenty-nine-foot long living room, she knew this was a size with which she felt comfortable. The width of the cottage was based on this dimension. On the floor above, the bedroom is the same luxurious size.

Since then the cottage has grown in two directions. A back porch, maid's room, and spiral staircase leading to a bedroom and bathroom—used for occasional visits mainly by Lil's sons Philip Isles, Jr., and Paul Groueff and his family—were added to the back of the house on the far side

THE 1890S FRANKLIN STOVE FIREPLACE (RIGHT) WAS USED IN A BLOOMINGDALE'S DISPLAY ROOM, BUT IT PRODUCES REMARKABLY EFFICIENT HEAT BECAUSE OF ITS HEATING COILS; ONLY A TINY PIECE OF COAL IS REQUIRED. FIGURED MIRROR GLASS DECORATES THE FRONT. OLD TOYS AND MINIATURES ORNAMENT THE MANTEL. THE ROSE PAINTING ABOVE CAME FROM A PARKE BERNET AUCTION. MOST OF THE ENGLISH EMBROIDERED SILK PICTURES CAME FROM PHILIP SUVAL. THE CARPET IS ENGLISH NEEDLEPOINT. ON A CHAIR TO THE LEFT IS AN APPLIQUED SOLDIER BOY. QUILTED CHINTZ, PATCHWORK CUSHIONS, AND A CHALLIS PAISLEY SHAWL FROM ROSE CUMMING COMPLEMENT THE ROOM. THE TWO CURTAINED DOORWAYS LEAD TO THE BATHROOM. THE GOLD WICKER CHAIRS CAME FROM THE RUE DE BAC APARTMENT AND WERE FOUND IN THE MARCHÉ AUX PUCES IN PARIS.

On the upstairs hall landing (ABOVE LEFT), the top of a captain's chest displays specimen tubes of flowers from the garden, a section from an antique patchwork quilt of houses, a woven straw hat, and a green oiled umbrella. On the wall above is an English 1807 collage of playing cards (the corridor holds more of these), theatrical figures, and some amusing drawings. The carpet is faux leopard with faded red trim.

A twenty-nine-foot-long luxurious bathroom (ABOVE RIGHT) leads out to a balcony. The Axminster carpet is in a rose pattern. An American hooked rug lies alongside the bathtub. In the foreground are a Lloyd Loom chair and hamper made in the 1940s. A cashmere shawl over a cotton damask cloth on a round table, and a shawl on the chaise longue both came from Yul Brynner's wife's shop in Gstaad. A portrait of the family dog by William Fielding is included in a melange of drawings of and by members of the family.

of the kitchen. In 1985 a sun room was added to the other end of the house, next to the living room. This enabled the Groueffs to indulge in a sumptuous bathroom and office above it with a balcony overlooking the swimming pool and rose garden.

The pool is "old-fashioned" as Lil describes it, being tiled in blue rather than the fashionable gray or black of the eighties. Surrounding it are clumps of herbs and perennials, casually but intentionally overflowing their boundaries like an English garden. Lil loves to garden. She applies the same visual talents to the garden as to a room. In the new sun room, for instance, there is a flower arranging sink.

Trained as an artist, and spending some of her life in Europe, Lil has been interested in decorating since childhood. She has a wonderful hands-on approach that, combined with her sophistication, produces intriguing and unusual effects. She is not afraid of handling paint or using her sewing machine or her imagination, so the results she achieves are unique and unexpected. Her ferreting eye finds treasures others miss.

Stephane Groueff was for many years the New York bureau chief of the French weekly, *Paris Match*. Much of the house reflects his intellectual European background. His study faces part of the garden that slopes down to an inlet.

At the entrance to the cottage, a bull's-eye window lights

BED HANGINGS ARE OF A FABRIC NOW OUT OF STOCK FROM BRUNSCHWIG & FILS. THE QUILT IS FROM THE ELDER CRAFTSMAN SHOP
BOUGHT AT LEAST TWENTY YEARS AGO. THE HEADBOARD IS COVERED IN "SEA CORAL" FROM COWTAN & TOUT. THE PAINTED TRUNK
WAS FOUND IN THE HAMPTONS. THE SLIPPER CHAIR IS COVERED IN A COLEFAX & FOWLER FABRIC WITH A CUSHION MADE BY CARRIE
MUNN. THE ROOM IS REFLECTED IN A NAPOLEON III CHEVAL MIRROR FROM LIL GROUEFF'S PARIS APARTMENT ON THE RUE DE BAC.

———

A BRICK TERRACE BY
THE POOL HOLDS
LOUNGING CHAIRS AND
SUN UMBRELLAS.
CLUMPS OF ELYSIUM
AND HERBS LINE THE
WALKWAYS AND FLANK
THE ENTRANCE TO A
ROSE GARDEN. ON THE
CHAISE IS A BIOGRAPHY
OF DAVID NIVEN, WHO
WAS A FRIEND OF THE
GROUEFFS.

LUNCH IS SET UP ON
THE BRICK TERRACE
OUTSIDE THE SUN-ROOM
(LEFT). SIMPLE
REDWOOD OR WHITE-
PAINTED METAL
FURNITURE IS
SURROUNDED WITH
POTTED GERANIUMS AND
MORNING GLORIES,
SHADED BY A MAPLE
TREE.

FLOURISHING CLUMPS
OF LAVENDER AND
ARTEMISIA BORDER THE
BRICK WALK AROUND
THE SWIMMING POOL.

up the hall. The large room to the left is lively even though it is painted brown. This is because Lil craved wood panels—of the best eighteenth-century English quality she couldn't afford—so she settled for brown paint and then ingeniously added wood details such as a piece of carving or a paneled wood door. By happenstance, the walls match a painted

screen, once used in her Paris apartment, that depicted a window hung with brown satin curtains.

For dinner parties, a round dark-oak table in the living room is used. This was found in the antiques department at Lord & Taylor, but it was recently given a formal finished surface, incidentally costing more than its original price. The

SEEN FROM THE ROSE GARDEN, THE POOL IS SECLUDED BY A DENSE HEDGE AND SURROUNDED BY OVERFLOWING BEDS OF HERBS AND LOW-GROWING PERENNIALS.

sun-room beyond takes on the role of a living room to be enjoyed before or after dining.

One of the great joys of the house is the lavish scale of the master bedroom and the added-on bathroom/study. These are more like living rooms in size and in décor and both are full of old-fashioned comfort.

Because the Groueffs live an interesting, cosmopolitan social life, this second home has more formality than, say, a renovated barn or a converted fishing shack. Yet the house like the owners has a welcoming and casual insouciance, a sort of nothing-should-look-too-new attitude typified in the way a truly elegant European woman puts herself together.

SEEN FROM A ROLLING HILL ABOVE THE HOUSE, THE MAIN PART OF THIS TYPICALLY PENNSYLVANIAN
STONE-POINTED FARMHOUSE WAS BUILT AT THE END OF THE EIGHTEENTH CENTURY. ADDITIONS AND
CHANGES INSIDE THE HOUSE ACCOUNT FOR THE SLIGHTLY UNSYMMETRICAL SET OF THE WINDOWS; THE
FRONT DOOR, FOR INSTANCE, IS NOT IN ITS ORIGINAL PLACE. THE GARLANDED WISTERIA CLINGING TO THE
FRONT OF THE HOUSE WAS PLANTED BY THE PRESENT OWNERS JUST FOUR YEARS AGO.

AUTUMN'S CROP OF
LADY APPLES AND
SECKEL PEARS FILL AN
EIGHTEENTH-CENTURY
FAMILLE ROSE CHINESE
BOWL IN A DINING ROOM
WINDOW.

Fieldstone Farmhouse

A RURAL BUCKS COUNTY RETREAT

Rolling fields and orchards form the landscape of this six-hundred-square-mile county, one of the original three of William Penn's Quaker commonwealth in the seventeenth century. Its undulating hills are dotted with simple fieldstone houses and barns—some of them almost three centuries old—built during prosperous years when the rich farmland provided wheat, corn, oats, and potatoes for a growing nation.

Crossing a picturesque Bucks County bridge (where in preautomobile days there stood a railroad station) and following an ambling lane to a fork leads one to a sign: Spring Hill Farm, 1779. It is here that a Scottish couple, Kenneth and Olive Bates, relax from their busy international but mostly New York-based life as purveyors of Scottish-made woolen textiles.

Pennsylvania, before it got its name, was claimed by the Dutch, Swedes, and English during the early decades of the seventeenth century. The Dutch based their ownership on the exploratory voyage of Henry Hudson (1609), who established trading posts along the Delaware River. In 1643 a party of Swedes founded the first permanent settlement within the territory. Called New Gottenburg, the colony was situated on Tinicum Island, near the site of modern Chester. This and the last-

A DROLL TOUCH TO THE FRONT DRIVE IS ADDED BY THE BRITISH TELEPHONE KIOSK (ABOVE LEFT) BROUGHT OVER BY THE BATESES,
"TO MAKE US FEEL AT HOME."

NEATLY CLIPPED TOPIARY TREES WERE PART OF THE GROUNDS BEFORE THE BATESES MOVED INTO THE HOUSE. AN ARCH FOR
CLIMBING ROSES HAS BEEN ADDED RECENTLY (ABOVE RIGHT).

named Swedish settlement, Upland, angered the Dutch so that in 1655, Peter Stuyvesant, governor of New Netherland (now New York) led an expedition against the Swedes giving the Dutch control over the area. The Dutch in turn lost their jurisdiction when the British seized New Netherland, renaming it New York.

In 1681 the British reformer and Quaker William Penn was granted the territory, including some of what is now New Jersey, in return for a debt owed his father by Charles II. Eventually Penn established a liberal constitution, attracting many English Quakers to his capital, Philadelphia, and to its neighboring counties.

The population increased during the eighteenth century, bringing many Scots-Irish and German settlers to parts of the area, although Bucks County was generally settled by the

English who came up the Delaware River from Philadelphia. Though the early settlers erected log houses, which were fast to build and at the same time helped clear the terrain, the land's agricultural bounty brought enough wealth to support more permanent fieldstone houses. The Germans introduced the two-storied barn; but it was the English who brought the distinctive Bucks County style of house. This crossbred the English architectural legacy of fieldstone cottages similar to those found in the English Cotswolds, particularly Wiltshire where many of the Quakers came from, and blended them with Georgian details of newly built Philadelphia. These houses were essentially simple, and usually based on the double-pile plan, adorned with symmetrical window placement, and topped with a lower, more classically pitched roof than their predecessors.

A BRICK TERRACE TO
THE SIDE OF THE HOUSE
WAS ADDED BY PREVIOUS
OWNERS. THE
AMERICAN-MADE
GARDEN CHAIRS ARE
METAL AND THE TABLES
ARE TOPPED WITH THICK
PIECES OF SLATE. A
DECORATIVE JAPANESE
CHERRY TREE WAS LEFT
IN PLACE TO PROVIDE
SPRING BLOSSOMS AND
SHADE IN THE SUMMER.

BEHIND A CUSHION-PILED SOFA IN THE LIVING ROOM IS AN ASSORTMENT OF PICTURES IN JACOBEAN-STYLE CREWEL, OR CROSS-STITCH NEEDLEWORK, EMBROIDERED BY OLIVE BATES AND HER DAUGHTERS. THE FOX FAMILY, HE IN RIDING CLOTHES, SHE IN A KILT, WERE CHRISTMAS PRESENTS. PHEASANT FEATHERS IN A GOBLET ON THE WALL ARE A REMINDER OF THE PREVIOUS OWNERS, WHO STOCKED PHEASANTS FOR HUNTING. THE COFFEE TABLE CAME FROM CARLISLE, PENNSYLVANIA.

AN OPEN FIREPLACE, SO LARGE IT HAS TWO SEPARATE FLUES, DOMINATES THE LIVING ROOM (LEFT). INSIDE THE GRATE IS AN EIGHTEENTH-CENTURY PENNSYLVANIA COPPER CONTAINER USED FOR MAKING APPLE BUTTER. ORIENTAL CARPETS, COMFORTABLE ARMCHAIRS—WITH CREWEL CUSHIONS EMBROIDERED BY OLIVE BATES—A RED-PAINTED ANTIQUE CHILD'S CHAIR, AND A LOW BOX ONCE USED FOR RAISING BREAD BUT NOW USED AS A COFFEE TABLE BESIDE THE ARMCHAIR, ALL ADD TO THE COZY ATMOSPHERE.

Geographically, Bucks County was a crossroad between the major cities of Boston, New York, and Washington, and it straddled coast and plain. By the time of the Revolution, Bucks had become the breadbasket of the Northeast, and therefore strategically important. The surrounding area is famous in American history not only because of the deprivations of Valley Forge, but later for the battle of Gettysburg, which decided the course of the Civil War.

Bucks County historian Charlotte Stryker describes the houses of this area as "a country style of building rather than architecture," a vernacular style similar to that of colonial Pennsylvania as a whole. And William Morgan, in *Bucks County*, says, "It is generally a conservative as well as additive building style. There is very little stylistic evolution; houses tended to grow larger when the standard of living permitted, rather than be replaced or remodeled according to more up-to-date fashions."

Among the early settlers was a Scottish couple, Samuel

89

Kirkbride and his wife, Mary. According to the fragment of an indenture now framed in Spring Hill Farm, they purchased the piece of land where the Bateses' farmhouse now stands in 1743 for forty shillings. It is not known if the Kirkbrides actually lived on Spring Hill Farm, though it is probable they had a log cabin or a more substantial stone house on the present foundation.

The earliest part of the house is dated 1779, and these early foundations survive in the present cellar. In 1805 a family named Bitts built most of the existing fieldstone house. They installed two Moravian-style pencil-carved mantels—one in the parlor, now the dining room, and the other in what is now a butler's pantry.

In the mid-nineteenth century, the house was bought by the Fackenthal family from Rotterdam. A granddaughter of the original Mr. Fackenthal, Etta Whitesell, now in her mid-eighties, recalls how her family lived there early in this century. There was then no indoor plumbing. An outdoor trough was filled by a Spring that flowed by gravity from two fields away. The Fackenthals added a kitchen, now the back living room; till then a separate outside cookhouse sufficed.

A later owner, John Meixel, a steel executive who worked at Bethlehem, was responsible for constructing all the built-in closets and shelves in the house. In a renovation that removed the house's central chimney, he eliminated one of the pencil-carved mantels, giving it to its present home, the Moravian Museum in Bethlehem.

The house had neither electricity nor indoor plumbing until the 1950s. The property passed through several hands until it was bought in 1974 by John and Mary Jane Shane, who used it as a working farm until 1977, thereafter for regulated shooting and hunting grounds and for breeding English pointers. Shane restored the barn; repointed the stonework of the house; added a new kitchen wing, a glassed-in porch room, a wine cellar, and a brick terrace; and converted the old outside cookhouse into a working summer kitchen. He sold the house to the Bateses in 1984.

Olive and Kenneth Bates came to America in 1955 for their honeymoon, and stayed. Kenneth Bates had been born in

THE OWNERS BEFORE THE BATESES ADDED THIS GLASSED-IN ROOM TO THE BACK OF THE STONE FARMHOUSE (ABOVE LEFT). A SELECTION OF CHEESES AND BREAD BAKED BY KENNETH BATES ARE LAID OUT ON THE NINETEENTH-CENTURY PINE NEW JERSEY TABLE. THE SET OF FOUR CHAIRS OF THE SAME PERIOD ARE FROM CARLISLE, PENNSYLVANIA.

IN THE "GLASS ROOM," AS THE BATESES CALL THIS GLASSED-IN PORCH, A WICKER CHAISE INVITES A LONG, LEISURELY READ ON THE WEEKEND (ABOVE RIGHT). ON THE SILL ABOVE BETWEEN THE WOODEN BLOCKS, ARE BIRDS' NESTS FOUND ON THE PROPERTY. THE ORIGINAL INDENTURE TO THE PROPERTY IS FRAMED ON THE STONE WALL THAT WAS ONCE THE OUTSIDE OF THE HOUSE.

Canada but at the age of two went to live in Innerleithen, in the border country between England and Scotland. It was here he learned about Scottish wool, which would become his trade. The Bateses had discovered the joys of Bucks County as a place to relax and live the country life some fourteen years before finding Spring Hill Farm, but had found that their first weekend house had over the years become suburban. Towns like New Hope, popular with artists and craftspeople, were becoming crowded. The Bateses wanted something a bit more rural and private, to be a contrast from their hectic New York City life. Spring Hill Farm fitted the bill to perfection. Since owning the house, they too have added, like the previous residents, their own improvements.

A swimming pool now sits on a slope below the house. A horse, a Shetland Pony, four sheep, and three friendly cats live in the barn. Wisteria, looking as if it has been there for centuries, has been trained over what has become the front facade. Garages, a cutting garden, and the odd jolt of a British red telephone kiosk—"to make us feel at home"—are outdoor features. In addition, they bought a few more acres so that their land included a trout stream, and a log cabin for extra guests.

Indoors, the Bateses have mixed English, Scottish, and Pennsylvania Dutch antiques to produce a cozy, relaxed weekend house. The "glass room" was given a new floor, becoming an ideal room for casual lunches. In the summer, a

TWO EARLY
NINETEENTH-CENTURY
SCOTTISH CHAIRS, LONG
OWNED BY THE BATES
FAMILY, FLANK A
NINETEENTH-CENTURY
PEDESTAL SEWING
TABLE THAT DISPLAYS
FAVORITE BIBELOTS,
INCLUDING A LITTLE
BLACK SCOTTISH CLOCK.
TWO GLAZED ANTIQUE
CHINESE JARS SIT ON
THE WINDOWSILL.

THIS GUEST ROOM IS TUCKED UNDER THE EAVES ABOVE THE OLDEST SECTION OF THE HOUSE. A FRAMED PIECE OF ANTIQUE PATCHWORK IS USED AS A PICTURE, AND ANOTHER OLD QUILT EMBELLISHES THE BED. THE MODERN RUGS WERE HAND MADE IN FRENCHTOWN, PENNSYLVANIA (LEFT).

THIS DRESSING TABLE COVERED WITH AN ANTIQUE QUILT ADORNS A GUEST ROOM IN THE MAIN SECTION OF THE HOUSE. THE OVAL ENGLISH LOOKING GLASS WAS FOUND IN VIRGINIA. THE TABLE IS ARRAYED WITH SILVER BRUSHES AND BOXES, FRAMED FAMILY PICTURES, DOLLS' CUPS AND SAUCERS AND TEAPOTS, DRIED FLOWERS AND POTPOURRI SACHETS (ABOVE LEFT).

A COLLECTION OF DIMINUTIVE OBJECTS IS DISPLAYED ON A SHELF UPSTAIRS (ABOVE RIGHT). TINY SCENT BOTTLES, JARS, AND A VARIETY OF METAL AND CERAMIC THIMBLES, INCLUDING MANY WITH MINIATURE PORTRAITS OF THE ENGLISH ROYAL FAMILY, HAVE ACCUMULATED OVER THE YEARS. THE THREE EBONY ELEPHANTS, GIFT-SHOP REMINDERS OF THE LAST DAYS OF THE BRITISH RAJ WHEN ALMOST EVERY BRITISH HOUSEHOLD POSSESSED A SET, ARE FROM INDIA.

---

perfect place for large groups is the brick patio, serviced by its nearby separate kitchen.

The house is visited often by their grown children, including three daughters and a college age son. The many bedrooms accommodate them with ease. None of this would be quite so simple without the help of full-time housekeeper-caretaker Lynne Weaver, who has been part of the family since they first ventured into Bucks County. She looks after the house, calls the plumber or electrician as needed, and feeds the animals, so that maintaining the place is not week-end drudgery. Time can happily be spent gardening, baking bread (Mr. Bates' favorite activity) or visiting and entertaining neighbors.

Though the house has been altered time and time again by each owner so that the once-balanced symmetry of the fenestration has been shifted, the house looks comfortably settled and well cared for. Trees are clipped and new walkways are being laid. The first Scottish couple, Samuel and Mary Kirkbride, would be well pleased to see how well their fellow countrymen are faring.

"Sheep, cats, and a horse have the run of the meadow by the barn."

96

THE TOPIARY TREES
FORM LONG SHADOWS
ON THE LAWN.

97

THE GREY GHOST, AS THIS HOUSE IS NICKNAMED, WAS RESTORED INSIDE AND OUT OVER A THREE-YEAR
PERIOD BY PENNSYLVANIAN FLOYD OHLIGER. THE HOUSE IS SURROUNDED BY A NEATLY PAINTED PICKET
FENCE ENCLOSING THE FRONT GARDEN NEWLY PLANTED BY ITS PRESENT OWNER, ANNE FRENCH
THORINGTON. TO THE LEFT CAN BE SEEN A GARAGE AND STORAGE SHED THAT HOUSES BICYCLES,
MAINTENANCE TOOLS, AND BEACH TOYS FOR HER FAMILY.

———

Steamboat Gothic

A CAPE MAY DUNES HOUSE

itting high up on the dunes, a house known colloquially as the Grey Ghost looks out over the Atlantic Ocean. Locals suggest that the ghost was a woman who once stared out to sea waiting for a lost husband. The house with its gingerbread trim can be viewed in the changeable seascape light as either inviting or foreboding, just like the cottage Hansel and Gretel encountered in the fairy tale by the Brothers Grimm. The impression is that the building has been wonderfully preserved. The typically Victorian color of the exterior paintwork has been beautifully executed, the woodwork scrupulously repaired, the front garden with its newly planted borders is in character, its hydrangeas neat and trim. The gravel path is well raked. Lace curtains discretely mask the interiors from the sun, and a picket fence warns the casual visitor that the owners prefer privacy.

Ten years ago the house was not in such good shape. Neighbors say they remember watching it fall on hard times, causing it almost to collapse in slovenly disrepair. A few decades before that the house was not even standing on its present spot, having been moved from two streets away, and, as far as can be discerned from maps and records, it had been moved even earlier, giving it three locations since it was first built. The present owner, Anne French Thorington, remembers from

PAINTED WICKER AND ROCKING CHAIRS ON THE FRONT PORCH EVOKE THE DREAMY SUMMERTIME OF THE LATE VICTORIAN ERA. FRESHLY PICKED CORN FILLS THE BICYCLE BASKET, AND SWEET ROUND WATERMELONS PROVIDE A SNACK, ALL FROM ONE OF NEW JERSEY'S RENOWNED ROADSIDE PRODUCE STANDS.

childhood the street where the Grey Ghost was located on its second move. That thoroughfare is now under water, and that particular stretch of ocean is unsafe for swimming because of the residual underwater pilings. This is true of many of the Cape's sandy beaches, and though Cape May is America's oldest seaside resort, its coastline loses ground every year.

Cape May is named for Captain Cornelius Jacobsen Mey. Captain Mey was not the first to discover the Cape; John Cabot in 1489, Giovanni da Verrazano in 1524, and Henry Hudson on his ship *Half Moon* in 1609, had arrived previously and found the region inhabited by a subtribe of the gentle, mediating Lenni-Lenape Indians called the Keche-

meches. Captain Mey, according to John T. Cunningham, author of *New Jersey: America's Main Road,* was a Dutch explorer for the United Netherland Company, who in 1620 sailed "along the coast, naming everything in sight for himself: today only the lower bit of New Jersey acknowledges the Mey vanity—and even that has been anglicized to Cape May." He became director general of the New Netherlands in 1623, and in the following year, he sailed up the Delaware River in his ship "Glad Tydings" and set up Fort Nassau on the East bank of the river near the present site of Gloucester. His colony disappeared, possibly destroyed by Indians. Captain Mey extolled the climate of the Cape, saying it was like

MOVED TWICE FROM ITS ORIGINAL SITE BECAUSE OF BEACH EROSION, THE CLAPBOARDED BLACKBURN HOUSE WAS BUILT IN THE 1870S AS A SUMMER RESIDENCE FOR A PHILADELPHIA FAMILY. IT IS CONSIDERED ONE OF THE FINEST EXAMPLES OF A SEASIDE CARPENTER GOTHIC COTTAGE IN THE CAPE MAY AREA.

101

SEEN FROM THE DUNES, THE GREY GHOST IS ATTRACTIVE AND WELL-MAINTAINED

that of Holland, so much so that two other company representatives, Godyn and Blommaert Samueals, purchased in 1630 a four-mile stretch of land along the bay from Cape May Point northwards and twelve miles inland in 1630. In *Gems of New Jersey*, New Jersey journalist-environmentalist Gordon Bishop writes that the first resident-landowner was a Dutchman, Davi Pieterson, who developed a prosperous fishing industry, chiefly whaling. As the English colonists expanded south from New England, they gradually took over the whaling business, then assumed general control, founding Town Bank, or Cape May Town. The coast became a stopping-off place for British men-o'-war and for pirate vessels,

for both types of boats were attracted by the fresh water found at Lily Lake between Cape May Town and Cape May Point. Captain Kidd was chased to this area by Colonel William Quary in 1699. The pirate Blackbeard (sometimes called Blackbird by New Jerseyites), frequented the region, according to George F. Boyer and J. Pearson Cunningham in *Cape May County Story*, and also seen there was the infamous Captain Shelly in his ship *Nassau*. During the War of 1812, local patriots dug a mile-long trench between the lake and the sea so that the British warships would only find briny, undrinkable water. The trench was later filled in and fresh water was eventually restored to the lake.

A BACK PORCH FACING SAND DUNES AND OCEAN IS A GOOD SPOT TO DRY BEACH TOWELS AND SWIMSUITS AND TO ENJOY CASUAL BARBECUES WHERE EVERYONE LENDS A HAND IN THE PREPARATION.

A WHALE WEATHERVANE ON THE GARAGE OVERLOOKS THE DUNES AND THE OCEAN.

The Delaware Bay became a heavily traveled waterway though its shifting shoals required cautious navigation. Cape May sailors became skilled pilots and soon began steering regular trips between their town and Philadelphia or Wilmington. The Cape's bracing sea air and sparkling, sandy beaches—dotted with Cape May "diamonds" (clear quartz pebbles abraded by rock and sand)—lured those who were interested in a novel form of social diversion—sea bathing. At the beginning of the nineteenth century wealthy southern planters, Baltimore businessmen, and federal officials from the newly formed capital of Washington, D.C. brought their families to these shores to escape the muggy, often fever-

ridden—inland towns in the summertime. To accommodate them, entrepreneurs built hotels. One of the earliest was Congress Hall (dubbed Tommy's Folly), built by Thomas Hughes in 1812 and rebuilt in 1816, 1853, and again in 1879 after a disastrous fire that destroyed much of Cape May Town. On the original site can still be found the large, now interestingly down-at-heel, evocative 1879 Victorian hotel, complete with high ceilings, louvered doors, and oversized natural wicker furniture.

Regular steamships connected Philadelphia to Cape May early in the nineteenth century, and by the 1830s train service began. During the Civil War, Cape May Point was used as a

THE FRONT PARLOR AT
GRANDMAMA'S HOUSE IS
THE PERFECT PLACE TO
PLAY. A SIMPLE,
FLOWER-SPRIGGED
WALLPAPER, CRISPLY
PAINTED WHITE WICKER,
AND STRAW MATTING ON
THE FLOOR ARE THE
MAIN INGREDIENTS IN
THIS SUMMER VACATION
ROOM.

link in the Underground Railway that enabled escaping slaves to reach New Jersey from the South. Because New Jersey had been settled by many Quakers who believed that slave holding was not consistent with their principles, many slaves sought their freedom here.

By the 1840s, Cape May had become known as the "playground of presidents," because so many came to the growing resort. Henry Clay, Abraham Lincoln, Franklin Pierce, James Buchanan, Ulysses S Grant, and Chester A. Arthur all visited Cape May. President Benjamin Harrison established his summer White House at Congress Hall Hotel in 1890 and 1891, though he himself stayed in nearby Cape May Point.

This adjunct to Cape May is not only where the Grey Ghost rests, but also, according to an advertising brochure put out by the West Jersey Railroad Company, "not a suburb of the city, but an independent settlement, based on a system of specific and restrictive regulations designed to render it a religious resort of a higher rank than any attempted heretofore, and the signal success attending the movement . . . has demonstrated the wisdom and sagacity of its founders and fulfilled their most ardent expectations." The area was originated in 1875 by Philadelphians connected with religious groups who obtained a charter from the State of New Jersey and opened up a settlement on an until then wild track of ground beyond Cape May itself. The plan was laid out with avenues radiating from a common center, each road named after eminent divines, religious centers of learning or local surroundings. Much of the original plan exists to this day, including the religious overtones, although some streets are now inundated by the sea, and the name Sea Grove is no longer used.

After the turn of the century, another resort on the Jersey shore began to attract summer visitors instead. This was Atlantic City. The decline in Cape May's popularity, however, is one of the reasons for its charm today. Like a house whose owners have never had enough money for drastic modernizations, Cape May still retains much of the authentic flavor of its late Victorian heyday, and has thus remained architecturally unique as a seaside resort. In addition, the town is one of a handful of cities to be designated a national historic landmark, granted in the 1960s to a seventeen-block area. This makes Cape May a living museum of over 600 buildings, most of them dating from 1879, following the big fire, to around 1910.

The houses built, or rather rebuilt "in a flurry of reconstruction" after 1878, were in "random, eclectic styles so fancied by the newly rich yet unsophisticated American entrepreneurs, reflecting their carefree, almost fairy tale view of the world," according to Gordon Bishop. Another author, Robert Santelli, idealizing the flourishing days of Cape May in his guidebook, *The Jersey Shore*, writes:

> The Victorian Age was an age when fancy gingerbread lace adorned verandas with rocking chairs on them; when the rest of the house was painted in bright, bold colors; when flower gardens hugged white picket fences; when the soft, dreaming light of gas lamps lit up the streets each evening; when gracious ladies and gentlemen socialized in rooms filled with ornate furnishings, or strolled walkways and paths and talked of Admiral Dewey's Great White Fleet and Teddy Roosevelt and his daring charge up San Juan Hill. The Victorian Age seemed inundated with niceties and a delectable romanticism that's difficult to find these days, except, of course, in Cape May.

Though such an idyllic life might be somewhat exaggerated, the Blackburn house could fit such a description. Set apart from the bustle of Cape May Town, the area where it stands belonged to a colonial landowner called Johnathan Pyne, who deeded the land to John Stites around 1710. For a while it was known as Stites Beach. It is now an unspoiled and peaceful resort community full of unpretentious old and new houses and churches. Moved twice from its original site because of beach erosion, the house now stands on the site of the old Centennial Hotel, which burned down early in the twentieth century.

The house is one of the largest and best preserved cottages in the Cape May area. A house with its unusual configuration shows on an 1878 map, which leads historians to believe the

Blackburn House was originally the S.M. MckIntyre cottage at the site now under the sea. Blackburn, who later acquired the house and owned it for a great many years, had cannily purchased land in Philadelphia. This property was sought after by John Wanamaker for his new department store, but Blackburn held onto his lot until he was made an offer he couldn't refuse. The Wanamakers at the time were fashionable frequenters of Cape May also. Some of the money Blackburn made from this deal in Philadelphia bought his Cape May house. No one knows who the builder or architect was. Blackburn and his sister used the house until she died, then he sold it.

Right after the big hurricane in 1962, the house was bought by the Qualls family. Eventually this couple divorced, and as they had bought some property on one side of the house that had belonged to the Presbyterian church, when they split up, Mr. Qualls got the land, while Mrs. Qualls was granted the house. Unfortunately she did not have the money to keep the house up, for frequent, careful painting is required to preserve the woodwork from lashing winds and corrosive salt water. This is when the house fell into disrepair.

In 1984 the beautiful but ramshackle building was purchased by Pennsylvanian Floyd Ohliger. He is mainly responsible for the house's rebirth. He spent three years painstakingly restoring the Grey Ghost to its former glory. The woodwork was expertly repaired by Schramm & Hallman, who specialize in fine woodwork and restoration in Cape May, and the exterior was painted and the inside modernized where necessary. Ohliger was careful to see that the original seaside Victorian charm of the house was maintained. Much of the interior decoration was organized by the Cape May decorating business, The Victorian Look. This firm supplied curtains, wallpaper, accessories, and advice.

When Anne French Thorington, usually known as Mimi, heard the Grey Ghost was on the market, she was immediately interested. Her primary residence is a horse-breeding farm near Philadelphia. As a horse breeder, she spends stretches of time in Kentucky or Ireland, but as other members of her family have summer houses on the Cape, she felt

106

SLATTED SWING DOORS LEAD FROM THE FRONT HALL INTO THE EAT-IN KITCHEN (TOP RIGHT). THE CUPBOARDS IN THE KITCHEN WERE INSTALLED BY PENNSYLVANIA FIRM, RUTT CUSTOM KITCHENS. ON TOP ARE A COLLECTION OF ANTIQUE AMERICAN CANISTERS.

BETWEEN THE KITCHEN AND BACK PORCH IS A SCULLERY USED FOR STORAGE, AN EXTRA FREEZER, UTILITIES, AND AS A PLAYROOM FOR MIMI THORINGTON'S TWO WELSH CORGIS. AN AMPLE SINK IS USEFUL FOR ARRANGING FLOWERS, CLEANING VEGETABLES, OR STRIPPING FRESH CORN. THE STAIRCASE LEADS TO A SITTING ROOM AND PORCH UPSTAIRS (MIDDLE RIGHT).

LEADING OFF THE BACK PORCH IS A SIMPLE WOOD-LINED CHANGING ROOM AND SHOWER STALL WHERE GUESTS CAN WASH OFF THE SALT AND SAND AFTER A DAY AT THE BEACH (BOTTOM RIGHT).

UNPRETENTIOUS FURNITURE OF LIGHT OAK COMBINE WITH STRAW CARPETING, LACE CURTAINS, AND REPRODUCTION VICTORIAN-STYLE LIGHTING FIXTURES IN THE DINING ROOM (FAR RIGHT).

SEA BREEZES STIR THE LACE CURTAINS OF THE MASTER BEDROOM (RIGHT). THE VICTORIAN-STYLE LIGHTING FIXTURE WITH ITS FAN IS A REPRODUCTION, BUT THE LIGHT-OAK CHEST OF DRAWERS IS LATE-NINETEENTH-CENTURY AMERICAN. THE WALLPAPER CAME FROM THE VICTORIAN LOOK IN CAPE MAY. THE QUILT AND LAMPSHADE (FOUND AT A CORGI DOG SHOW) WERE ADDED BY MIMI THORINGTON.

AN OLD-FASHIONED BATHTUB FITS UNDER THE EAVES OF THE GUEST BATHROOM (FAR RIGHT). THE WALLPAPER (FROM THE VICTORIAN LOOK) HAS A NOSTALGIC FLAVOR TO GO WITH THE WOODEN TOWEL RACK, PAINTED FLOOR, AND WASHABLE COTTON RUG.

that this house, with its spectacular view of the ocean, would give her a wonderful place to go and relax during the summer months, and to entertain her children and grandchildren. In 1987 she bought the house, fully furnished and ready to be used. As she explains, not all of its interior decoration is exactly to her taste, but she has everything she needs and can gradually change anything as she feels fit. For instance, the pictures in the parlor are, she points out, *not* what she would have chosen, but they will fill the wall until the right thing comes along.

108

The two-and-a-half-story Carpenter Gothic-style house is built on a T-plan with a front parlor. Constructed on masonry piers, the clapboard exterior boasts gables with curved bargeboards and has pierced wood porches on two stories, embracing, on the bottom floor, most of the house's exterior.

The house is situated on a corner and surrounded by a neat fence. The two sides that face the road have a manicured garden—barely one year old—laid out by Mimi Thorington. To one side of the house is a garage and shed. Two other sides face the dunes and beyond is the ocean. On the porch are

FANCIFUL WICKER BEDS ARE TUCKED UNDER THE EAVES IN THIS GUEST BEDROOM. OUTSIDE IS A DECK OVERLOOKING THE STREET. SIMPLE COTTON BEDSPREADS, A COTTON RUG, AND A MIXTURE OF OLD AND NEW WICKER ARE THE INGREDIENTS OF THIS NAIVE BUT INVITING ROOM.

rocking chairs, but in this day and age, they have to be chained to the floor. On the more private porch to the side facing the dunes, there is a charcoal broiler, tables and benches, and a changing room with a shower for those coming in from the beach.

Inside, the well-polished floors are covered in casual straw matting. Most of the furniture is light oak, much of it made in the 1880s and 1890s, probably in Philadelphia, Baltimore, or New York. As Mimi Thorington contends, they're not quite antiques, but they are more than adequate for a summer home by the sea. She has added the odd quilt or lampshade, or changed some of the window valances, but the house is

much as she found it. This suits her, for she is herself still new to the house as it is to her. As the years go on the house will take on the patina of its owner.

On the ground floor off the entrance hall is a large front parlor, an ample dining room, a practical kitchen adequate for most casual meals, and a back scullery or mud-room with sink, freezer, closets, and washing facilities. A second, smaller staircase leads up to a sitting room with its own porch that overlooks the sea. This is an ideal place to sit and contemplate the view, or to move indoors and watch television. A small well-equipped bar with a sink and refrigerator makes it a good place to serve drinks in the evening. A master bedroom,

CARVED BARGEBOARDS, IN SEASIDE CARPENTER GOTHIC-STYLE ADORN THE GABLE SEEN FROM THE FENCED-IN DECK OUTSIDE A TOP FLOOR GUEST BEDROOM.

and a large bedroom ideal for Mimi Thorington's visiting family (including a handsome light-oak crib for the new grandchild), together with accompanying bathrooms, can be found on this floor. Reproduction Victorian ceiling fans keep the rooms cool in the summer months, as do natural ocean breezes. On the floor above are more smaller bedrooms with single beds and a bathroom with an inviting bathtub tucked cozily under the eaves for guests and family members.

The Grey Ghost looks out on a soothing view of ocean and quiet beaches. Even on the hottest days, cool sea breezes stir the lace curtains at the windows. Given its locale on the fragile shoreline, however, this may not be the last site for the Grey Ghost. Each year the land shrinks as the sea moves in. Many methods have been tried to prevent erosion—as Boyer and Cunningham write in *Cape May County Story*, such as "pilings, sandbags, snow fences, enormous boulders. Some have been partially successful, others have failed completely. Coastal residents have learned it is difficult to outwit the sea."

The present owner is happy with her Steamboat Gothic-style second home on the cape despite these forbodings. Having survived—and never looked better—for over a century, the Grey Ghost will no doubt make its presence felt wherever it goes.

111

The concept of second-home-living developed early in the South. Rich plantation owners frequently maintained a town house as well as "the big house" on the plantation. Because during the summer so many low-lying coastal towns were prey to the then-killer diseases of malaria and yellow fever, the "gentle folk" often headed for another refuge in the hills for health reasons. Many southerners still go to the mountains to elite enclaves like Blowing Rock, Flat Rock, Highland, or Roaring Gap, where the Old Guard still maintain traditional second homes.

The charms of sun and beach did not become generally popular until the twentieth century, when a "healthy" tan became fashionable. In the previous century a tan was considered suitable only for farm laborers, but by the 1920s, a tanned skin was the hallmark of those who could afford to get away for the "cruise" season in winter. And, if one couldn't afford the Riviera, one went to Florida. America's "Last Resort" is the charming but maverick town of Key West, where today, artists and writers and nonconformists from the North maintain their second homes. With little room here for grandiose houses or pompous behavior, the town with its diminutive gingerbread-carved Conch cottages possesses a raffish style all its own.

Though most women were happy to lounge around on the beach and show off their newly emancipated figures, many men craved something more sporty. Once Papa Hemingway had made deep-sea fishing stylish, this became the perfect masculine pastime. Alabamians and Mississippians discovered sleepy fishing villages on the Gulf Coast where they built their second houses; North and South Carolinians "roughed it" on the Outer Banks in fishing shacks.

THE EARLY SUN LIGHTS UP THE ATLANTIC OCEAN FROM THE PORCH.

116

Fishing Shack

A BEACH HOUSE IN NAG'S HEAD

t the height of summer, when dawn breaks before six in the morning, the red sun ascends, scattering pink sparkles in a path across the ocean. Pelicans flying from their roosts at Hatteras form V-shaped chorus lines and glide gracefully down to the waves, dipping their claws in the water, rise, and move on. A jogger with his dog passes by the foam's edge, silhouetted against the emerging light. At Robert and Betty Howisons' house in Nag's Head, day is beginning.

Nag's Head is around the midpoint of North Carolina's Outer Banks. This fragile arc of roughly 170 miles of sandy islands comprises many romantic-sounding communities such as Corolla, Duck, Kitty Hawk (where the Wright Brothers first launched their flying machines), Kill Devil Hills, Pea Island, Rodanthe, and the more remote wildlife areas of Hatteras Island, Ocracoke Island, and Cape Lookout. From there southward, the islands hug the shore all the way to Cape Fear, which is close to the South Carolina border.

Directly inland from Nag's Head is Roanoke Island, the site of the first English attempt to colonize America. In 1584, two English explorers commissioned by Sir Walter Raleigh anchored off the coast. Prompted by their enthusiastic description of the terrain, an expedition sailed from Plymouth the following year. On July 22,

SEEN FROM THE SAND DUNES WITH THEIR LEGALLY PROTECTED GRASSES, THE HOUSE REQUIRES CONSTANT REPLACEMENT OF SHINGLES, SHUTTERS, AND PORCH DUE TO THE HARSH SEA AIR. A ROW OF CONCH SHELLS COLLECTED OVER THE YEARS DECORATES THE TOP RAIL OF THE PORCH, WHILE A HAMMOCK LAZILY SWINGS (TOP LEFT).

TYPICAL IN THIS PART OF THE WORLD, SHUTTERS SWING OUT FROM THE WINDOW, PROVIDING SHADE IN THE MIDDLE OF THE DAY WITHOUT BLOCKING THE CROSS-BREEZES (MIDDLE LEFT).

UNDER THE SHADE OF A FLAG, A CASUAL LUNCH IS SERVED ON THE PORCH. THE TABLE IS FASHIONED FROM A WOOD CABLE-WIRE REEL THAT WAS WASHED UP ON THE BEACH (BOTTOM LEFT).

1587, another group of 120 men, again commissioned by Raleigh and led by John White, established a colony. White returned to England for supplies, but when he came back to Roanoke in 1590 the colony had disappeared—one of the unsolved mysteries of American history. This story is celebrated every summer on Roanoke Island with America's oldest outdoor drama, *The Lost Colony.* Raleigh's name is perpetuated by Raleigh Bay on the Outer Banks as well as by the town of Raleigh, capital of the state.

When first sighted by explorers, the Outer Banks were covered with trees to the water's edge, a refuge for birds and wildlife. Early settlers began to cut the trees to use for building and firewood, thus starting the erosion that the islands have suffered over the last few hundred years.

Stories abound that during the eighteenth and nineteenth centuries, sailing ships would be deliberately lured to the treacherous sandbanks. Supposedly Nag's Head acquired its name from lantern-bearing horses, or nags, being paraded along its shores at night to entice cargo-bearing ships. Once the vessels ran aground, salvagers or pirates moved in. The infamous pirate Blackbeard used Ocracoke farther south as a rendezvous point.

In the 1850s Nag's Head began to be used as a summer resort to escape from the mosquito-infested interior. The only access was by boat, landing on the sound side of what is now Old Nag's Head. The original small beach houses were described as bright white cabins against dark foliage still on the beaches. The first hotel was ordered to be burnt down to prevent its use by Yankees in the War Between the States, but was quickly replaced by a 200-room hotel, destroyed by fire in 1903. A hundred-foot dock accommodated the growing number of steamship vacationers.

By the 1880s the ocean side at Nag's Head began to acquire vacation houses. Betty and Robert Howison's house, the Winston-Wales cottage, was built in 1883, and it is one of the earliest houses still standing. In one pre-twentieth-century photograph of the house, a cow is tied to the corner post. Livestock was brought along for the summer as well as family servants, so that those in residence could be self-sufficient.

UNPAINTED ROCKING
CHAIRS LOOK OUT OVER
THE BEACH. AN ANTIQUE
IRONING BOARD SERVES
AS AN OUTDOOR TABLE.
EARTHENWARE POTS
FILLED WITH SAND
PROVIDE ASHTRAYS.

119

THE LIVING ROOM IS EQUIPPED—SECOND-HOMES STYLE—WITH CAST-OFF FAMILY FURNITURE (ABOVE). EASY-CARE, INEXPENSIVE FABRICS, ABLE TO WITHSTAND THE ONSLAUGHTS OF SAND, SALT AIR, AND ACTIVE CHILDREN, HAVE BEEN USED FOR UPHOLSTERY. BAMBOO, WICKER, OR JUST PLAIN OLD-FASHIONED DEPARTMENT STORE CHAIRS MINGLE WITH SHELL COLLECTIONS, PICTURES BY LOCAL ARTISTS, AND STORE-BOUGHT CURTAINS.

IN THE KITCHEN, A SALAD FOR LUNCH IS IN PREPARATION ON A LONG-OWNED TABLE (RIGHT). AN EARLY SEARS-ROEBUCK CHAIR THAT HAS SEEN BETTER DAYS SITS UNDER A SHELF HOLDING EVER-NECESSARY FLASHLIGHT AND BUG SPRAY. A LOCAL CALENDAR, AND KITCHEN TOWELS WITH HAND-CROCHETED HOLDERS FOUND AT A LOCAL CHURCH SALE HANG NEARBY. THE VINYL FLOOR IS IN IMITATION SEA-GRASS SQUARES.

Few people then countenanced the idea of bathing in the ocean, and sunbathing, at a time when a pure white skin was highly desirable, was out of the question. The Outer Banks had their year-round people who to this day speak an unusual version of archaic Cockney, a legacy of the original English settlers. According to Mason Peters in an article *"The Carolina Coast"* for *The Virginian-Pilot and Ledger-Star,*

these settlers, in colonial times were " 'The Bankers, a hardy mixture of Eastern shore Marylanders and Virginians who trickled down to what is now the Nag's Head area to farm and fish and mind their own business."

The Howisons' house is one of some twenty-five now occupying a half-mile stretch of private beach. Dubbed the "Unpainted Aristocracy" by Raleigh editor Jonathan Daniels,

A GUEST BEDROOM BOASTS A WASHBASIN HIDDEN BY A COLORFUL SCREEN. A TENNESSEE WILLIAMS-STYLE LIGHT HANGS OVERHEAD (RIGHT).

A NARROW PASSAGE LEADING FROM THE DINING ROOM SERVES AS A BAR. OILCLOTH COVERS THE SHELVES FULL OF THE NEAR-TO-REACH PLASTIC GLASSES THAT ARE SAFE TO USE BY THE BEACH. A FEW REAL GLASSES FOR THE GROWNUPS ARE ON THE TOP SHELVES. A TINY ENAMELED SINK IS USED FOR WATER. A HATCH OPENS ONTO THE KITCHEN (TOP RIGHT).

BEDROOM CLOSETS ARE IMPROVISED FROM PLYWOOD WITH THUMBTACKED CURTAINS (FAR TOP RIGHT).

A DOWNSTAIRS BATHROOM IS EXTEMPORIZED WITH A GALVANIZED WASHBASIN AND OUTDOOR FAUCETS. A WICKER MIRROR AND PLASTIC SOAP-DISH COMPLETE THE DÉCOR (BOTTOM RIGHT).

A SET OF GOLF CLUBS RESTS IN A SCREEN-DOORED PASSAGE THAT OVERLOOKS THE NEXT-DOOR NEIGHBOR (FAR BOTTOM RIGHT).

the cluster has been called "Drab Town" by others. The cottages still look much as they did when first built, though many have acquired additions, been frequently repaired, and moved further inland as the beach has worn away. Charlie-Martin Johnson, a septuagenarian of the Outer Banks, helped to build some of them. He recalls that in those days there wasn't another house between them and Virginia Beach.

Mason Peters goes on to credit a "bantam-sized Elizabeth City carpenter who more than anyone was responsible for the unique architectural style that now distinguishes the 'Unpainted Aristocracy.' The builder was John Samuel J. Twine who had no formal training in design but displayed a sure hand for form and function." He died in 1973 at age ninety-nine. Many of the old cottages are listed on the National Register of Historic Places, due to their one- and two-story architectural configuration, their attractively rough shingled texture, their weather-beaten coloring, and their functional details, all of which relate to the sea-swept landscape.

Twine was also responsible for building the present St. Andrew's Episcopal church, where Betty Howison's son is on the vestry. The timbers of the original church of St. Andrew's were moved in Civil War times by the Yankees to build a house for black people. The town was eventually awarded money—only $700—to build another church. Services meanwhile were held in the Howisons' house and she remembers the organ left from those days in the cottage.

Most of the Unpainted Aristocracy share certain architectural features. The sloping roofs that overhang extra-wide porches at the front, back, and often the sides give a skirtlike effect. Often the vertical balustrades of these porches are interrupted by built-in porch seats whose backs slope outward and overhang the edge of the porch. Many of the outer doors are shuttered. Most of the window shutters open in a single piece to be propped open from the bottom, providing both shade and cross-breezes.

All the houses are perched on wooden stilts so that the

BY EACH ENTRANCE, A PLASTIC BASIN IS PROVIDED TO WASH OFF SANDY FEET.

huge waves of the winter season can wash underneath without destroying the structures. It is interesting to note that during the Ash Wednesday gale of 1962, dozens of newer, supposedly "better" cottages were destroyed and vanished, but these old-timers stood firm.

Betty Howison was two months old when she was first brought to the Winston-Wales cottage. She has many childhood memories of coming to the house. The family would arrive from their home town of Edenton—a charming town full of early houses some ninety miles away on the Albemarle Sound. Most of the people who built their summer homes in

this part of Nag's Head came from North Carolina towns like Elizabeth City, Williamston, Hertford, Windsor, and Edenton, all in the Albemarle area. The children of these families would form friendships over the summer vacations and frequently intermarried.

The family came by steamer, docking at the more inhabited sound side of Nag's Head where there were stores. A two-wheel horse-drawn cart manned by one of the local grocers would drive the family to the house. In the mornings, Betty Howison recalls, the grocery store would send around the horse and cart to receive their grocery orders, which

would be delivered that afternoon. Local people brought fish, or a block of ice, so in those days, "one didn't have to leave the porch to shop." Eventually horses and buggies gave way to trucks with big balloon tires that could drive in the sand. The house had protective corner posts to prevent these trucks from slicing corners from the porch.

Robert Howison's family also came to Nag's Head in the twenties when they began to find their usual summer spot, Virginia Beach, getting too citified. The isolation and simplicity of Nag's Head then held great charm. It wasn't until the early 1930s that connecting roads and bridges were built,

bringing a large influx of summer people to Nag's Head. The Winston-Wales cottage was moved several times before taking up its present position—twice in two successive years before 1920, when the encroaching sea lapped at the front steps. The foundation of the original house is about a hundred yards out in the ocean. At times, storms and hurricanes have stripped off its porches. Though most of it was built by Betty Howison's grandfather, the nucleus started as a fisherman's one-room shack. Built of cedar like most of these cottages, present-day replacements—porches, window and door frames that warp and stick—are often of compressed

125

ON ONE SIDE OF THE BUILDING AN OUTDOOR SINK IS USED FOR CLEANING FISH (ABOVE). HERE IS A SELECTION OF LOCALLY
CAUGHT FLOUNDER, SPANISH MACKEREL, CLAMS, AND TWO BLUE "JIMMY" (MALE) CRABS.

THE SIDE ENTRANCE BY THE OUTDOOR SINK IS SUPPLIED WITH A LINE FOR DRYING SWIMSUITS. A FISHING ROD, BUCKET FOR FISH,
AND WHITE HOLDER FOR THE FISHING ROD IN THE SAND IS HANDY BY THE STEPS (RIGHT).

wood, which is less affected by the harsh sea spray and sand. Heavy-duty maintenance is all on the exterior. Furnished unpretentiously as a place to relax and kick off shoes, the interior is low-key and housekeeping nowadays minimal. The main part of the interior is still much as it was in 1883, though rooms have been added as the family grew. The two servants' rooms are now used by visiting family and as storage. Though personal, none of the furniture is precious. Details are improvised: a door handle is concocted from a piece of ship's rope held by nails, or the pull string for a bare light bulb ends with a shell. The house can sleep eleven. Closets in the bedrooms are mere racks hidden by tacked-up curtains. Bathrooms have been added but these are practical, summer-camp style, and hardly luxurious. The kitchen has been up-

dated recently with natural wood, white-knobbed cupboards, and a new dishwasher.

Things that *are* precious include fishing, wildlife, and long walks along the dunes. Delightful lighthouses, painted plain, vertically, or diagonally striped, dot the islands. But much of modern man's contribution to the Outer Banks has been neither so decorative nor so benign. Fines now have to be imposed for disturbing the scant sea grass along the beach. Over the last few decades, Nag's Head's natural beauty has unfortunately been prey to cluttered development, shopping malls, motels, restaurants, and asphalt parking lots that cause destructive runoffs in the winter months. However, the lure of Nag's Head remains. The Howison children, who spent their summers here, now live with their families in the area.

126

FROM THE QUAY CAN BE SEEN THE SLOPING ROOF OF THE HOUSE AND THE ANGLE OF THE MASTER
BEDROOM BALCONY. BECAUSE THE HOUSE IS RAISED HIGH FROM THE WATER, THE EVER-PRESENT THREAT
OF HURRICANE DAMAGE IS LESSENED.

———

Seventies Style

A GULF COAST FAMILY HAVEN

The westernmost section of Florida's Gulf Coast is dominated by three main themes: hurricanes, naval air bases, and fishing. Periodically—usually several times in a century—Mother Nature shows who is boss by striking the coast with vehemence. The need to find shelter in protective bays, inlets, and harbors is evident and the geographical mainspring for most of this region's communities. Pensacola, the largest town in the area, was settled originally by Europeans because of its natural harbor protected by the long arm of Santa Rosa Island. Though the town was once dubbed "The Mother-in-law for the U.S. Navy," it is more accurately "The Cradle of Naval Aviation." Its surroundings reflect the presence of the Pensacola Naval Air Station, manifested by neat roads, installations surrounded by well-maintained landscaping, and the buzz of airplanes.

The McMillan family have built their getaway house in the small town of Destin on an extension of Pensacola's sheltering Santa Rosa Island. Buildings far more haphazard than the military complexes line the highway leading to Destin. These range from massive developer condos to mom-and-pop T-shirt stands and honky-tonk "museums" decked out to attract the growing tourist business.

Pensacola was at one time the old colonial capital of West Florida. The bay was

SET BEHIND HIGH HEDGES, THE FRONT DRIVE MADE OF CRUSHED OYSTER SHELLS LEADS TO THE MAIN ENTRANCE. FROM HERE CAN BE SEEN ARCHITECT HEFFERNAN'S DESIGN USING JUXTAPOSED TRIANGLES, CIRCLES, AND SQUARES, CONTRASTING GRAINS OF CEDAR WOOD, AND STRUTS OF WHITE METAL TUBES.

shaped by glaciers that receded as the last great ice age ended and the North American continent developed. Its idyllic white sand beaches are formed of clear silica. Pensacola Indians inhabited the area when the first Spanish explorers probed the Gulf coastline. According to local lore, in his quest for the fountain of youth, Juan Ponce de Leon (about 1460–1521) is credited with the discovery of what he christened *La Florida* because of its abundant vegetation. Three years after his discovery, two other explorers, the Miruelos, an uncle and his nephew, scouted the Gulf coastline. In 1528 a further exploration led by Panfilo de Narvaez landed near Tampa Bay and penetrated as far as Tallahassee. In an attempt to find Mex-

ico, his by now starving band of explorers built boats of logs and sailed along the Gulf Coast. Two of their party, a Greek named Teodoro and a friendly Indian (or he may have been a Negro), went ashore for water and provisions, then disappeared. Years later, a dagger belonging to Teodoro was found near Pensacola. A more complex expedition took place in 1539 when Hernando de Soto landed near Tampa and marched north. One of his parties, led by Diego Maldonado, explored the Pensacola area and described the magnificent bay, then called Ochuse. Because Spain's increasing number of treasure ships were harassed by pirates or sunk by disastrous weather, a haven became essential. As Ochuse was the

THE ARCHITECTURAL PLAY OF TRIANGLES AGAINST SQUARES CAN BE SEEN FROM THE BACK OF THE HOUSE WHERE THE POOL NESTLES BETWEEN THE MCMILLANS' HOUSE AND THE HOUSE NEXT DOOR THAT BELONGS TO ROBERT MCMILLAN'S SISTER. WHITE PLASTIC-COATED LOUNGING CHAIRS AND STOOLS ARE PROVIDED FOR FAMILY MEMBERS AND THEIR GUESTS, AND A STRING HAMMOCK SWINGS IN THE ZEPHYROUS WIND.

best port in the Indies, an ambitious settlement was attempted in 1559 under Tristan de Luna. This time Spain attempted a colony rather than exploration and conversion of the heathen, but it failed. The fine harbor was ignored by Europeans for 125 years.

As Spain, France, and England jockeyed for position in Florida, each tried to dominate the Gulf Coast. Finally Andrew Jackson won it for the Americans in 1822, and he became governor. He lived with his wife, Rachel, in Pensacola. Annual meetings were held either at St. Augustine or Pensacola until it became more practical to choose a place between the two. Tallahassee was chosen as Florida's capital,

and Pensacola became the site of the naval, and later naval aviation establishment.

Destin, less than an hour's drive from the heart of Pensacola, is called "The Luckiest Fishing in the World." Until recently Destin was a sleepy fishing village, and a rustic sign proclaiming this sobriquet graced the bridge leading to the sandbar facing the Gulf. Habitués would gather on the docks at the end of the day and compare catches. Everyone knew everyone else and it was all very relaxed. Since the 1970s this has changed. The sign now, as one old-timer said, is "practically in neon!" Fishing has always been Destin's main attraction. With the development of refrigerated railroad cars in

131

CONSTRUCTED OF CEDAR, THE CENTER OF THE BREEZEWAY BECOMES A SMALL COURTYARD OPEN TO THE SKY (ABOVE). SITTING ON A BED OF STONES, TERRA-COTTA POTS HOLD PALMS. TERRA-COTTA TILES FROM MEXICO FORM THE REST OF THE FLOORS. WEATHERED NATURAL WICKER AND WOODEN LOUNGING CHAIRS MAKE IT A COMFORTABLE PRIVATE PLACE TO PAUSE FOR A DRINK OR A QUIET READ IN DAYLIGHT WITHOUT TOO MUCH OF THE HARSH FLORIDIAN SUN'S EXPOSURE.

AT THE ENTRANCE, FOOTWEAR FOR THE WHOLE FAMILY CAN BE ACQUIRED OR DISCARDED IN HANDY SHOE RACKS. A WEATHER-WORN LOUNGING CHAIR ADDS TO THE RELAXED ATMOSPHERE (TOP RIGHT).

NATURAL CEDAR CHANGING ROOMS AND SHOWER ARE NESTLED BEHIND AN OUTDOOR BAR BESIDE THE POOL (BOTTOM RIGHT).

the nineteenth century, fishing became an important industry in the Pensacola area. Red snapper was the first and main fish to be shipped north, but others followed. Fishing boats were built with open wells that were filled with seawater to keep fresh-caught seafood from spoiling. The smacking sound of water in these wells is why these boats were called "fishing smacks."

With the twentieth century, the concept of resort life took hold. Wealthy town dwellers in the South (like the "rusticators" of the North) began to look around for places where they could live a simpler life. The Gulf Coast was untouched by the formality of Atlantic resorts like Palm Beach. Businessmen from growing inland towns in Florida and Alabama were drawn to Destin like New Yorkers to the Adirondacks.

Up until then, fishing had been a means of making a living. Now it became a sport. Charter boats of all sizes became available. At first small fish were sought, but with the popularization of Papa Hemingway's novels, deep water fishing became predominant. Grouper, barracuda, amberjack, muttonfish, tuna, bonito, dolphin, hammerhead shark, kingfish, tarpon, and sailfish (that can go eighty miles an hour) are all hunted, as well as smaller catches such as mackerel, squid, mullet, shrimp, snapper, and grunts.

Destin was still an unsophisticated spot, rattled every now and then by tremendous hurricanes that destroyed vulnerable houses. For several generations, the McMillans had driven for an hour and a half from Brewton in southern Alabama to Destin. The family had profited from Alabama's oil and timber industries in the earlier part of the century, and had since then expanded into real estate and ranching.

Robert McMillan's father had been a Destin habitué. Anticipating rising land values, he bought the town's hotel and some property overlooking Destin's natural inlet harbor where the fishing boats berthed. He was able to give each of his three sons and two daughters land or houses where they could come and ease up on weekends or long vacations.

These houses form a row on a high bluff that is as safe from hurricanes as anything can be in the area. Though contemporary in concept, they are all different in design. Robert

A THIRTY-FOOT-SQUARE LIVING ROOM (LEFT) WAS A PREREQUISITE FOR THE HOUSE—A PLACE WHERE THE FAMILY COULD GATHER, INCLUDING THE SISTERS AND BROTHERS FROM THE NEIGHBORING HOUSES. LOUVERED FRENCH WINDOWS LET IN COOL BREEZES OR SHIELD THE ROOM FROM TOO MUCH SUN. NATURAL WICKER FURNITURE HAS CUSHIONS OF BRIGHT WATERPROOFED COTTON FROM QUADRILLE SO THAT THE YOUNG CHILDREN CANNOT HARM THEM EVEN WHEN THEY ARE IN WET SWIMSUITS.

RATTAN CHAIRS FROM WILLOW AND REED, NEW YORK, WITH SEATS UPHOLSTERED IN PRACTICAL VINYL-COATED FABRIC, SURROUND A CIRCA 1878 PENNSYLVANIA SAW-BUILT TABLE OF BUTTERNUT AND PINE. MODERN FIXTURES THROW LIGHT ON THE TABLE, NOT ON THE GUESTS (ABOVE).

———

DESIGNED BY CANDY McMILLAN AND ARCHITECT ROBERT HEFFERNAN, THIS JUNGLE GYM OF BUNK BEDS CAN SLEEP THE TWO YOUNGEST BOYS AND UP TO FOUR OF THEIR GUESTS. SIMPLE FOAM MATTRESSES CAN BE COVERED WITH A VARIETY OF COVERS, AND THE COMPLEX USED FOR PLAY OR SLEEP. THE LARGE, ANGLED WINDOW CAN BE SHADED WITH LOUVERED BLINDS.

McMillan's was the last to be completed, having been built in the 1970s.

Robert McMillan met his wife, Candy, at the Brewton High School. As she describes it, "I was two years older than him, so of course I took *no* notice of him then!" After school their friendship blossomed enormously. They were married and produced a daughter, Brett. When Mr. McMillan senior presented them with the land for their Destin house, they knew there would soon be more children, so the house was designed with this in mind.

Its building was, in many ways, a first for everyone concerned. For the Robert McMillans it was their first Second

Home. To design it they turned to an in-law, Robert Heffernan, who had just been awarded his architectural degree. This was his first professional commission, though he has since gone on to carve out a successful practice in Pensacola. To decorate the house, Candy McMillan turned to one of her friends from Brewton, Richard Keith Langham, who was then studying interior design at the Fashion Institute of Technology in New York. He worked with her during his vacations, selecting colors, fabrics, paintwork, and furniture. Langham was talented enough to land a job with decorator Mark Hampton, and later became part of the Irvine & Fleming decorating team.

The house is hidden behind a high hedge and shaded by trees. All four houses share a common entrance with a driveway formed from crushed oyster shells. Architect Heffernan was given the brief of building the house around one large living room area where the family, including siblings and friends, would have space to gather comfortably. Heffernan was very taken with geometric shapes, squares, circles, and triangles. Flush with architectural school enthusiasm, he put all of these into his plans.

While the house was being constructed, the McMillans stayed in the local family-owned hotel so they could keep an eye on the proceedings. This made the transition easier on everyone—there are few things more agonizing than living on the site. This also enabled the family to have more input as they watched the house develop. For instance, when Bob McMillan saw the rising triangular shape of the roof, he thought it looked like a ship's sail. He was the one who suggested the motif be carried even further, and that the walkways be enhanced with canvas lashed by rope onto the railings. For this, a deep-blue plastic-proofed fabric was chosen, with white rope embellishment.

No proper southern house should be without its breezeway, so the house's entrance forms a corridor that runs through the structure with a glimpse of the sea beyond. The gate to this is a heavy metal grill designed by an artist using abstract shapes that suggest the sails of boats. This gate is seldom locked, though lockable doors branch off the breezeway. Forming a right angle is another corridor that leads into the dining and living room areas, and continues to the kitchens and the staff or guest wing. Halfway down the breezeway is a patio area that is open to the sky. To the right of the breezeway is a guest suite consisting of two bedrooms that share a spacious bathroom. Climbing stairs that turn, turret style, to the second floor, one reaches more bedrooms, including one designed for the two young boys, and a master bedroom with a secluded balcony that overlooks the inlet and ocean beyond.

The large living room can be divided into several areas. In one corner is a games table. In another two lounging chairs flank a side table, perfect for quiet reading. A wicker sofa and easy chairs provide a place for conversation. Children's toys are kept in an open basket, with plenty of space on the floor for play. All the furniture is cushioned in cotton with a vinyl finish so that no harm can come from wet swimsuits. Upholstery and slipcovers were made by Williams Upholstery in Fort Walton Beach, Florida, and the fabric was laminated by Custom Laminations in Paterson, New Jersey. French windows border two sides of the living room. One side leads directly to the pool area, and the other to a roofed-in loggia set about with potted flowers.

In keeping with the casual running of the house, the kitchen and dining room are divided only by a bar, enabling whoever is cooking to converse with family or guests. Many of the meals are eaten out of doors on a picnic table. The pool forms a link with the house next door, and is used by Robert's brothers, sisters, nephews, and nieces. To shield it from the front drive, a roofed-over bar, changing rooms, shower, and shed for the pool's filter works are constructed in the same wood—cedar—as the body of the house.

When the property was first acquired by Mr. McMillan senior, in the days when he would come to fish at Destin, there were no more than half-a-dozen houses on the sandbank opposite the inlet. In the intervening years, Destin has

BEYOND THE HARBOR INLET ARE DUNES AND THE GULF (ABOVE LEFT).

STEPS FROM THE HOUSE LEAD TO THE WOODEN BOARDWALK AND QUAY WHERE BOATS CAN BE MOORED IN THE PEACEFUL INLET (BOTTOM LEFT).

CONTEMPORARY WOODEN DAYBEDS FROM WICKER WORK, SAN FRANCISCO, HAVE MATTRESSES AND CUSHIONS COVERED IN WATERPROOFED COTTON, MAKING THEM FOOLPROOF FOR THE CHILDREN DURING THE DAY, AND COMFORTABLE FOR GROWNUPS TO RECLINE IN AND READ IN AT NIGHT (ABOVE).

———

A LARGE AWNINGED
PORCH AT THE BACK OF
THE HOUSE IS ONE OF
THE MOST POPULAR
SPOTS, WHETHER FOR
BREAKFAST, LUNCH, OR
EVENING DRINKS.
CANDY-STRIPED COTTON
COVERS CUSHIONS ON
THE WHITE-PAINTED
WOOD FURNITURE FROM
GROSFILLEX, READING,
PENNSYLVANIA, WHILE
POTTED PLANTS AND
SHELLS PROVIDE THE
ONLY OTHER
DECORATION NEEDED.
THE VIEW OF THE INLET
DOES THE REST
(RIGHT).

SUNSET AND PALM
TREES ARE A PERFECT
BACKGROUND FOR A
CASUAL OUTDOOR
SUPPER. A SANDCASTLE
DECORATES THE TABLE,
A SHELL HOLDS PAPER
NAPKINS FROM BLOWING
AWAY, AND BECAUSE OF
THE PROXIMITY OF THE
POOL AND THE
LIVELINESS OF THE
CHILDREN, DRINKS ARE
OFTEN SERVED IN
PLASTIC BEAKERS (FAR
RIGHT).

become a developer's dream, and an old-timer's dread. Now the buildings are almost edge to edge, the town is bustling, and during the latter part of his life, Robert's father and his friends seldom visited the place. The younger McMillans don't find the influx of so-called civilization a problem. Once they arrive at their house, they more or less stay put. When

they do leave the house, it is usually by boat, as most of the good restaurants and gathering spots are accessible by water. At the back of the house, steps lead down the bluff to their own dock, and the family shares boats used for fishing, sailing, or visiting. For the McMillans, Destin is indeed the perfect getaway.

THE PORCH IS PAINTED A DISTINCTIVE SHADE OF GREEN, SELECTED BY JACKSON, A COLOR THAT BLENDS
WELL WITH THE LOCAL VEGETATION. SHUTTERS ARE USEFUL IF HURRICANES STRIKE.

Conch House

A KEY WEST COTTAGE

Whether they drive across Overseas Highway, the causeway that links the many islands of the Florida Keys, or arrive by air, "snowbirds"—a local term for Northern escapees—are likely to be dazed by Key West's languid, tropical tempo. Here one is nearer to Cuba than Miami. Trees and hedges of exotic flora—bougainvillea, hibiscus, frangipani, and oleander—fringe the streets. At midday, dogs lie on shaded sidewalks. Cats, seeking shade, peek out from under cars. These are very Key Westish animals, linked to the Hemingway legend; his house swarms with supposed descendants of his cats. Parrots squawk remarks from perches at passers-by. At nightfall, music of all varieties pours out from the doors and windows of doll-sized houses that were once built for Cuban cigar makers. The locals are dubbed "conchs," pronounced "conks" (after the twisted mollusk shells found in the area). They, and vacationers, weave by on their bicycles, the tiny town's favorite means of transport.

Everything in Key West is called conch, including the native houses. One of the earliest conch cottages belongs to writer-artist David Jackson and is the winter haven of acclaimed American poet James Merrill. Jackson started life in the Black Hills of South Dakota where his grandfather ran the Homestate Gold Mine, and at

A ROOFED ARBOR PROVIDES THE MOST-USED EATING PLACE OF THE HOUSE. IN THE FAR CORNER CAN BE SEEN THE SWIMMING POOL WITH ITS REFLECTING MIRROR DRAPED IN SPANISH MOSS.

THE SWIMMING POOL IS SURROUNDED BY A BRICK TERRACE (RIGHT), A PRACTICAL MATERIAL SELECTED BECAUSE IT NEITHER BURNS THE FEET LIKE STONE, NOR GETS SLIPPERY WHEN WET. BETWEEN THE CRACKS CAN BE SEEN SOME OF THE MARBLES PRESENTED TO MERRILL BY HIS STUDENTS.

sixteen, Jackson was a prodigy concert pianist, a career he never seriously pursued. Merrill has won almost every literary prize around, including the Pulitzer, the National Book Award in poetry twice, the Bollingen Prize in poetry, and the Oscar Blumenthal Prize. While still a senior at Lawrenceville, Merrill wrote his first book of poems, which was published by his father, a founder of Merrill Lynch. He courted controversy later by using a Ouija board, with partner Jackson, in forming some of his finest epic poetry. Though James Merrill has an apartment in New York, his primary house is in Stonington, Connecticut. He and Jackson used to share a second home in Greece, but now they prefer Key West as the place to retreat and relax.

Billed as "The Last Resort," Key West sits at the southernmost tip of the United States, only ninety miles from

THE OLDEST PART OF THE HOUSE IS CENTERED ON A GENEROUS HALL PASSAGE. THE LOUVERED DOORS EMPHASIZE THE HALL'S FUNCTION AS A BREEZEWAY. A TINFOIL BIRD DECORATION HANGS FROM A LIGHTING FIXTURE, AND CHINESE SANDALS STAND BY THE HALL SETTLE.

THE LIVING ROOM (ABOVE LEFT) HAS SIMPLE MOUNTAIN-ASH WALLS AND CEILING STAINED WALNUT AND WAXED. FRENCH WINDOWS LOOK OUT ONTO THE GARDEN. WICKER FURNITURE WITH ITS COTTON-COVERED CUSHIONS WAS BOUGHT IN KEY WEST. THE PICTURE ABOVE THE SOFA IS FROM A LARGE PAINTING IN MUNICH BY GERMAN ARTIST ARNOLD BOECKLIN. THIS REPRODUCTION—A PERIOD LITHOGRAPH OF THE ORIGINAL—WAS BOUGHT AT AUCTION IN GREECE. A SIDE TABLE TO THE RIGHT IS COVERED WITH CONTEMPORARY CHINESE TRINKETS BROUGHT FROM BEIJING BY A FRIEND WHO DECADES EARLIER HAD KNOWN MAO TSE-TUNG. THE GILT BALLROOM CHAIR CAME BY ROUNDABOUT MEANS FROM THE ROYAL PALACE IN ATHENS.

A WICKER TABLE TOP HOLDS A MELANGE OF SHELLS, MINERALS, MARBLES, KALEIDOSCOPES AND OTHER ACCUMULATED OBJECTS (ABOVE RIGHT).

silks and lace, wine, and precious jewels were auctioned, drawing buyers from Havana, Mobile, Charleston, and New York. In the 1830s, Key West became a boom town, the largest city in Florida, and for a while, the wealthiest city per capita in the United States.

In 1852 the first lighthouse was erected at Carysfort Reef. Others followed, creating a chain of lighthouses along the reefs. That, and the growing use of steamships instead of sailing vessels, finished wrecking as a lucrative profession.

Meanwhile another moneymaking business started due to trouble in Cuba. Throughout the nineteenth century Cuba had been struggling for freedom from oppressive Spanish rule. Trade tariffs, revolutions, and brutal assassinations

brought many Cubans to Key West. The Cubans brought their old-world culture and the skill of cigar making. The town of Key West expanded as rows of cottages were built to accommodate these cigar makers. The cigar trade continued in the present century, but declined in the twenties. Once more the town dwindled into a poor fishing town—and the ideal place for individualistic artists and writers.

The Jackson-Merrill house is described by Lynn Mitsuko Kaufelt in her delightful *Key West Writers and Their Houses* as one of about ninety so-called island houses, supposedly built in the Bahamas, dismantled, brought over on barges, and reconstructed in Key West. It is difficult to trace the accuracy of this, or the quoted 1840 date. Historian Thomas L. Ham-

A BASIC, PRACTICAL KITCHEN SHARES SPACE IN THE LIVING ROOM AREA BUT IS SEPARATED BY A WALL CONTAINING SHELVES. HERE POET JAMES MERRILL INDULGES IN COOKING, ONE OF WHAT HE CALLS HIS "MANUAL THERAPIES."

bright, Director of the Key West History Department, suggests that as the street was not settled until the last third of the nineteenth century, the house may be of later date. Its street was named after Elizabeth Rodman Rolch of New Bedford. She was the wife of Francis Rolch, who, as father-in-law to John Fleeming, helped to finance Fleeming's purchase of his quarter of the island. The house is built close to the highest part of the island, Solares Point, and is therefore fairly safe from devastating hurricanes that periodically wreak havoc on the zone.

150

The cottage sits behind a picket fence and a small, densely packed front garden. Neat brick pathways and gravel walks help keep the lush vegetation at bay. The house has a tin roof typical of Key West, and a decorative front gable. Fancy gingerbread woodwork on the porch was added towards the end of the nineteenth century. Like most Key West houses, it stands on pilings made of rocks, a precaution against flood damage, and a deterrent to earth-crawling termites: "a crop of shanties built on blocks,/On air, on edge for, any day,/ Water and wind to sweep them clean away"—to quote James

A TABLESCAPE OF
OBJECTS—SACRED AND
PROFANE—INCLUDES A
PYRAMID AND PART OF
AN ICON. A PAINTING BY
ROBERT ARNER,
CHINESE FIGURINES, A
TANAGRA FIGURE, AND A
FAVORITE CHRISTMAS
CARD PAINTED BY ELSA
GETZ PERCHED ATOP
THE LAMPSHADE ARE
OTHER COMPATIBLE
INGREDIENTS IN THIS
CORNER OF THE LIVING
ROOM.

Merrill in *Clearing The Title*, a poem he wrote about purchasing the house.

Inside, the plan is based on a central corridor that can be used, Southern style, as a breezeway. The front door has optional louvered doors to facilitate this. However, at a later date, probably in the thirties or forties, an addition was built onto the house at the back, adding a living room and kitchen area. When Jackson bought the house in 1979, plans were made to pierce the back of the house with a series of French doors. He discovered that under the wall-to-wall carpets of the previous owner the floorboards were so riddled with termites that the whole of the back addition had to be rebuilt from the floor up.

The front and oldest part of the house was built of hard, termite-resistant wood. Once believed to be Bahamian mahogany, it is, according to Hambright, more likely to be of Dade County pine from the mainland of Florida, a wood no longer available. In some buildings this wood has become so hard over the years that renovators have to use screws rather than nails when making alterations. Due to saturation by salt

151

air, it has been found to be fireproof. The only time termites take a bite is when repairs include the use of newer wood.

Though the house looks diminutive from the road, amply sized rooms (those nearest the street would have probably been used as parlors) sprout from the central hallway. On one side now is a large bedroom, study, and bathroom used by Jackson, the more permanent occupant. On the other is a guest bedroom (with a tiny bathroom cunningly converted from a closet), and Merrill's suite. His study is divided from the bedroom by a large bookcase.

The hall ends in a large living room. About a third of the living room is taken up by kitchen space, partly separated by a wall that contains shelves on the kitchen side. French windows on two sides of the living room look out onto the back garden. One French window leads off the kitchen to a roofed-in arbor used as a setting for most meals. This arbor is shielded from the next-door neighbor's garden by a heavy canvas curtain. Though the curtain was once painted with trompe l'oeil jungle vegetation by Jackson, the Key West climate cracked the paint so the curtain is now unadorned.

IN THE HALLWAY (NEAR RIGHT), TWO OPEN DOORS CATCH THE MORNING LIGHT.

A KEY WEST RITUAL IS TO WATCH THE SUNSET (RIGHT). HERE, ON THE SOUTH SIDE OF THE ISLAND, THE SUN CAN BE SEEN SETTING BEHIND COAST GUARD INSTALLATIONS.

More sleight of hand and eye has gone into the pocket-handkerchief-sized garden at the back. A swimming pool takes up most of the space, with barely room for a walkway around two of its sides. The owners were fortunate to glean advice from noted English garden designer, John Codrington. He was on his way back from a working trip to Australia, breaking his return with a week of leisure in Key West. He had traveled, by bus, in indefatigable English style, all across America, at the age of ninety-two—and nearly exhausted his friends with his energetic partying during his visit. While there, Codrington suggested schemes for planting the garden. He even painted a charming watercolor, now hanging above the piano, which has a device loved by landscape designers; by pulling a cord one can change the shape of the boscage, rather like moving the wings of a toy theater. The idea of setting a large reflecting glass catty-cornered at the far corner of the pool resulted from his counsel. This gives the impression of water stretching beyond the boundaries of the garden. Brick terraces border the pool. The observant visitor might catch sight of an odd glass marble or two caught between the bricks. This is an intended reference to a literary anecdote

about Lady Diana Cooper who, when memory failed her, would flash her charming smile and say, "Another marble gone." The marbles were a witty gift to Merrill, who captured this anecdote in one of his poems, from his students.

Furnishings throughout the house are gleaned from travels or previous domiciles, picked up by chance, or given by friends. These run the gamut from erudite to kitsch, which is a fair echo of Key West's attitude. It is a town that has attracted writers for many years, big guns like Hemingway, Tennessee Williams, John Dos Passos, and Robert Frost, as well as many prominent contemporary writers. Richard Wilbur, Poet Laureate for 1988, and his wife Charlee live only half-a-block away in a compound that includes houses owned by John Hersey and Ralph Ellison. What lures them to this town is not merely the tropical climate but also the human scale of the town and its houses, the support of congenial fellow artists if needed, the freedom to be unconventional in this most accepting of American towns, the legacy of adventure, and the possible chance of discovering one's own place in, as Merrill describes the Key West sunset ritual, the "immense pink spotlight and the scene."

The Central States

A CLOSEUP OF ONE OF NANCY WILLIAMS' NEEDLEPOINTED CHAIRS SHOWS THE CUDAHY HOUSE,
SURROUNDED BY A DECORATIVE BORDER OF OAK LEAVES AND ACORNS.

Summer-style Queen Anne

A HOUSE ON MACKINAC ISLAND

The clip-clop of horses' hooves and the whir of bicycles are the distinctive street noises of Mackinac (pronounced "mackinaw") Island. History has it that in 1896, a car—then a toy for the rich—was brought from the mainland and driven along Main Street. The noisy vehicle scared the horses so badly they bolted. The hackmen got together and petitioned the council, where a resolution was passed banning automobiles. Ever since then, ambulances and fire trucks have been the only motors permanently allowed on the island; even the police give chase on bikes!

Mackinac Island's reputation as a summer place goes back to the time of the Chippewa and Ottawa Indians. They would come to the island—which they called *Michilimackinac*, or "Big Turtle"—in the summer, set up their lodges on the shore, and fish for sturgeon, trout, and whitefish in the Strait that joined the Great Lakes of Huron and Michigan. In winter the Indians returned to the mainland where they found more abundant hunting and crops.

When French explorers and Catholic missionaries arrived in the 1660s, they brought the fur-trade industry. Fort Michilimackinac was built on the south side of the Strait near what is now known as Mackinaw City. The stockaded fort became a rendezvous point for fur trappers. The fort was moved by the British at the time of

161

A SERIES OF THIRTY BALUSTRADED STEPS LEAD TO THE FRONT ENTRANCE. THE LOWER STEPS ARE CONCRETE, BUT THE UPPER WOODED ONES HAVE BEEN COVERED WITH HARD-WEARING PRUSSIAN BLUE CARPETING (ABOVE LEFT).

A VIEW FROM THE CORNER OF THE PORCH SHOWS THE HORSE-DRAWN CARRIAGES THAT CLIMB THE ROAD, AND FERRIES THAT PLY THE LAKE (ABOVE RIGHT).

A TYPICAL EXAMPLE OF THE GRANDER TYPE OF SUMMER COTTAGE ON THE WEST BLUFF OF MACKINAC ISLAND, THIS HOUSE WAS BUILT IN 1888. ITS SOUTH FACADE, FACING THE LAKE, IS SET ON A FIELDSTONE BASE THAT SUPPORTS THE HOUSE BUILT WITH A VARIETY OF WOOD PATTERNS—DIAGONAL, HORIZONTAL, FISHSCALE, TRELLIS, SHINGLE ROOF, AND BALUSTRADES (RIGHT).

the American Revolution to the more defensible locale of Mackinac Island, where it is now a tourist attraction.

Summer people had always used the island, but it wasn't until just after the Civil War that tourism really began to thrive. Like most of America, families in the Midwest wanted to escape city life in summer, first because of the havoc caused by the Civil War, and secondly because of growing urban industrialization. A private cottage community was built on Mackinac in an area called "The Annex," but by 1875 the United States government decided to reserve part of the Island as Mackinac National Park, a preservation move to make the beauties of nature available for all the people.

Within this plan they made provision for two more cottage communities— the West Bluff and the East Bluff. Construction of dwellings on these sites began in 1885, and by 1895 all the choice lots were taken. In 1895 the park was transferred to the state of Michigan, and the land is now leased from the state. Strict rules apply about the use of the land, including a fifty dollar fine for picking a wildflower.

Wealthy families began to gather on Mackinac for the summer, bringing their entourages of servants. A new surge came with the building of the Grand Rapids and Indiana Railroad, which pushed its line north up to Mackinaw City in 1881. Further impetus came from the construction of the

GOVERNOR WILLIAMS' WIFE NANCY, A HIGHLY REGARDED NEEDLEPOINTER, DESIGNED AND EMBROIDERED THIS FIRESIDE BENCH. IT DEPICTS VARIETIES OF HORSE-DRAWN VEHICLES USED ON MACKINAC ISLAND, INCLUDING FOUR CARRIAGES CURRENTLY IN THE CARRIAGE HOUSE AT THE BACK OF THE HOUSE.

TYPICAL OF THESE SECOND-GENERATION MACKINAC ISLAND SUMMER COTTAGES WAS THE "LIVING HALL," A LARGE, CENTRAL FAMILY ROOM LEADING OFF THE PORCH (LEFT). IT USUALLY SPANNED THE WIDTH OF THE HOUSE, HAD A STAIRCASE LEADING OFF IT TO THE BEDROOMS, AND A DINING ROOM TO THE OPPOSITE SIDE. A FIREPLACE WAS NECESSARY TO WARM CHILLY ISLAND EVENINGS. THE CARPET IS ORIGINAL TO THE HOUSE. THE FANCY PINE PANELING HAS BEEN FINISHED IN A SHINY TOFFEE-COLORED TONE. WALLS WERE ORIGINALLY CANVAS PAINTED DARK BLUE, BUT THEY SHOWED TOO MUCH WEAR AND TEAR, SO THEY WERE PLASTERED AND PAINTED A NEUTRAL PARCHMENT COLOR.

Grand Hotel in 1887, one of the most impressive resort hotels in America. Prosperous meat packers from Chicago—Armours, Swifts, and Cudahys—patronized the Grand Hotel, and eventually John, Michael, and Edward Cudahy all built houses on the island. John Cudahy's house, which cost the exorbitant amount of $5,000 in 1888, is one of the second-generation cottages on the West Bluff. These were much larger and grander than the modest first cottages of The Annex. Built in fashionable Queen Anne style, these cottages were designed by trained architects rather than in the vernacular contractor-built tradition. Neighboring houses were rebuilt in order to keep up with the new, affluent character of the West Bluff enclave, forming a row of magnificent residences overlooking the lake.

AT THIS STAIRWELL LEADING OFF THE LIVING HALL CAN BE SEEN THE METICULOUS PINE PANELING FASHIONED FOR THESE SUMMER COTTAGES (LEFT AND ABOVE LEFT).

DECORATIVE TONGUE-IN-GROOVE PINE PANELING WITH A HIGH-GLOSS FINISH IS IN EVIDENCE ALL THROUGH THE SECOND-FLOOR HALL AND BEDROOMS. HERE A SMALL SITTING—DRESSING ROOM AT ONE END OF A CORRIDOR SHOWS THE DIAGONAL AND VERTICAL CARPENTRY (ABOVE RIGHT). THIS ROOM, WAS ONCE AN OPEN CORRIDOR.

The John Cudahy house is mentioned in a book, *View from the Veranda,* by town historian Phil Porter. The cottage's official designation is "The Pines," but no one uses that name. On horse-carriage guided tours it used to be known as "Soapy William's house"—Soapy being the affectionate nickname given to Democratic Governor Gerhard Mennen Williams, scion of the family who started the Mennen toiletries company.

Now the house belongs to Richard and Linda Kughn. Tour guides point it out as belonging to the family that owns Lionel Trains—only one of many businesses owned by the Kughns. When the Kughns (who are Republicans) bought the house from the Williamses (who are Democrats), instead of letting politics get in the way, they agreed to negotiate as Episcopalians—both Richard Kughn and Governor Williams had lay positions in the Episcopal Church. As the Mennens knew the Kughns would restore the house sensitively, they were inclined to make the transaction easy. The whole deal—house including belongings—was consummated in a record fifteen minutes. The only point of contention was the seats of eight dining room chairs which had been designed and needlepointed by Governor Williams' wife, Nancy, depicting eight different Mackinac landmarks. Her husband suggested they be signed, framed, and brought back to the Detroit area, or donated to the governor's residence on Mackinac. Nancy Kughn felt they should remain in the very room for which

167

they had been designed, for their colors were picked out from the dining room carpet. The seats are there to this day.

The typical architectural scheme of these cottages—the John Cudahy house is a prime example—included a large front porch attached to a "living hall." During the summer, the amenities were moved onto the porch, including oriental carpets, potted ferns, silver, and good china, creating luxury in an informal semioutdoor setting. John Cudahy also owned a seventy-foot boat, the *Gerald C.* used for parties and informal gatherings. Like summer houses, boat decks would be lavishly decorated with wicker chairs and oriental rugs. In other parts of America, most Queen Anne houses were built for the containment of heat, but here on Mackinac Island they were constructed for the flow of fresh air. This Summer Queen Anne is particularly pleasing and suits the casual life of the island. It has a certain amount of interior finish—fancy carpentry in particular—but the living hall, located right in the center of the house, is a frequently-used family room, unlike the rather stiff, less utilized parlors of later more formal revival houses.

The Kughns learned that each owner after the Cudahys used the house for about a quarter of a century, and each family left its mark. A family from the Detroit area was responsible for adding a glassed-in room to the end of the

porch. After them, Commander McDonald, founder of the Zenith Corporation, summered in the house. Though it is not known for sure, he may have been the owner who installed indoor bathrooms, for the original house had none. Nancy Williams said that when they first arrived, she found a multitude of chamber pots. Because Mennen Williams had enjoyed summering in the governor's house on Mackinac, he and Nancy bought the Cudahy House during his last term as governor, and they came to the house regularly until they sold it

to the Kughns. Because the house was sold with its belongings, many of the furnishings date from before the twentieth century. In a series of William Gardner photographs taken around 1900, the very same tables, wicker porch chairs, huge living hall carpet, and many accessories in use today can be identified, including the Steinway and its stool! Though some pieces may not be in current taste, instead of throwing these things out for fashion's sake as happens in many summer homes, each owner has successfully incorporated

170

ON THE THIRD FLOOR THREE CHARMINGLY SIMPLE BEDROOMS HAVE BEEN PAINTED IN FONDANT COLORS. THIS BLUE BEDROOM (ABOVE RIGHT) LEADS TO THE WIDOW'S WALK. FURNITURE IS TYPICALLY SECOND HOME VARIETY—PAINTED TIN CABINETS, ODD CHAIRS, OR CAST-OFF CHESTS OF DRAWERS. THE PAINTING IS BY POPULAR TURN-OF-THE-CENTURY ARTIST MURIEL HUMPHRIES. SHE WAS THE MOTHER OF HUMPHREY BOGART, AND TRADITION HAS IT THAT THIS IS HIS PORTRAIT AS A VERY YOUNG CHILD.

the house's accumulated history without letting the house look in the least like a museum. The Kughns found themselves the owners of much bric-a-brac, from linens with the Williams monogram and signed books that were Christmas or birthday presents, to Meissen, Royal Dalton, and Haviland china and Tiffany, Waterford, and just plain carnival glasses. The inventory is still incomplete, and discovering new finds is always thrilling.

The Kughns' first brief was to jack up the house and install a proper concrete base to replace rotting wood. This in turn necessitated new plumbing and electric wiring. They were lucky to find hands-on local contractor Barry BeDour. Speeding about the island on his own pontoon aircraft, BeDour would sit at the table with Richard Kughn as they both solved engineering problems to enable the outside of the house to retain its distinctive flavor.

The kitchen area posed a complex problem. The original house was composed of two buildings—the house proper

171

172

THIS AREA WAS ORIGINALLY PART OF
THE OPEN PORCH (ABOVE). IT WAS
GLASSED IN BY THE SECOND OWNERS
OF THE HOUSE, WHO USED THEN-
FASHIONABLE FANCY STAINED GLASS
AND LEADED PANES. MANY OF THE
FURNISHINGS WERE HERE IN
GOVERNOR WILLIAMS' DAY BUT HAVE
BEEN REFINISHED OR RECOVERED BY
THE PRESENT OWNERS. THE
REPRODUCTION TIFFANY LAMP WAS
ADDED TO BLEND WITH THE BLUE
GLASS IN THE WINDOWS.

and a back cookhouse where wood-burning stoves were used. This was often the scheme with wood houses to prevent fires spreading. A previous owner had joined the two houses with a breezeway. This was later walled in to become a passage. The Kughns proposed to enlarge the passage and create a spacious kitchen, complete with extra storage, outlets, and counter space designed by Linda Kughn, together with a back living room, laundry area, office, and extra bed and bathrooms for a live-in, house-sitting family.

At the same time, it was decided that the house should be given adequate insulation and a forced-air heating and air-

FROM A QUEEN ANNE-STYLE, TURRETED WIDOW'S WALK CAN BE SEEN MACKINAW BRIDGE, THE LONGEST SUSPENSION BRIDGE IN THE WORLD.

conditioning system for year-round use. Winters are fierce in this part of Michigan and the lakes freeze over, so most houses are only used in the summer months. The Williamses had added supplementary heat in their time, but a fire and a good sweater was supposed to take care of the rest. As the house had been originally built with balloon-frame construction, the Kughns were able to blow insulation into the walls fairly easily. They also installed brand new Therma-paned made-to-measure windows following the exact dimensions of the originals.

In 1984, the year the Kughns took possession, the water system on the island was overhauled. Until then, it was

strictly a summer place with no water available on the bluff from November 1 until May 1. The Kughns opted for a deep tap water supply so that they can use the house to entertain at Thanksgiving or Christmas. Amazingly none of this work is visible from the road.

Apart from the kitchen area, most of the interior has remained much as it was a hundred years ago. Fabric has worn out and been replaced, and the look is less cluttered than the late Victorians decreed, but the woodwork is still in excellent shape. In the living hall, walls that were once covered in dust-catching somber blue canvas have been lightened with parchment-colored paint. Of the five bedrooms on the second floor,

174

THE FAVORITE PLACE IN THE HOUSE IS THIS FRONT PORCH, HIGH OVER THE ROAD. HERE IS A BREATHTAKING AND CONTINUALLY CHANGING VIEW OF EARTH, SKY, AND WATER. ALL THE ORIGINAL WICKER STILL IN USE IS FROM CUDAHY'S TIME.

two are master bedrooms, elaborately paneled in stained pine. One originally had an open sleeping porch, but this was enclosed to enlarge the space. The other three bedrooms are painted in lighter colors, each with a coordinating bathroom.

On the top floor three servant's rooms were painted in the Williams time in sugar-almond colors, and are now used for visiting family. Each bedroom has a desk, and each bureau gets a well-laundered embroidered runner from the plentifully supplied linen closets. The quilts are from the governor's mansion while the mattresses are of horsehair. A playroom with toys and a blackboard has been painted vivid fire-engine red.

On the exterior, the Queen Anne asymmetric turrets and roofs have been reshingled with cedar shakes and sealed with copper. Porches and railings have been repaired, and the fieldstone foundation refaced. The gardens have been landscaped with an irrigation system and planted with flowers by the house sitter to take the most advantage of northern Michigan's short but vigorous summers.

Like most of the West Bluff cottages, The Pines looks as fresh as when it was built. Most of these houses have been through major renovations, and their owners can now sit on their porches and relax watching the ever-changing, shimmering lake.

175

At one end of the living room two rustic daybeds with a pickled-green paint finish can accommodate extra guests if necessary. These are covered with an American Indian-inspired cotton print and scattered with chintz and needlepoint, or balsam-filled cushions. On the wall are Curtis photographs of Western Indians. The rag rug is made from scraps of the room's upholstery and cushion fabrics.

———

THE CRYSTAL CLEAR
STREAMS OF MONTANA
ARE IDEAL FOR TROUT
FISHING.

Log Cabin

A MONTANA FISHING RANCH

asterners arriving at Billings Airport find the Stetsons and cowboy boots worn by Montanans somewhat startling. However, as one drives westward, these clothes become more seemly, and by the time you reach the Crazy Mountains—a forty-mile ridge named because they were tipped upside down by the earth's movement many eons ago—western gear makes total sense. Leaving the highway for dirt roads bordered by wildflowers, hayfields, and grazing deer and bounded by majestic mountains carved by crystal streams with golden eagles circling in The Big Sky above, one drives over metal cattle guards, passes monolithic ranch gateways, and prepares for the first greeting of "Howdy, pardner!"

Montana is the third biggest, but most sparsely populated state in the union. The Heminway's getaway ranch lies between the state's two major types of terrain—the undulating Great Plains on the east and Rocky Mountains on the west. Montana's fauna includes moose, elk, black bear, grizzlies, mountain sheep and goats, coyotes, cougar, antelope, and, making a slow comeback, herds of buffalo. Ducks, geese, and grouse abound. But it is the trout fishing, commonly described as blue ribbon, the best in the West, that brings the Heminway family and their guests to this American arcadia.

FISHING RODS ARE READY FOR ACTION GROUPED ON THE OUTSIDE PORCH, WHICH IS SCREENED TO KEEP OUT FLYING INSECTS.

Before Europeans actually arrived in Montana, their presence had been felt. Indians from the East had been forced to move west in a kind of domino effect, tribe by tribe. Montana Indians included Shoshonis, Flatheads, Pend Oreille, Sioux, Crow, Kutenais, and the warlike, Algonquin-speaking Blackfeet. The Indians near the Heminway ranch were called the Absarokas (or Apsaroke), a branch of the Crow tribe who were of Siouan linguistic background—the "Bird People." They had become nomadic plainsmen by 1800 and roamed the Yellowstone region of upper Wyoming and lower Montana. Though frequently at war with their neighbors, particularly the Sioux, they remained at peace with the whites— mainly because they needed them as allies against their Indian enemies. They are commemorated in the Heminway house by one of a series of much-collected Curtis photographs of the Absaroka Indian, Medicine Crow.

With the discovery of America by Europeans, the hope was to find a "northwest passage" through to the coast. The lucrative fur trade in this part of the continent soon became

178

SET BY A TROUT STREAM IN A LUXURIANT VALLEY, THIS RANCH HOUSE WAS BUILT IN THE EARLY PART OF THE CENTURY. NEW JACKLEG FENCES (A PRACTICAL, STRADDLE-LEGGED TYPE OF BARRIER IDEAL FOR THIS ROCKY TERRAIN), ROOF SHINGLES, FRENCH WINDOWS AND SCREENED-IN PORCH HAVE GIVEN THE OLD LOG HOUSE A MODERN FACE-LIFT (RIGHT).

enticing. British, French, and Spanish, jockeying for footholds in America, vied for supremacy. The French in 1682 were the first to claim Montana as a portion of the Louisiana Territory, which included land west of the Mississippi Basin. However as France's vision of controlling the New World slipped away with the loss of San Domingo, by the beginning of the nineteenth century Napoleon felt safer disposing of the territory of Louisiana to the newly-constituted Americans rather than letting it fall into the hands of France's traditional enemy, the British. In 1803, with what turned out to be the real estate deal of the century—the Louisiana Purchase—Montana officially became part of America's holdings.

A year later Lewis and Clark set off on their famous expedition, reaching Great Falls, Montana by 1805. After having traversed some 8,500 miles of unknown Indian territory they returned to St. Louis in 1806.

For the next few decades, fur-trapping companies—the best known being John Jacob Astor's American Fur Company—established trading posts. Due to the change in fashion from beaver to silk hats, fur trapping declined, leaving a legacy of romantic memories.

The second half of the nineteenth century brought social and physical upheavals to Montana, mostly caused by man's greed. Gold, discovered in 1852, brought mining speculators.

181

This couple lived in the house during the 1930s. In gutting the outer shed now used as an office, the Heminways found one of the commander's calling cards. From Massachusetts, he worked as an amateur still photographer and used the office as his darkroom.

Though the stream always boasted some natural fish, which the Indians would catch, in the 1920s and 1930s, when the ranch became a place for sport more than survival, it was stocked with trout. To emphasize this aspect, when enclosing the compound with jacklegged fences, Hilary Heminway persuaded a local carpenter, Chuck Defandorf, to make a gate designed in the minimal form of a fish with a tail and fin. Nonfishers can head off on trails up the aspen, lodgepole pine, and cottonwood-covered mountains—but they have to take a bell devised especially to warn off bears.

Hilary Heminway was no stranger to Montana as her family owns another, larger ranch in the northern part of the state. She and her brother John acquired their Montana fish-ing ranch in 1984. As a decorator with a business in Connect-icut, she has skillfully fixed up the log house and its satellite cabins using a unique combination of western material and eastern taste. During the process she rooted out numerous talented local artisans, inspiring her to open a decorating practice in Montana—an idea that has overjoyed many of her friends and neighbors.

The welcoming tone of the house is immediately visible on the front porch, where painted wicker furniture softened with printed cotton pillows mingles with fishing tackle. The front door leads into the room used for dining, with banquette and a table in one corner. The table, fashioned from a solid piece of wood set on river driftwood, was worked out by the owner with artist and furniture maker Ken Siggans. The banquette is loaded with pillows, some made from tea towels with fishes woven into the design, and some, tubular in shape, made from the stuffed legs of blue jeans. Rare botanical prints of fishes have been framed and hung on the wall. Window cur-

185

CHAMOIS BUCKSKIN HELD ON ANTLERS FORM WINDOW CURTAINS IN THIS CORNER OF THE DINING ROOM (ABOVE). HOOKS HOLD HIKING POLES, FOUL-WEATHER GEAR, A WATER BAG THAT USED TO BE ISSUED TO DRIVERS ENTERING YELLOWSTONE PARK IN CASE THEIR CARS RAN OUT OF WATER, FISHING TACKLE, STRAW HATS AND A MOOSE HAT, AND A LONG-HANDLED FRYPAN. KITES ARE KEPT IN A WOODEN TUB. A CITRONELLA CANDLE BY THE FIREPLACE WARDS OFF INSECTS.

Bedrooms are found at either end of the house: the master bedroom to the left and two more bedrooms on the right. For additional accommodations, independent log cabins for guests are within the compound. These are equipped with their own bathrooms, kitchens, and log-burning stoves.

The one-time darkroom has been turned into a communications center, complete with modern electronic computer, fax machine, and video monitor. This equipment is amusingly juxtaposed against the log cabin wall, longhorn cattle horns, and burlap drapes.

The essence of the complex lies in its deceptively easy, casual style. A closer examination reveals that a lot of refinement has gone into the planning, collecting, and assembling of this unpretentious but imaginative home away from home.

189

The West

merica's Northwest is one of the fastest-growing areas of the country. The climate is generally temperate and the grass is almost always green. Northwestern town dwellers, though they tend to live a far more sporty, open-air life than easterners, still like to escape to remote places. An alluring group of islands, the San Juans, attracts ferryloads of Seattlites, as well as weekenders from Oregon. On these islands, where it almost never snows or becomes unbearably hot, ambitious young couples can build their weekend houses, and then use them year round while they tend their gardens, watch nature, or enjoy the sea.

San Francisco is packed with people. Some escape north to find a second home among the art colonies of Mendocino County. Others go south to the ranch-dotted mountains of Santa Barbara, mingling with the rich, famous, and ex-Presidential. The West Coast boasts incredibly variegated terrain within driving distance—beaches, islands, snow-topped mountains, inland lakes. According to their desires, city dwellers can head off in many different directions for their second homes.

For some the journey out of town takes no more than an hour. Malibu's beach is idyllic for those beautiful bodies seeking the perfect wave. Although beach houses practically sit right on top of each other, ingenious architects have built them with a semblance of privacy. The golden sand, the balmy weather, and the great Pacific Ocean provide a perfect summer place all year round.

OVERLOOKING THE STRAITS OF JUAN DE FUCA WITH THE OLYMPIC MOUNTAINS OUTLINED IN THE FAR
DISTANCE, THE PORCH IS A WONDERFUL PLACE TO SIT WITH BINOCULARS AND WATCH THE CIRCLING BIRDS.

BUILT IN THE NINETEENTH CENTURY AS A LIFE SAVING STATION ON NEAH BAY, THE HOUSE WAS FLOATED ON A BARGE TO ITS PRESENT LOCATION ON LOPEZ ISLAND IN THE 1960S. REMODELED IN THE 1980S THE SHINGLED EXTERIOR WILL EVENTUALLY ACHIEVE A MELLOW PATINA.

Converted Coast Guard

A REFUGE ON THE SAN JUAN ISLANDS

bout halfway between Seattle and Vancouver, a Washington State ferryboat carries passengers from the town of Anacortes to San Juan County, which consists of a group of islands called the San Juans. This cluster of islands lies between three bodies of water: the Strait of Georgia to the north, the Strait of Juan de Fuca in the southwest, and the Puget Sound to the southeast. The islands enjoy a surprisingly moderate climate because they lie in the rain shadow of the Olympics, a range of mountains pushed up by geological upheaval. Inland, to the east, are the Cascade Mountains, which are volcanic in origin. The San Juans draw vacationers and weekenders who seek relaxation, solitude, and unspoiled nature.

These islands are formed from the tips of sunken mountains that were once part of the continent that joined Vancouver Island to the mainland. Glacial drift scoured out fiordlike bays and channels from the old bedrock, and they are now covered for the most part with a thin layer of soil. At low tide over 700 islands have been seen, though only 175 warrant official names. Ten of these are state marine parks. The four main islands are Orcas, Lopez, San Juan, and Shaw.

Before Euro-Americans ever landed on the San Juans, Indians of the Salishan Nation used them. In *Know Your County: San Juan, Washington,* a book pub-

THE FRONT DOOR OF THE HOUSE LEADS INTO A PASSAGE WITH A COAT CLOSET, THE HALL STAIRS AREA, AND THE ORIGINAL LIVING ROOM SEEN HERE (LEFT). THE HORIZONTAL AND VERTICAL LINES LEADING UP THE STAIRS ARE PART OF THE REMODELING DONE IN THE 1960S. RUGS, FURNITURE, LAMPS, AND PICTURES WERE ALL FAMILY POSSESSIONS, INCLUDING THE GLASS-TOPPED TABLE THAT CONTAINS ANTIQUE WATCHES, SCRIMSHAW, JEWELRY, AND FAMILY PHOTOGRAPHS.

AN AMERICAN NINETEENTH-CENTURY SUITE OF BEDROOM FURNITURE THAT BELONGED TO GALE MCCALLUM'S GREAT-GRANDMOTHER SHARES THE MASTER BEDROOM WITH A CHEST OF DRAWERS THAT BELONGED TO HER HUSBAND'S GRANDMOTHER.

lished by the Orcas Island League of Women Voters in 1988, it says:

> In the summers (the Indians) would reef net salmon, gather clams and plants, hunt deer and other animals. In the Fall they would leave for winter villages, canoeing back to Bellingham Bay and Vancouver Island. The peace-loving Lummi remained and wintered here, living in cedar plank houses or long houses. Remnants of their settlements have been found at West Sound, Eastsound, Fisherman's Bay, Garrison Bay, and Stewart Island.

By the end of the eighteenth century, Europeans had started to explore the coastal areas of this northwestern territory. In 1792, separate expeditions of both Spaniard Captain Francisco Eliza and the representative of British King George III, George Vancouver, navigated and named bays, waterways, and islands in the region. Homesteaders, British and American, soon followed, settling in the islands. An out-

post of the Hudson Bay Company, which had a monopoly on the fur trade granted by the king, established an outpost on San Juan Island despite the American claim to the islands. In 1846 a treaty was signed by Britain and America establishing the forty-ninth parallel as the dividing line of ownership. This was described as "between the channel that separates the continent from Vancouver Island." As there are two channels, Haro and Rosario, with the San Juans between them, the wording was ambiguous. Both countries claimed the San Juans. The border dispute was aggravated by tax claims and counterclaims, and, when tensions ran at their highest, an American homesteader, Lyman Cutler, shot a pig belonging to the Hudson Bay Company. This act sparked The Pig War—fortunately a conflict with no bloodshed except that of the innocent pig. Eventually the matter was settled in 1872 by the newly-elected Emperor Wilhelm of Germany who decided, it is suspected with a politically biased opinion, that the San Juan Islands should belong to the United States.

A DETAIL IN THE DINING ROOM SHOWS A PICTURE BY CLEVELAND ROCKWELL, A MARINE SCIENTIST AND SURVEYOR WHO PAINTED LANDSCAPES (ABOVE LEFT). AN ENGLISH NINETEENTH-CENTURY PLATTER, A VICTORIAN DECANTER, AND THE FAMILY SILVER TEA SET ADORN THE SIDEBOARD.

AN ACCUMULATION OF FAMILY CHINA FILLS A CUPBOARD IN THE DINING ROOM (ABOVE RIGHT). A TOLE TRAY, ONCE USED BY THE OWNER'S GREAT-GRANDMOTHER FOR PARCHING CORN, NOW SITS ON A SIDE TABLE.

Washington had been established as an American territory in 1853. San Juan County, which included the whole group of islands, was formed in 1873, with Friday Harbor on San Juan as the county seat. The main islands have differing physical characteristics. Orcas is hilly with Mount Constitution rising to 2,409 feet; Lopez boasts a rolling, agricultural landscape; while San Juan, with the only incorporated city, combines qualities of town and country.

Lopez is the first stop on the Washington State ferry, a journey taking about three quarters of an hour. The island covers forty-seven square miles. The road from the dock at the northern tip to the McArdle Bay at the south is lined with fields, farmhouses, and trees—Douglas fir, grand fir, and shore pine. On a high bluff overlooking the Straits of Juan de Fuca, with the Olympics silhouetted on the distant mainland,

sits a newly shingled house belonging to retired surgeon Dr. Gene McCallum and his wife, Gale.

Their house actually started life on the mainland, at the mouth of the Straits. Some say the very first structure was built on Waahdah Island in 1877, and was moved later, but a smudged photograph is the only documentation of this. A later owner, JoAnna Anderson, believed the house was built in 1886 at Neah Bay. This is right near the tip of the mainland on the Pacific coast, close to Cape Flattery.

The house belonged to the commandant of the Life Saving Station, which later became known as the Coast Guard. A photograph taken in the late 1800s shows a lifeboat of gallant Life Savers, oars aloft, their mascot dog in the prow, and, in the background, the house situated next to the lighthouse. Neah Bay is an Indian reservation, belonging to the Macah

THE BLACK-WALNUT
DINING ROOM
FURNITURE CAME FROM
A GERMAN RELIGIOUS
SECT IN AMANA, IOWA.
THE CARPET IS
NINETEENTH-CENTURY
TURKISTAN. A BELOVED
BABY SITTER, BERTHA
PARADIS, CROCHETED
THE LACY TABLECLOTH.
CUT-GLASS
WINEGLASSES ARE
WATERFORD.

———

Indians who make distinctive, traditional baskets using whale and canoe motifs.

When the Coast Guard and Life Saving Station were rebuilt in the 1950s, the commandant's house was considered expendable. However, the structural engineer in charge, a colorful character named H.A. Anderson, could never resist a bargain. Instead of destroying the house, he had it barged down the Straits to Lopez Island, where it was dragged on skid logs to its present location. The entire moving bill came to a total of $875.

In the 1960s, around the time of Seattle's World's Fair, the house underwent some remodeling that made it more habit-

able but far less aesthetically pleasing to our current tastes. Aluminum siding (in three different shades!) replaced wood shingles, and metal frame windows opened up the view. When Gale McCallum first saw the house in 1971 from a boat in the bay, she was convinced it was far too ugly to consider purchasing.

Once inside, the charm of its history became seductive. The timbers were held in place with square-shaped hand-forged nails. The scale was perfect as a second house. The location—just far enough from Gene McCallum's practice in Oregon—was practical. As members of the Audubon Society, this couple found the view, patrolled by circling bald

BASKETS, KITCHEN
IMPLEMENTS, RECIPES,
AND CANNED GOODS FILL
THIS CORNER OF THE
PANTRY.

eagles, appealing. The bucolic simplicity of the island promised a restful contrast to their working life.

Lopez Island proved to be the ideal place, so much so that the McCallums bought more land in a different spot, anticipating building a larger house for their own retirement and enjoying frequent visits from grown children and a number of grandchildren. The ghosts of the past, however, exerted a lure. Their children persuaded them that nothing could beat the splendid view. Eventually they decided to stay in the commandant's house and undertake a thorough renovation.

The McCallums were lucky to be able to consult their son Tom, an architect with a practice in Seattle. He entered the project with enthusiasm, paying attention to their desires and giving cohesion to the project. Much of the work involved tidying up the exterior, removing siding and replacing it with wood shingles, realigning and replacing the metal-framed windows with wood frames, and using porch space to extend the original living room. But the major thrust of the job was adding an extended wing to include a large stove-warmed study with built-in bookcases, a downstairs master bedroom with bathroom, a utility room and workroom, back staircase, and storage rooms above. This wing extends beyond the present dining room, continuing the slope of the ceiling so that it is difficult to tell where the old ends and the new begins. As

201

IN A *RECHERCHE DE*
CHILDHOOD FANTASY,
ARCHITECT TOM
MCCALLUM USED A
CLOSET SPACE OFF THE
KITCHEN AS A HIDING
PLACE FOR THE DELIGHT
OF VISITING
GRANDCHILDREN—SEVEN
AT LAST COUNT. HERE
THEY CAN PLAY PRIVATELY
BUT SAFELY IN A SPACE
THAT A GROWNUP CAN
BARELY SQUEEZE INTO.

FAMILY HAND-EMBROIDERED LINENS HAVE BEEN CAREFULLY PRESERVED AND PAINSTAKINGLY LAUNDERED OVER THE AGES. THE ANTIQUE DOLL HAS A CHINA HEAD AND LEATHER HANDS AND FEET, AND IS CALLED RUTH. ALL HER CLOTHES ARE EXQUISITELY HANDMADE AND EMBROIDERED. HER NECKLACE IS CARVED IVORY AND WAS WORN BY GALE MCCALLUM AS A CHILD.

part of the renovations he moved the hundred-year-old windows, replacing them at the end of the new wing so that both ends of the house would be consistent.

Always one of the most crucial rooms in the house, the kitchen area required the toughest decisions. Gale McCallum knew she would need a pantry with plenty of shelves to hold homemade preserves from the fruits and vegetables they intended to grow as part of their "back to nature" life. She also knew she wanted a high shelf encircling the kitchen to display her collection of stoneware. If it was to be an open kitchen

where she could see guests while she was cooking, she also felt the need of some sort of barrier so that she could cook without feeling as if she were doing a demonstration. Tom addressed all these requirements and together they worked out solutions. The kitchen was completely revamped using dark-blue tiles for the counters, stainless steel for the sinks, and cabinet work fashioned by a skilled Lopez Island cabinet-maker, Greg Starkman. The raised surround to the counter space gave additional shelving and is more pleasant than having culinary chores in full view. An overhead rack holds a

COMPLETELY REMODELED, THE KITCHEN (LEFT) WAS THE MOST DIFFICULT PART OF THE HOUSE TO DESIGN. HIGH SHELVES WERE AN ESSENTIAL TO HOUSE THE OWNERS' COLLECTION OF STONEWARE, PLATTERS, AND CONTAINERS. TILE-COVERED COUNTER SPACE HELPS DELINEATE THE KITCHEN AREA WITHOUT CUTTING OFF COMMUNICATION. VEGETABLES BY THE SINK ARE HOMEGROWN, A TRIBUTE TO THE TEMPERATE CLIMATE, HAVING BEEN PICKED IN THE MIDDLE OF JANUARY.

gleaming set of polished copper pots and pans that dangle within easy reach.

As the plans for the kitchen progressed, a tiny space, no bigger than a coat closet, evolved. Tom, who has a young daughter and a feeling for youthful sensibilities, proposed making it into a hiding place for visiting children. Here they can play in controlled privacy and never be underfoot. It has become their favorite room.

The earliest part of the house included a living room. This has been extended by taking over part of the adjoining porch. A fireplace—its gaudy Seattle World's Fair tiles replaced with more subdued brickwork—holds an efficient wood-burning stove, supplied by the McCallum's own fir trees. This living room has become an old-fashioned American parlor, with its plush-covered sofa and needlepoint footstools. Almost all the furnishings have some age and came from some branch of the family. Lamps, with leanings towards art nouveau, an-

STILL BANKS OF CAST IRON, TIN PENNY BANKS, AND POTTERY PIGGY BANKS, ARE PART OF A COLLECTION
ACCUMULATED OVER THE YEARS.

tique memorabilia—an aunt's jewelry, a grandfather's watch —chairs remembered from great-grandmother's house, pictures that tell stories, such as a landscape given in lieu of money to a pharmacist great-grandfather, a piece of art by a sculptress daughter—all add ambience to the well-rooted family surroundings.

Navajo blankets decorate the walls by the staircase. The guest bedroom is filled with a wealth of hand-embroidered pillow slips, runners, and hand towels—all treasured family heirlooms. Silver repoussé hairbrushes and mirrors ornament the dressing tables. A prized collection of penny banks—still banks of pressed iron, tin banks, and pottery piggy banks— fill a corner cupboard. An antique doll dressed in hand-

embroidered clothes is another cherished family possession. A tiny but delightful upstairs bathroom is used primarily by the grandchildren, which means its tub is filled with toy ducks.

Because of the temperate climate—a bit like the British Isles where you get *weather* rather than a predictable climate—gardening has become an enjoyable and useful hobby. The kitchen garden provides vegetables all year long. Swings and a jungle gym find a place on the spongy, knolled and lichen-covered land surrounding the house. A garage-toolroom provides shelter for vehicles. Because the house is remote, a certain self-sufficiency is necessary. Gradually the McCallums are being absorbed into the Lopez community of both old-timers and newcomers.

THE BACK STAIRS
LEADING FROM A UTILITY
ROOM AND WORKROOM
UP TO ATTIC STORAGE
SPACE SPORTS A
MELANGE OF COLLECTED
PICTURES, MAPS,
ANTIQUE SHOE LASTS,
AND DIPLOMAS.

———

A PORCH ON THE GUEST HOUSE OVERLOOKS THE SAN RAFAEL MOUNTAINS. IT IS FURNISHED WITH WICKER
FURNITURE FROM THE OWNER'S GRANDMOTHER'S DAY.

California Casual

A SANTA BARBARA RANCH

Just north of the affluent town of Santa Barbara—known for its old world charm, fine beaches, distinguished Victorian houses, and Spanish-inspired buildings with red-tiled roofs—a steep road leads inland and high into the Santa Ynez mountains. This road meanders through the San Marcos Pass, a place of spectacular, chaparral-covered heights and dizzying drops. Beyond the summit, spectacular ranch lands spread as far as the eye can see, luring the rich and famous, horse breeders, Los Angeles celebrities, and even ex-presidents, all seeking some version of the bucolic life. One family, the Odells, have found, in the historic Rancho San Marcos, an idyllic second home.

Before Portuguese navigator Juan Cabrillo, sailing for Spain, passed through the Santa Barbara Channel in 1542, the region was peopled by various tribes of Indians with differing languages and cultures, all in fairly close proximity. According to Vivian Thompson in an article "Rancho San Marcos; Gateway to the Santa Ynez Valley" from the *Santa Ynez Valley News*, these Indians' common heritage was probably a mixture of Aztec and Shoshone. The local Chumash were a gentle and affectionate people, makers of intricate baskets and distinctive pottery. Those in the Channel were dubbed Canalinos. They were skillful sailors, navigating unique craft

A VINTAGE LEATHER SUITCASE USED BY ROBERT ODELL DURING THE DAYS OF TRAIN TRAVEL IS NOW FILLED WITH HIS GRANDSON'S POSSESSIONS: SHIRTS, TIES, GLOVES, FAMILY PHOTOGRAPHS—HIS FATHER ON A PAINT (TWO-COLOR) HORSE, HIS PARENTS AT THEIR PREVIOUS RANCH IN UKIAH—AND FIRST EDITION RAYMOND CHANDLER AND DASHIELL HAMMETT MURDER MYSTERIES.

THE LARGE BUT SIMPLY DECORATED LIVING ROOM (RIGHT) IN THE GUEST HOUSE IS WHERE BIBLIOPHILE JOSHUA ODELL KEEPS A PORTION OF HIS BOOK COLLECTION. OVER THE MANTEL IS A PAINTING OF FIGUROA MOUNTAIN, A LOCAL BEAUTY SPOT BY SANTA BARBARA ARTIST EDWARD HICKS. THE PAINTED-WOOD HEREFORD COW BY THE SOFA WAS FOUND IN SANTA BARBARA.

of lashed planks, or in quieter waters, balsas—rafts made of tule rushes found in the Southwest. Sometimes their boats were huge woven baskets, or canoes hollowed out of logs.

Cabrillo had been sent to probe the western side of California in the hope of finding rich land and a connecting passage to the Atlantic. Though unsuccessful in the latter, his two vessels, *San Salvador* and *La Victoria,* found haven in the Santa Barbara Islands. Cabrillo broke his arm disembarking from a boat in 1543 and died from the injury. He lies on San Miguel Island in an undiscovered grave.

On Saint Barbara's Day, December 4, 1603, Sebastian Vizcano entered the Channel and named the region Santa Barbara. Spain set up a *presidio,* or outpost, around which grew the town of Santa Barbara.

A chain of twenty-one missions was established up the coast. Indians were recruited as workers, and attempts were made to convert them to Catholicism. A mission was founded in Santa Barbara in 1786—the only one of California's missions never abandoned by the Franciscans. The Mission of

210

Santa Ines over the mountains in the Santa Ynez Valley was established a few years later. Because the journey between the two missions was arduous, a way station or *asistencia* was established in 1804, some eight leagues (one league equals about 4,400 acres) from Santa Barbara. This place of sojourn was named San Marcos after a mission priest, Father Marcos Amestoy. The *asistencia* offered board and meals, a small chapel, farm animals, a granary, and a threshing corral. Padres in charge irrigated the land, and traces of a flume—an artificial channel—that diverted water from Hot Spring Canyon, is still visible. It was this *asistencia* that became the Rancho San Marcos.

After Mexico overthrew the Spanish in 1822, plans proceeded for the secularization of the missions. Huge tracts of mission lands were granted to the cattle farmers, known as rancheros; the owner of a ranch was called the Don. Indian land claims were largely ignored, and gradually the Indian population disappeared—either being defeated by force or succumbing to diseases brought by whites. When Rancho

212

A GUEST BEDROOM, LIKE MOST OF THE BEDROOMS, HAS A HUGE PICTURE WINDOW OVERLOOKING LAKE CACHUMA AND THE SAN RAFAEL MOUNTAINS. THE WICKER CHAIRS REMAIN FROM MRS. ROBERT ODELL'S TIME. SIMPLE, DOUBLE-FACED TARTAN BLANKETS DRESS THE BEDS (FAR TOP LEFT).

AT RIGHT ANGLES TO THE MAIN HOUSE IS A WING THAT INCLUDES A FIVE-CAR GARAGE, SERVANTS' QUARTERS, AND THIS BUILT-IN DOG-HOUSE WITH DOORWAYS FOR TWO FAVORITE DOGS DESIGNED BY HOTELIER AND ENTREPRENEUR ROBERT ODELL. THE PITCHFORKS, FASHIONED FROM SINGLE BRANCHES, CAME FROM SPAIN. THE WOODEN SETTLE IS FILLED WITH THE FAMILY'S WORK BOOTS (NEAR LEFT TOP).

A BRICK PATIO OUTSIDE THE MAIN RANCH HOUSE IS A GOOD SPOT TO SIT AND READ (FAR LEFT BOTTOM).

THIS GUEST HOUSE, SET BELOW THE MAIN FAMILY HOUSE, WAS ORIGINALLY BUILT BY DWIGHT MURPHY FOR HIS DAUGHTER. IT BECAME KNOWN AS THE GUEST HOUSE IN ROBERT ODELL'S DAY (MIDDLE BOTTOM LEFT).

ONCE USED AS A MAID'S ROOM, THIS ROOM WITH A VIEW HAS BEEN CONVERTED INTO CAPRA PRESS PUBLISHER JOSHUA ODELL'S STUDY (NEAR LEFT). ON THE DESK IS A REPLICA OF THE MALTESE FALCON USED IN THE MOVIE OF THE SAME NAME BASED ON THE RAYMOND CHANDLER NOVEL. THE TWO LION BOOKENDS ARE MINIATURES OF FAITH AND FORTITUDE, THE LIONS THAT FLANK THE ENTRANCE TO NEW YORK'S 42ND STREET LIBRARY.

San Marcos was secularized, its livestock included 948 sheep, ninety-two cattle, ten tame horses, and seven mules. In a 1958 article in *Noticias*, Santa Barbara's Historical Society journal, former owner of the San Marcos ranch Dwight Murphy wrote: "Although the structure of the asistencia is now in ruins, the size of the building can be determined." In 1843, the administrator of Mission Santa Barbara leased to naturalized Irishman Nicholas A. Den, his physician brother Richard S. Den, and Daniel Hill, a prominent Santa Barbaran, all the property of the mission, including the San Marcos ranch, for $1,200 per year. In 1845, Captain John Charles Freemont, marching through the San Marcos Pass against the Mexicans, stayed with Don Nicholas Den, who eventually owned the Santa Barbara mission lands that then covered 35,573 acres.

By the early part of the twentieth century, this considerable property had been divided and subdivided many times. In a November 1968 article in *Noticias*, Selden Spaulding tells how Dwight Murphy came to Santa Barbara just after the turn of the century and served as a forest ranger in the back country before becoming a rancher. As owner of the San Marcos Ranch, Murphy became famous not only as a public benefactor but also as a horse breeder, developing the Palomino—a Spanish breed of golden horses, with distinctive

213

IN THE AFTERNOON, SUN STREAMS THROUGH THE WINDOWS OF THIS LONG GALLERY (LEFT). THIS IS A GREAT PLACE TO BROWSE THROUGH A SCRAPBOOK, PLAY BACKGAMMON, OR JUST CURL UP WITH A BOOK.

BIBLIOPHILE JOSHUA ODELL COLLECTS MODERN FIRST EDITIONS OF AMERICAN PROSE AND POETRY. HERE CAN BE SEEN SOME OF THE BOOKS, PROTECTED IN THEIR TRANSPARENT JACKETS. THE SIGNED HEMINGWAY, *FOR WHOM THE BELL TOLLS,* WAS A GIFT FROM HIS GRANDMOTHER, AND STARTED HIS COLLECTION.

blond tails and manes, that were once called "Isabellas" after the Queen of Spain.

In the 1940s, finding his adobe ranch house too cumbersome, Murphy, by then a highly respected and philanthropic member of the Santa Barbara community, decided to build a modern house for himself, and another nearby for his daughter. To find just the right location in the foothills, he hired a man to camp out and watch dawn and dusk on various parts of the mountainside before settling on a site. Famed architect Chester Carjola was engaged as designer. The two houses, spaced one about fifty feet above the other, are joined by a secluded, landscaped path. They nestle in the lower reaches of the national forest. Both enjoy scenic views of the Santa Ynez Valley and the San Rafael range. Below is Lake Cachuma, at 4,000 acres the largest man-made body of

water in southern California, completed in 1953. In the 1950s, the ranch was sold to entrepreneur Robert Odell. The Odells' primary home was in San Francisco. Among his business enterprises, Robert Odell was the original owner of the Clift Hotel in San Francisco, and he ran a flagship hotel, the renowned Santa Barbara Biltmore. He knew and loved the Santa Barbara area, and he was no stranger to ranching, having owned a ranch in Ukiah in northern California. When he bought the Rancho San Marcos, he and his family used the upper, larger residence as their second home, while the smaller house below became known as the guest house—self-contained quarters for friends or other branches of the family. The ranch consisted of just under 700 acres, the last remaining portion of the original land grant. A herd of Herefords used the pastures for grazing, mules

A TINY, INTIMATE BAR IS DECORATED WITH AN AMUSING 1950S WALLPAPER AND LIPSTICK-RED ACCENTS (ABOVE).

ONE CORNER OF THE LARGE LIVING ROOM IN THE MAIN HOUSE FEATURES A FULLY EQUIPPED WET BAR THAT CAN BE CLOSED OFF DURING THE DAY AND OPENED FOR COCKTAILS AT NIGHT. CLOSE BY IS THE GRAND PIANO WHERE FRIENDS CAN GATHER FOR A SING-ALONG. AUDUBON PRINTS ADORN THE WALLS (RIGHT).

were bred, and horses were maintained for herding and recreational riding.

When patriarch Robert Odell lived in the house, his wife filled it with antiques. Her children, in turn, maintained the place as a second home. Now, in her grandchildren's and great-grandchildren's generation, many of her antiques have been dispersed among family members. The house is currently filled with unpretentious, practical furniture, though some pieces, especially the wicker, date from Grandmother Odell's time.

Of all the descendants, the most constant resident is Joshua Odell, a grandson of the hotelier. On his shoulders falls much of the maintenance of the two houses. The feeling of the décor is contemporary, with an eye on practicality. A publisher of Joshua Odell Editions/Capra Press and a bibliophile, Odell collects first editions of modern American and British literature. He is a member of the distinguished New York book collectors club, the Grolier, and his love of books is evident throughout, particularly in the guest house where he usually

216

THE GUEST HOUSE
KITCHEN WAS DESIGNED
IN THE FORTIES AND HAS
REMAINED ALMOST
UNCHANGED SINCE
THEN. A JUICER OF THE
SAME VINTAGE IS STILL
IN USE.

A CORNER OF THE GUEST HOUSE LIVING ROOM FORMS THE DINING AREA (ABOVE LEFT). THE TWO SEPARATE TABLES PUT TOGETHER ARE WALTER LAMB FURNITURE MADE OF BRASS TUBING THAT CAME FROM SHIPS IN PEARL HARBOR. THE HAND-BLOWN GREEN GLASS IS PART OF A VAST SET BOUGHT IN VENICE BY MR. AND MRS. ROBERT ODELL.

THIS BATHROOM/DRESSING ROOM IS PART OF A RECENTLY ADDED WING (ABOVE RIGHT). AMONG ITS COMFORTS ARE A SPACIOUS SHOWER WITH A BUILT-IN WOODEN BENCH, A HEATED TOWEL RACK, A WELL-LIT DRESSING TABLE, AND COPIOUS CLOSETS AND DRAWERS.

stays. He started collecting in college because of an interesting incident: When his grandfather was flying back from Europe in 1940, he protested to someone behind him on the airplane who kept bumping his seat. He suggested they'd do better sitting side by side. The culprit turned out to be Ernest Hemingway. The two became friends. Hemingway gave Robert Odell a signed first edition of *For Whom the Bell Tolls.* Joshua's grandmother gave him the book, and it was this that originated his now extensive collection.

Joshua Odell is responsible for the relaxed, comfortable look of the two houses. The upper residence is a single-story stucco house, long and spacious in design, with a distinctively Californian feel—from the graveled courtyard with servants' quarters and five-car-garage wing, covered entrance and lanai area (Hawaiian name for a porch), and doors that lead out onto brick patios, to the sunny interiors with painted beam ceilings. The living-dining room is generous enough to entertain a sizable crowd, but works equally well for just a handful. It boasts a large brick fireplace, and easy, comfortable armchairs break up the room into conversational groups. At one end a grand piano sits next to a fully equipped wet bar. Audubon prints decorate the walls. A wall of sliding glass doors lead out to a roomy screened porch that offers a breathtaking view of Lake Cachuma and the San Rafael Mountains.

In character with the older part of the house, a recent wing has been added at the west end of the ranch house. This wing includes two more bedrooms (making a total of five in the house itself), a den, dressing room, and three bathrooms. An east wing contains kitchen services—butler's pantry, sizable kitchen with two-oven stove and white-tiled counters, breakfast space, walk-in closet, service porch, and a luncheon area with windows on three sides, again overlooking the impressive scenery.

A Long drive leads
high above Lake
Cuchama to the
Rancho San Marcos.

When he was a child, Joshua Odell and his family stayed in the guest house so that he and his brothers and sister could, if necessary, be out of their grandparents' way. The guest house is still his favorite domicile, the place where he keeps his books and office. During his period of responsibility, Joshua Odell has had the comfortable armchairs reupholstered in casual, functional fabrics. He has removed dated wall-to-wall carpets, exposing and buffing the attractive wood floors enhanced by interesting rugs. The guest house, though slightly smaller—four bedrooms and baths, and only a three-car garage with a studio and storage room—has great charm, and equally staggering views. The living room and its adjoining porch look out immediately onto a pasture frequented by the family's horses, who pace right up to greet one. The dining area has tables by Walter Lamb, a designer from Honolulu who later had a design studio in California and whose furniture is much collected today. Here the kitchen, almost untouched from the forties, has a special period charm with its curved counter. The essential bar, lined in an amusing 1950s wallpaper, is minute. Its two red bar stools give it a zany, romantic atmosphere.

The working part of the ranch is on meadowlands further down the hill and on the opposite side of the highway. Here can be found dwellings for the foreman, a bunkhouse for ranch hands, four double-fenced corrals, chain-linked paddocks, a chicken building, and a dairy barn (used at the moment for storage). An exceptional horse barn is finished inside with varnished natural wood, with a brick walk-through floor. It includes six dirt-floor stalls with sliding doors, a tack room, feed room, and an office. The ranch is primarily used now for the raising of hay and cattle, and it operates in conjunction with other lands that surround Lake Cachuma.

Surrounding the Rancho San Marcos are many other ranches, some of them elegant showplaces. With the confidence of long-established tenure, the Odells have no need for show. Their enjoyment of the family gathering place is based on an awareness of the peace and vitality of old California and an unaffected love of nature.

A LARGE LIVING ROOM IS DECORATED IN THE SOUTHERN CALIFORNIA STYLE. COMFORTABLE SOFAS AND
ARMCHAIRS ARE UPHOLSTERED IN HEAVY, TEXTURED COTTON. BUILT-IN CUPBOARDS BY THE FIREPLACE
AND BENEATH THE STAIRS ARE USED FOR THE STEREO SYSTEM AND SPEAKERS. THE COFFEE TABLE IS OF
UNFINISHED IVORY TRAVATINE.

West Coast Contemporary

A MALIBU BEACH HOUSE

Malibu! The name conjures up a melée of impressions—Beach Boys, Barbie Doll glamor, Hollywood stars' lavish getaways. Anyone who saw Judy Garland in *A Star Is Born* will recall the luxurious, idealized, pure 1953 Malibu house she shared with James Mason before he slowly walked out into the Pacific. The set decorator got it absolutely right; most Malibu homes try to be on the cutting edge of southern California style.

For twenty-three miles Malibu Beach and its glorious surfing waves stretch northwards from Los Angeles, with the Pacific Coast Highway and the Santa Monica Mountains paralleling and sometimes almost touching the shoreline. A variety of dwellings, sumptuous and expensive, are packed closely along the ribbon of sandy beach with hardly room for an alley between them. Lots are shoehorned between lots, and building still goes on. Spreading over two prime lots and constructed in 1987—and still being fine-tuned—is an opulent state-of-the-art Malibu beach house belonging to a thriving computer engineer (*the* decade's profession) and his German-born wife.

Malibu was not always this crowded nor as competitive. As resorts go, Malibu is a bit of a late starter. The climate, however, was always perfect even in the days of the

A DINING AREA LEADS OFF THE KITCHEN AND OVERLOOKS THE LIVING ROOM (**ABOVE LEFT**). THE DINING TABLE, AN ART PIECE, IS FORMED FROM A SLAB OF GRANITE, WITH ONE ROUGH-CUT EDGE, SET ON ASYMMETRICALLY PLACED MARBLE AND SLATE SUPPORTS. IT WAS DESIGNED BY CASIGLIANI "AMBIGUITA." THE LITHOGRAPH IS BY SAM FRANCIS.

THE COUPLE WANTED A SPECTACULAR ENTRANCE, SO THEY DESIGNED THIS HALLWAY USING GLASS BRICKS TO ENCLOSE A CANTILEVERED SPIRAL STAIRCASE (**ABOVE RIGHT**). THE FLOOR AND STEPS ARE OF POLISHED, PALE PINK-BEIGE LIMESTONE, AND THE BANISTERS ARE STEEL WITH A SATIN FINISH. ORCHIDS AND PALMS ARE PERFECT EMBELLISHMENTS.

Chumash Indians—who appear to have lived an agreeable life, not unlike the surfers of today. They were skilled at handling their unique red-plank boats; they made distinctive baskets and pottery; they were friendly, and, one gathers, somewhat "laid back." There was a Chumash settlement at the foot of present day Malibu Canyon where they lived in circular houses with a hole in the center of the roof to let the light in. According to Judge John J. Merrick in *The Malibu Story*, a publication by the Malibu Lagoon Museum, the Indian name for the area was *Humaliwo*, which means "where the surf sounds loudly." Their culture, Judge Merrick says, was based on the use of asphaltum, a natural bituminous substance the Indians used to caulk their canoes, seal their water baskets, and glue arrowheads to their spears.

Though they were considered the most advanced Indian group in California, the Chumash were corralled into Spanish missions as workers and converts. They didn't take wholeheartedly to the Roman Catholic religion, and after the missions were secularized, they wandered off and gradually died from diseases brought by white men.

One Chumash Indian, according to the Malibu Chamber of Commerce (though it's difficult to find written corroboration), became a successful ranchero in the region. His name, Umalibu, means "place on the mountains" in the Chumash language.

Malibu remained ranchlike and mostly uninhabited for much of the nineteenth century. In *The Malibu Story*, Thomas Doyle tells how one of the region's first farmers was

224

A FIREPLACE IS BUILT INTO THE LIVING ROOM WALL. ABOVE IT IS A LITHOGRAPH BY JUAN MIRÓ.

STEEL DECK RAILINGS WITH A SATIN FINISH FORM AN ABSTRACT PATTERN AGAINST THE OCEAN BEYOND (ABOVE LEFT).

A GARDEN FACING THE SEA HAS BEEN CAREFULLY PLANNED AND PLANTED BY THE OWNER'S WIFE IN ORDER TO DISPLAY FLOWERS ALL YEAR LONG (ABOVE MIDDLE).

José Bartolome Tapia, who had journeyed from Mexico to California as a young man. He came in an overland expedition with Juan Bautista de Anza in 1775, the intent being to settle the California coast before the English or the Russians got the idea. Tapia never followed the legal procedures to get clear title to the land he farmed, making great complications for his heirs. Eventually, after the instant prosperity of the Gold Rush, when real-estate prices started to slump, his descendants were able to sell the three square leagues (about 13,330 acres) for roughly ten cents an acre to Irishman Mat-

thew (Don Matteo) Keller. In 1892, Keller's son Henry sold the ranch to a wealthy man from Massachusetts named Frederick Hastings Rindge. It became one of the biggest and most valuable real-estate holdings in the United States.

Rindge, a philosopher, philanthropist, and writer of an 1898 book called *Happy Days in Southern California,* foresaw Malibu as an "American Riviera." He died at 48, but his widow, May Knight Rindge, took over his business affairs. She spent much of her life trying to prevent the Pacific Coast Highway from passing through her lands. Determined to

A DECK OUTSIDE THE LIVING ROOM IS PERFECT FOR A LEISURELY BREAKFAST AND THE SUNDAY PAPERS. HERE THE OUTDOOR FURNITURE AND THE STEEL RAILINGS ARE ALL SELECTED TO WITHSTAND THE HARSH EFFECTS OF SAND AND SEA AIR (ABOVE RIGHT).

keep her own realm by the ocean intact, she was dubbed "Queen of the Malibu." Twenty-two years of bitter court battles passed before the United States Supreme Court granted a road easement to the state of California through the Malibu ranch. That was the end of Malibu's isolation. The advent of the automobile did the rest.

It wasn't long before the idyllic coast was discovered by those made newly rich by "The Industry," as the Los Angeles movie business is called. Popular stars like Clara Bow built beach houses there in the twenties. Others soon followed. The resort was convenient, just over an hour's drive from the city. Yet even in the forties much of the property had not been developed. The postwar years saw the area boom. In an attempt to get the perfect view of the Pacific, builders perched houses on the sides of mountains or wedged them into handkerchief-sized plots on the ever-eroding shoreline.

This disintegration of such expensively bought land was the first problem that our couple addressed. They had found a lot on a private road, amazingly still empty, but would it gradually erode away? Both of them are people with practical

AFTER THE OWNERS PURCHASED THE FIRST LOT, ANOTHER LOT NEXT DOOR BECAME AVAILABLE, ALLOWING THEM TO LANDSCAPE A MORE EXTENSIVE GARDEN. A PAVILION OVERLOOKING THE FISH POND WAS DESIGNED WITH CANVAS SIDES THAT CAN BE LET DOWN IN INCLEMENT WEATHER. THIS PAVILION IS A PERFECT SPOT FOR LUNCHEONS OR FOR DRINKS IN THE EVENING. THE CUSHIONS ON THE BANQUETTES ARE COVERED WITH PLAIN, EASY-CARE COTTON CANVAS.

———

and scientific minds, so they put time, research, and effort into the proper buttressing of the sloping lot.

Having ensured that the land would not be pulled out from under them, they then spent a year deciding what sort of house to build. With the exception of the front entrance hall, which they agreed had to be a knock-out, to begin with both had totally different ideas. But as they planned and discussed, their thoughts melded. They realized that salt air, sand, and exposure to sea winds were all destructive to many building materials. Exploring the possibilities they chose polished limestone in a soft pink-beige as the floor-covering of the entrance hall and living area. To complement it, pale pine, pickled to a whitened beige, was selected for cabinet and woodwork. An almost indestructible material was chosen for rails and banisters—steel—but this has been softened with a satinlike finish. The flash they required for the entrance was perfectly satisfied by the choice of glass brick, for it was translucent, impervious to the destructive weather conditions, and possessed a glamorous radiance. Gradually they decided that the core of the building should be a cantilevered spiral staircase enclosed in a tube of glass bricks.

Their lot sloped down sharply from the existing private dirt road. Essentials like a garage and security gates had to be addressed. The tiny tilted drive they installed is similar to many of those found on sloping terrains as in Beverly Hills, where every inch, even if it is vertical, counts. The wide garage door is, in fact, the first thing one sees of the house between the bars of the electronically secured gate. It became obvious that the house's windows should face the ocean. For this reason, the front—the side facing the road—is generally uninteresting. A shaped window of green glass above the garage brings light to the indoor greenhouse, but otherwise there are few windows or architectural details.

From this unremarkable exterior, the entrance hall plan became all the more spectacular, with the spiral staircase as focal point. A large living room was designed to lead off to the

THIS SEEMINGLY SIMPLE MASTER BEDROOM (ABOVE LEFT) WITH ITS UNADORNED HORIZONTAL LINES REVEALS IMMACULATE HOUSEKEEPING. PURE WHITE BED-LINEN FROM PRATESI IS EMBELLISHED WITH SUBTLE HEMSTITCHING ON THE DUVET AND PILLOWS. A BLACK MARBLE CLOCK BESIDE THE BED IS FROM BLOOMINGDALE'S. TWO DAYBEDS MATCH THE HOUSE CATS; ONE IS SOFT, SANDY BEIGE, AND THE OTHER (WITH ITS MATCHING CAT BENEATH) IS IN PATTERNED GRAY SUEDE.

THE SLEEK, CONTEMPORARY KITCHEN (ABOVE RIGHT) WAS PLANNED METICULOUSLY FOR THIS COUPLE WHO HATE CLUTTER. BLACK GRANITE COUNTERS AND BLACK ANODIZED ACCESSORIES PUNCTUATE THE NEAT WHITE TILES. GLASS BRICKS BELOW THE CUPBOARDS GIVE DIFFUSED LIGHT WHILE CONCEALING THE NEXT-DOOR HOUSE, WHICH IS ONLY AN ALLEY'S SPAN AWAY.

right down a few stairs. Green tinted-glass windows were selected in order to cut the glare and heat but retain a remarkable view of the sea. Here the furnishings were to be unadorned, practical, and able to stand up to the continual sunshine. They selected cotton and linen upholstery, wicker chairs, and a rough ivory travertine coffee table.

The kitchen to the left of the hall was planned to be the woman-of-the-house's dream. Hating clutter, she chose clean white tiles, polished black granite, black anodized gadgets, and all the latest equipment. A glass-topped table in a corner facing the ocean suffices for breakfast and lunch, but for more formal dinner parties, a dining area between the kitchen and living room was planned.

Deciding that it would be preferable not to have guest suites too close to their own quarters, they resolved after much discussion to put themselves one floor up from the reception rooms, and put guests on the floor below. Because of the slope, guests would have their own doors leading to the garden and the beach. Two self-contained guest wings were planned with separate entrances, and set far enough apart to have complete privacy. The guts of the house—water heaters, sprinkler system, under-floor heating, and Jacuzzi equipment—were confined to an area called the "machine room." Half of this area is given over to a small workshop, a laundry room with a stacked washer/dryer and wash-up sink, and a toilet to be used by service people or by those coming in from

In a corner of the kitchen is a round glass table used for breakfasts or luncheons. Its wide beveled edge and heavy base of polished stone give it great style. Wedge-shaped place mats are designed to conform to the circular table.

———

IN MALIBU, THE BEACHES ARE COMMON PROPERTY, THOUGH ACCESS IS NOT ALWAYS EASY. THESE STEPS LEAD DOWN FROM THE HOUSE TO A SECURE GATE THAT OPENS ONTO THE BEACH (ABOVE LEFT).

BUILT ON A SLOPE LEADING TO THE SEA, THE GARDEN IS CAREFULLY LANDSCAPED TO ENHANCE THE UNEVEN TERRAIN. THESE STEPS LEAD UP TO A SIDE GARDEN ENTRANCE (ABOVE RIGHT).

the beach. There is also storage room for surf boards, beach shoes, towels, and snorkling equipment.

Their own quarters had to include an office, a large bedroom, well-equipped bathroom, masses of closet space, and the obligatory work out room. In addition they designed space for a greenhouse for growing orchids and other plants. Each needed a room-sized walk-in closet, one with a well-lit vanity table, and additional closets in the bedroom could be fitted into the circular shape formed by the staircase enclosure. This also could hold a mammoth television screen opposite the bed. The office, which they would share was to be a plain natural oak wood workroom with his and her computers. Throughout the house, easy maintenance was the goal. Both owners lead busy lives in Los Angeles and abroad.

232

Exotic fish live in the fish pond constructed from locally found rocks (above left).

Built on a steep slope that required engineered bracing, the back of the house extends down to accommodate two separate, self-contained guest quarters below the main living floors (above right).

Finally their initial planning was complete. They found an architect to draw up the blueprints, hired a general contractor, and work began.

Around this time they discovered that the lot next door was for sale. It was too late to redesign the house—they would have made it bigger if they had known sooner—but instead they planned far more elaborate landscaping around the house. This included a simple gazebo with pull-up canvas sides, and a fish pond formed from natural rocks. As the wife is an avid gardener, planting has been planned as meticulously as the architecture so that flowers bloom in every part of the yard all year long.

Eight months into the job, the couple found the contractor's work unsatisfactory and fired him. This is not so unusual

THE LIVING ROOM (RIGHT) LOOKS
OUT ONTO THE DECK AND OCEAN
THROUGH GREEN-TINTED GLASS
WINDOWS AND A SLIDING DOOR. PALE
COTTON RUGS AND WICKER
FURNITURE WITH COTTON-COVERED
CUSHIONS STAND UP TO THE SUN AND
SALT AIR.

given the emotional turmoil of building one's dream house. What is atypical is that the couple were able to finish the work themselves, hiring subcontractors as needed. As an engineer, the owner was able to solve many practical engineering problems himself. For instance, constructing the spiral staircase posed difficulties. Each stair is a shell of steel filled with concrete and topped with a slice of polished limestone. The sheer weight, supported by the central pillar, is mammoth, but this problem was addressed and resolved by the owner.

The result is a very personal house, though the materials used—glass, limestone, steel, and stucco, might be considered cold and impersonal. Now that the house is completed and the garden planted, the couple are able to enjoy their second home. Though the Pacific Ocean continually batters, and earthquakes constantly threaten, this house is likely to weather very well.

Because of the changing nature of commerce, no source list can ever be complete despite every effort at accuracy. Here, therefore, is a somewhat quirky, gleaned-along-the-way listing of goods and services that may be of use to readers. An asterisk (*) appears next to those listings that deal only through architects or decorators.

ANTIQUES AND COUNTRY ACCESSORIES

America Hurrah Antiques
766 Madison Avenue
New York, NY 10021
(212) 535-1930
Great collection of antique American quilts; American folk art and antiques including country furniture, decoys, Indian artifacts, and weather vanes.

American West
2110 N. Halstead Street
Chicago, IL 60614
(312) 871-0400
Contemporary Southwestern art.

Angel House Designs
Route 158
Brookfield, MA 01506
(617)867-2517
Reproduction country furniture.

Don Badertscher Imports
716 North La Cienega Boulevard
Los Angeles, CA 90069
(213) 655-6448
Dressers, fireplaces, garden furniture, kitchen accessories, overmantels, and sideboards, mostly late nineteenth and early twentieth century, many imported from Europe.

236

Balasses House Antiques
Main Street
Amagansett, NY 11930
(516) 267-3032
Pine farm tables, corner cupboards, sideboards, Windsor chairs, brass lamps, antique kitchenware, and hanging light fixtures.

Bardith Ltd.
901 Madison Avenue
New York, NY 10021
(212) 737-3775
English porcelains.
1015 Madison Avenue
New York, NY 10021
(212) 737-6699
Eighteenth- and nineteenth-century furniture and accessories.
31 East 72nd Street
Nw York, NY 10021
(212) 737-8660
Country furniture and sets of porcelain.

British Country Antiques
Route 6
Woodbury, CT 06798
Polished pine country furniture from England or the Continent; unusual early paint-decorated armoires; large collection of country accessories.

Bull and Bear Antiques
1189 Howell Mill Road, N.W.
Atlanta, GA 30318
(404) 355-6697
Eighteenth-century furniture; Staffordshire figures.

Richard Camp
Montauk Highway
Wainscott, NY 11975
(516) 537-0330
Bamboo and pine furniture, platters, bowls, and country antiques.

Cape Island Antiques
609 Jefferson Street
Cape May, NJ 08204
(609) 884-6028
Victorian antiques, collectibles, and furniture.

Carriage Trade Antique Center
Route 7 North
Manchester, VT 05254
(802) 362-1125
A center for local dealers. It offers a wide selection with an occasional great find.

Charterhouse Antiques Ltd.
115 Greenwich Avenue
New York, NY 10014
(212) 243-4726
small pieces of antique furniture and artifacts, mostly English

Croft Antiques
11 South Main Street
Southampton, NY 11968
(516) 283-6445
Antique country furniture and artifacts.

Danby Antique Center
Main Street
Danby, VT 05739
(802) 293-9984
A center for local dealers. Occasionally a real find emerges.

English Heritage
8424 Melrose Place
Los Angeles, CA 90069
(213) 655-5946
Country and formal furniture and fine Georgian silver.

Equinox Antiques
Route 7a
Manchester, VT 05254
(802) 362-3540
Fine quality eighteenth- and nineteenth-century American antiques.

Evergreen Antiques
1249 Third Avenue
New York, NY 10021
(212) 744-5664

120 Spring Street
New York, NY 10012
(212) 966-6458
Scandanivian country antiques and accessories.

Malcome Franklin, Inc.
15 East 57th Street
New York, NY 10022
(212) 308-3344

126 East Delaware Place
Chicago, IL 60611
(312) 337-0202
Fine eighteenth-century furniture and accessories including clocks and mirrors.

Patty Gargarin
975 Banks North Road
Fairfield, CT 06430
(293) 259-7332
Early American antiques and folk art, specializing in fine painted furniture.

Francis Gibbons
1119 South La Brea Avenue
Los Angeles, CA 90019
(213) 937-0452
Country furniture, accessories, and gifts.

Harry B. Hartman
Marietta, PA 17547
By appointment only
(717) 426-1474
Pennsylvania antiques and folk art.

Hayward's of Santa Barbara
1025 Santa Barbara Street
Santa Barbara, CA 93101
(805) 965-0011
Antiques and gifts.

Ken Heitz
Box 161
Indian Lake, NY 12842
(518) 251-3327
Adirondacks rustic furniture.

James II Galleries, Inc.
15 East 57th Street
New York, NY 10022
(212) 355-7040
Antique candlesticks, glass, ivory, miniatures, papier-mâché, pillboxes, picture frames, porcelain, pottery, silver and silverplate; small pieces of antique furniture including bamboo pieces, hat stands, and chairs.

Jenkintown Antiques
520 Route 32 South
New Paltz, NY 12561
(914) 255-8135
American antiques and folk art, specializing in Hudson River artifacts and furniture. Decorating service also.

Howard Kaplan Antiques
827 Broadway
New York, NY 10003
(212) 674-1000
French and English country antiques and furnishings.

Kentshire Galleries
37 East 12th Street
New York, NY 10003
(212) 673-6644
Antique furniture, mostly English; antique accessories, small objects, and jewelry. And a shop also at Bergdorf Goodman.

The Lamplighter
South Street
Middleton Springs, VT 05757
(802) 235-2306
A great source for kerosene lamps in original condition.

J. Garvin Mecking, Inc.
72 East 11th Street
New York, NY 10003
(212) 677-4316
Primarily nineteenth-century furniture and decorative accessories including antique needlepoint, bamboo and twig furniture, lacquerware, majolica, papier-mâché, objects with animal motifs, tole, decorative folk art, and painted country furniture.

Mill House Antiques
Route 6
Woodbury, CT 06798
(203) 263-3446
Antique walnut, pine, and mahogany furniture, Welsh dressers, hunt boards, and desks.

Ann Morris Antiques
239 East 60th Street
New York, NY 10022
(212) 755-3308
Formal and country antique furniture; billiard lights, various lighting fixtures including eighteenth- and nineteenth-century chandeliers; vitrines, large cabinets, shop cases, tables, kitchen crockery, and more.

Old Spa Shop Antiques
Village green
Middletown Springs, VT 05757
(802) 235-2366
An antique shop specializing in nineteenth-century furniture.

Florian Papp
962 Madison Avenue
New York, NY 10021
(212) 288-6770
Fine antique furniture.

Pine Street Antiques
Pine Street
Southampton, NY 11968
(516) 283-6339
Country antiques.

Trevor Potts
1011 Lexington Avenue
New York, NY 10021
(212) 737-0909
Mostly English antiques.

Ralf's Antiques
807 North La Cienega Boulevard
Los Angeles, CA 90069
(213) 659-1966
Seventeenth-, eighteenth-, and nineteenth-century country furniture, copper and brass accessories, bronze figurines, and pictures.

ARCHITECTURE AND BUILDING

Architectural Heritage
62 Glebe Point Road
Glebe NSW 2037, Australia
(02) 398 1403
Restoration.

Architectural Paneling, Inc.
979 Third Avenue
New York, NY 10022
(212) 371-9632
Handcarved mantels, fireplaces, wood paneling, and moldings, woodwork made to order.

Architectural Salvage Warehouse
337 Berry Street
Brooklyn, NY 11200
(718) 388-4527
Architectural salvage.

Bedour Construction
Box 194
Mackinac Island, MI 49757
(906) 847-6221
General contracting for house restoring, renovation, or building.

Delmer Steele
100 Sierra Vista Road
Santa Barbara, CA 93108
(805) 969-2122
General contracting with own staff of carpenters, cabinet makers and window makers.

Fellenz Antiques
439 North Euclid Avenue
St. Louis, MO 63108
(314) 367-0214
Architectural artifacts.

Great American Salvage Co.
34 Cooper Square
New York, NY 10003
(212) 505-0070
Building materials and artifacts from another time. Call for information about other stores.

Knox-Uriu, Inc.,
189 Vanderbilt Avenue
Brooklyn, NY 11205
(718) 858-2946
General contracting.

Joseph Pell Lombardi
55 Liberty Street
New York, NY 10005
(212) 349-0700
Architectural restoration.

Tom McCallum
1932 First Avenue, Suite 702
Seattle, WA 98101
(206) 441-1596
Architecture and architectural restoration.

Harold R. Norton
Box 1142, RD 1
Schuyerville, NY 12871
(518) 695-3560
General contractor for house renovation and remodeling.

Nostalgia
307 Stiles Avenue
Savannah, GA 31401
(912) 236-8176
Architectural antiques.

Schramm & Hallman
723 Spring Lane
Cape May, NJ 08204
(609) 884-5797
Builders and contractors specializing in fine woodwork and restoration including carpentry and painting.

Traditional Line
143 West 21st Street
New York, NY 10011
(212) 627-3555
and
35 Hillside Avenue
Monsey, NY 10952
(914) 425-6400
Architectural restoration.

Urban Archeology
137 Spring Street
New York, NY 10012
(212) 431-6969
Architectural remnants and artifacts.

DECORATORS

Paul Arnold
1065 East Prospect #102
Seattle, WA 98102
(206) 328-7945
Contemporary interior design with traditional influences.

Lee Barrett
Pleasant Street
Dover, MA 02036
(617) 785-1618
Interior decorating.

Bilhuber, Inc.
19 East 65th Street
New York, NY 10021
(212) 517-7673
Mainly contemporary interior design.

Mario Buatta
120 East 80th Street
(212) 988-6811
Traditional interior decorating.

Anne Close
4875 South Fairfax Lane
Littleton, CO 80121
(303) 771-0216
Interior design.

Colefax & Fowler, Inc.
39 Brook Street
London, WIY2JE, England.
011.44.1.493-2231
Traditional English decorating, including their own range of decorative fabrics, and workrooms.

Gary Crain Associates, Inc.
211 East 70th Street
New York, NY 10021
(212) 734-7847
Traditional interior designing.

Gregory Evans, Inc.
509 North Robertson Boulevard
Los Angeles, CA 90048
(312) 275-9040
Interior design.

Georgina Fairholme
By appointment only.
(212) 410-4035
Traditional English decorating.

Lil Groueff
139 East 66th Street
New York, NY 10021
(212) 737-7707
Traditional decorating.

Anthony Hail
1055 Green Street
San Francisco, CA 94133
(415) 928-3500
Classical interior decoration with northern European influence.

Mariette Himes Gomez Associates, Inc.
241 East 78th Street
New York, NY 10021
(212) 288-6856
Interior decoration with emphasis on natural fiber bed and table linens.

Mark Hampton, Inc.
654 Madison Avenue
New York, NY 10021
(212) 753-4110
Traditional decorating.

Harry B. Hartman Interior Designs
Marietta, PA 17547
By appointment only
(717) 426-1474
Interior design and restoration.

William Hodgins, Inc.
232 Clarendon Street
Boston, MA 02116
(617) 262-9538
Interior decorating with leanings to traditional style.

Irvine & Fleming
19 East 57th Street
New York, NY 10022
(212) 888-6000
Traditional interior decorating with an English bias.

Jean Jongeward
119 Tower Place
Seattle, WA 98109
(206) 285-3338 or 284-1999
Contemporary interior design using skilled local metalworkers, painters, and craftspeople.

Gloria Kaplan
245 East 63rd Street
New York, NY 10021
(212) 758-3524
Interior design.

Sheila Kotur
229 East 79th Street
New York, NY 10021
(212) 737-0386
Interior design.

Richard Keith Langham
50 East 81st Street
New York, NY 10028
(212) 744-4415
Contemporary interior design with traditional influence.

Leah Lenney
1019 Esplanade
Pelham Manor, NY 10803
(914) 738-5302
Interior design.

Ann Maloney: A.S.M.
1659 Milford
Houston, TX 77006
(713) 524-6605
Interior design.

McMillen, Inc.
155 East 56th Street
New York, NY 10022
(212) 753-6377
Traditional and contemporary decorating, both corporate and residential.

Kevin McNamara, Inc.
541 East 72nd Street
New York, NY 10021
(212) 861-0808
Traditional interior decorating.

Victoria Melian de Marsans
315 East 51st Street
New York, NY 10022
(212) 371-6250
Interior design.

Parish—Hadley Associates, Inc.
305 East 63rd Street
New York, NY 10021
(212) 888-7979
Traditional interior decoration.

John Ragsdale
95½ Broad Street
Charleston, SC 29401
(803) 722-1838
Neoclassic high-style interior design.

John Saladino, Inc.
305 East 63rd Street
New York, NY 10021
(212) 752-2440
Interior designing using classical motifs.

Gary Zarr
150 Columbus Avenue
New York, NY 10023
(212) 877-1992
Contemporary interior design with traditional overtones.

PAINT WORK

William Horgan
1083 Shunpike Road
Cold Spring, NJ 08204
(609) 884-4970
Painting contractor.

*Pat Cutaneo, Inc.
(718) 987-4560
Fine painting and specialty finishes.

Robert Jackson
498 West End Avenue
New York, NY 10024
(212) 873-1920

Lewis Group Painters
8 Carter Street
Randwick NSW 2031, Australia
(02) 398 1403
Paintwork.

Michael Tyson Murphy Studio
346 West 56th Street
New York, NY 10019
(212) 502-0178
Decorative paint work including trompe l'oeil, murals, faux bois, glazes, and stencils.

Serious Surfaces
2530 Clinton Avenue
Minneapolis, MN 55404
(612) 874-0580
Fancy paint finishes for walls and furniture.

FABRICS AND TRIMMINGS

*Robert Allen Fabrics
979 Third Avenue
New York, NY 10022
(212) 759-6660
Contemporary decorative fabrics.

Laura Ashley
(800) 223-6917
Stores nationwide providing fabrics, household linens, and decorative accessories.

Bergamo Fabrics, Inc.
37–20 34th Street
Long Island City, NY
(718) 392-5000
Contemporary decorative fabrics.

*Boussac
979 Third Avenue
New York, NY 10022
(212) 421-0534
Sixteen stores throughout the country showing decorative fabrics and wallpapers.

*Carleton V
979 Third Avenue
New York, NY 10022
(212) 355-4525
Fabric and wall covering. Call for information on showrooms.

*Clarence House
211 East 58th Street
New York, NY 10022
(212) 752-2890
Showrooms nationwide. Fabrics, wallpapers, and trimmings.

Conran's
160 East 54th Street
New York, NY 10022
(212) 371-2225
Call for information in other stores. For mail order only:
4 South Middlesex Avenue
Cranbury, NJ 08512
(609) 655-4505
Furnishing fabrics and coordinated wall coverings; contemporary furniture and kitchen systems.

*Cowtan & Tout
979 Third Avenue
New York, NY 10022
(212) 753-4488
Other showrooms nationwide. Fabrics and wall coverings.

*Rose Cummings Chintz, Ltd.
232 East 59th Street
New York, NY 10022
(212) 758-0844
Nationwide showrooms offering documentary chintzes. Antique furniture and accessories sold to the trade at the New York showroom; also interior decorating.

Decorator's Walk
245 Newton Road
Plain View, NY 11803
(516) 249-3100
Represents many companies with a variety of fabrics and wallpapers.

Descamps
723 Madison Avenue
New York, NY 10021
(212) 355-2522
Bed linens

*Donghia
979 Third Avenue
New York, NY 10022
(212) 935-3713
Furniture and fabric, mostly in a contemporary or neoclassic vein. An interior design division can be reached at (212) 838-9100 for residential work.

*Eaglesham Prints, Inc.
979 Third Avenue
New York, NY 10022
(212) 759-2060
Custom hand-printed furnishing fabrics, with coordinating wall coverings.

*Ernest Studio, Inc.
207 East 84th Street
New York, NY 10028
(212) 988-4900
Workroom for interior decorators making curtains and upholstery.

* Fonthill
979 Third Avenue
New York, NY 10022
(212) 924-3000
Marbelized and stried chintzes and wallpapers; hand-blocked documentary chintzes.

The Ground Floor
John Ragsdale
95 Broad Street
Charleston, SC 29401
(803) 722-1838
Tassels and pulls for curtains in a variety of styles that can be colored to go with fabrics.

* Guido de Angelis, Inc.
312 East 95th Street
New York, NY 10028
(212) 348-8225
Upholstery and drapery.

* Hinson & Co.
979 Third Avenue
New York, NY 10022
(212) 475-4100
Wallpapers and fabrics.

David Jones (Aust) Pty Ltd.
(02) 266 5544
Stores in Sydney, Melbourne, Adelaide, Brisbane. Household linens.

Ralph Lauren Home Collection
Shops in fine department stores and selected Polo/Ralph Lauren shops throughout the country. Call for up-to-date listing (212) 930-3200.
Household linens, fabric, furniture, and accessories.

* Jack Lenor Larsen
41 East 11th Street
New York, NY 10003
(212) 674-3993
Contemporary decorative fabrics.

* Lee—Jofa, Inc.
979 Third Avenue
New York, NY 10022
(212) 688-0444
Showrooms nationwide. Decorative fabrics, wall coverings, and trimmings.

Liberty of London Shops, Inc.
3222 M Street NW
Georgetown Park No. 249
Washington, DC 20007
(202) 388-3711
Shops also in New York, Armore PA, and Chicago. Printed fabrics, sheets and duvet covers (through Martex, Inc.), picture frames, and gift objects.

Maison Belle Pty Ltd.
34 John Street
Lidcombe NSW 2141, Australia
(02) 649 2973
Drapery.

Elinor Merrell
By appointment only.
New York, NY
(212) 288-4986
Antique European fabrics.

François Nunnalle
By appointment only.
New York, NY
(212) 246-4281
Antique linens and lace; large selection of decorative antique tiebacks.

Order Imports
139 Murray Street
Pyrmont NSW 2009 Australia
(02) 660 3799
Fabric.

Pierre Deux Fabrics
350 Bleeker Street
New York, NY 10014
(212) 741-7245
Mail order department:
147 Palmer Avenue
Mamaroneck, NY 10543
(800) 8-PIERRE. In New York State call (800) 992-2998 or (914) 698-0555.
Boutiques nationwide. French country printed fabrics; faience, pewter, glassware, floor tiles, and other accessories.

* Randolph & Hein
101 Henry Adams Street
Galleria Design Center, Suite 101
San Francisco, CA 94107
(415) 864-3550
Showrooms nationwide. Upholstery fabrics made of natural fibers, especially silks.

* Quadrille
979 Third Avenue
New York, NY 10022
(212) 753-2995
Fabrics and wallpapers.

* Scalamandre
950 Third Avenue
New York, NY 10022
(212) 980-3888
Showrooms nationwide. Decorative fabrics, wall coverings, trimming and carpets.

Sea Port Fabrics
Route 27
Mystic, CT 06355
(203) 536-8668
Home decorating fabrics at a fraction of the regular price.

* Sonia's Place
979 Third Avenue
New York, NY 10022
(212) 355-5211
Wall coverings and decorative fabrics representing many manufacturers.

* Stroheim & Romann, Inc.
155 East 56th Street
New York, NY 10022
(212) 691-0700
Showrooms nationwide. Decorative fabrics for upholstery and curtains.

Vermont Country Store
Route 100
Weston, VT 05161
(802) 362-2400
A wide selection of merchandise of solid quality with a country background.

* Waverly, a division of F. Schumacher & Co.
Call (212) 704-9900 for locations.
Traditional country prints and patterns from Victorian styles to the 1930s and 1940s.

Wolfman, Gold & Good Company
116 Greene Street
New York, NY 10012
(212) 431-1888
Household fabrics, mostly white or neutral, lace, toweling; white pottery; pine country furniture.

* Woodson
979 Third Avenue
New York, NY 10022
(212) 684-0330
Showrooms nationwide.
Wall coverings and fabrics of a mainly contemporary nature.

FLOOR COVERINGS

Country Floors, Inc.
15 East 16th Street
New York, NY 10003
(212) 627-8300
Large variety of tiles.

*Doris Leslie Blau Gallery, Inc.
15 East 57th Street
New York, NY 10022
(212) 759-3715

E.J. Horst
120−b West Canon Perdido
Santa Barbara, CA 93101
(805) 966-1330
Custom rugs, creative carpet sculpting.

Fred Pazotti
64 Moncur Street
Woollahra NSW 2025, Australia
(02) 32 9221
Floor coverings.

*Stark Carpet Corporation
979 Third Avenue
New York, NY 10022
(212) 752-9000
Showrooms nationwide. The largest selection in the world of fine antique and custom-made carpets.

Sybella
By appointment
(516) 283-6888
Carpets and floor covering.

Topalian Trading Company
281 Fifth Avenue
New York, NY 10016
(212) 684-0735
Antique Oriental carpets.

WALL COVERINGS

Bradbury & Bradbury Wallpapers
P.O. Box 155
Bernicia, CA 94510
(707) 746-1900
Silk-screened wallpapers and borders.

Decortex Wallcoverings & Fabrics Pty Ltd.
22 Rosebery NSW 2021, Australia
(02) 663 0521
Wallcoverings.

*Charles R. Gracie & Sons, Inc.
979 Third Avenue
New York, NY 10022
(212) 753-5350
Specialists in Orientalia including hand-painted scenic panels.

*Katzenbach & Warren, Inc.
979 Third Avenue
New York, NY 10022
(212) 751-4470
Authentic reproductions of documentary wallpapers.

Scalamandre
950 Third Avenue
New York, NY 10022
(212) 980-3888
Will reproduce wallpaper from fragments.

Norman Shepherd
458 Jackson Square
San Francisco, CA 94111
(415) 362-4145
and at:
Montauk Highway
Water Mill, NY 11976
(516) 726-4840
Antiques from around the world

Territory
6907½ Melrose Avenue
Los Angeles, CA 40038
(213) 937-4006
Decorative arts and paintings of the Old West.

Washington Square
Washington Street
Cape May, NJ 08204
(609) 884-3338
Antiques, crafts, and gifts.

The Wicker Garden
1318 Madison Avenue
New York, NY 10128
(212) 410-7000
Large selection of wicker furniture, including Victorian and Art Deco; also brass and iron beds and accessories.

Winsor Antiques
53 Sherman Street
Fairfield, CT 06430
(203) 255-0056
Country furniture from late seventeenth century to Victorian, including stripped pine, French Provincial fruitwood, Georgian, and English oak; also decorative antiques, early ironware, prints, baskets, American decoys; specializes in English Windsor and ladderback chairs.

Thomas K. Woodward
835 Madison Avenue
New York, NY 10021
(212) 988-2906
American antiques, quilts, rag runners; accessories including baskets and pottery: Custom rugs made to order.

Bibliography

BOOKS

Andrews, Peter; Dunning, Jennifer; and Tower, Whitney. *Saratoga: The Place and its People.* New York, NY: Harry N.Abrams, 1988.

Artman, L.P., Jr. *Key West History.* Key West, FL: L.P. Artman, Jr., 1969.

Banks, Ronald F. *Maine becomes a State* Middletown, CN: Published for the Maine Historical Society by Weslyan University Press, 1970.

Bayles, Richard M. *Suffolk Country, and its Towns, Villages, Hamlets, Scenery, Institutions and Important Enterprises.* Port Jefferson, NY: published by the author, 1874.

Beacon, Seward E. *Pulpit Harbor: Two Hundred Years.* North Haven, ME: North Haven Historical Society, 1985.

Beveridge, Norwood P. *The North Island: Early Times to Yesterday.* North Haven, ME: 1976.

Bishop, Gordon. *Gems of New Jersey.* Englewood Cliffs, NJ: Prentice-Hall, 1985.

Bookbinder, Bernie. *Long Island: People and Places: Past and Present.* New York, NY: Harry N. Abrams, 1983.

Boyer, George F., and Cunningham, J. Pearson. *Cape May County Story.* Egg Harbor City, NJ: The Laureate Press, 1975.

Britten, Evelyne Barrett. *Chronicles of Saratoga.* Woodridge, CN: Research Publications, 1975.

A Brief Historical Sketch of Vinalhaven. (No author credit found), MN: 1889.

Browne, Jefferson B. *Key West: The Old and The New.* Gainesville, FL: University of Florida Press, 1973.

Calkins, John. *Michigan.* New York, NY: Doubleday, (no date).

Camarillo, Albert. *Chicanos in a Changing Society.* Cambridge, MA: Harvard University Press, 1979.

Cape May. New York, NY: West Jersey Railroad Company, 1877. (No author credited on this pamphlet to promote the railroad.)

Catton, Bruce. *Michigan: A History.* New York, NY: W.W. Norton, 1976.

Cox, Christopher. *A Key West Companion.* New York, NY: St. Martin's Press, 1983.

Cunningham, John T. *New Jersey: America's Main Road.* New York, NY: Doubleday, 1966.

Duvall, Ralph G. *The History of Shelter Island 1652–1932, with a Supplement 1932–1952 by Jean L. Schladermundt.* Shelter Island Heights, NY: 1952.

Ellsworth, Lucius, and Ellsworth, Linda. *Pensacola: The Deepwater City.* Tulsa, OK: Continental Heritage Press, Inc., 1982.

Espsito, Frank J. *Travelling New Jersey.* Union City, NJ: Wm. H. Wise, 1978.

Faust, Langdon, ed. *Fodor's California.* New York and London: Fodor's Travel Guides, 1987.

Fisher, Sydney G. *The Quaker Colonies.* New Haven, MA: Yale University Press, 1919.

Gilborn, Craig. *Adirondacks Furniture in the Rustic Tradition.* New York, NY: Harry N. Abrams, 1987.

Gillis, Mabel R. *California, the WPA Guide to California.* The Federal Writer's Project of the Works Progress Administration for the State of California. New York, NY: Pantheon Books, 1939.

Graham, Frank, Jr. *The Adirondack Park: A Political History.* Syracuse, NY: Syracuse University Press, 1978.

Kaiser, Harvey. *Great Camps of the Adirondacks.* Boston, MA: David R. Godine, 1982.

Kaufelt, Lynn Mitsuko. *Key West Writers and their Houses.* Englewood and Fort Lauderdale, FL: Pineapple Press and Omnigraphics, 1986.

Lancaster, Clay; Stern, Robert A.M.; and Hefner, Robert J., ed. *East Hampton's Heritage: An Illustrated Architectural Record.* New York, NY: W.W. Norton & Company in association with The East Hampton Ladies Village Improvement Society, 1982.

Malone, Michael P.; and Roeder, Richard B. *Montana: A History of Two Centuries.* Seattle, WA: University of Washington Press, 1976.

McCurdy, James G. *By Juan de Fuca's Strait.* Portland, OR: The Metropolitan Press, Binsford & Mort, 1937.

McDermott, Charles J. *Suffolk County, N.Y.* New York, NY: James H. Heineman, 1965.

McKee, Russell, ed. *Mackinac: The Gathering Place.* Michigan Heritage Series, Volume II. Lansing, MI: Woolly Bear Productions, 1981.

Merrill, James. *The Seraglio.* New York, NY: Knopf, 1957. *From The First Nine: Poems: Clearing The Title.* New York, NY: Atheneum, 1982.

Michigan, A Guide to the Wolverine State. Michigan: The Writer's Program, 1941.

Morgan, William, and Siskind, Aaron. *Bucks County: Photographs of Early Architecture.* New York, NY: The Bucks County Historical Society: Horizon Press, 1974.

Murray, Keith A. *The Pig War.* Tacoma, WA: Washington State Historical Society, 1968.

Newberry, Lida. *New Jersey: A Guide to the Present and Past.* New York, NY: Hastings House, 1977.

Nutting, Wallace. *Pennsylvania Beautiful.* New York, NY: Bonanza Books, 1924.

Parks, Virginia. *Pensacola: Spaniards to Space Age.* Pensacola, FL: Pensacola Historical Society, 1986.

Petersen, Eugene T. *Mackinac Island: Its History in Pictures.* Mackinac Island, MI: Mackinac Island State Park Commission, 1973.

Piljac, Pamela A., and Piljac, Thomas M. *Mackinac Island: Historic Frontier, Vacation Resort, Timeless Wonderland.* Portage, IN: Bryce-Waterton Publications, 1988.

Porter, Phil. *View From The Veranda: The History and Architecture of the Summer Cottages On Mackinac Island.* Mackinac Island, MI: Mackinac Island State Park Commission, 1981.

Prokopoff, Stephen S., and Siegfried, Joan C. *The Nineteenth-Century Architecture of Saratoga Springs: Architecture Worth Saving in New York State.* New York State Council on the Arts, 1970.

Rattray, Everett T. *The South Fork: The Land and People of Eastern Long Island.* New York, NY: Random House, 1979.

Richardson, David. *Pig War Islands.* Eastsound, WA: Orcas Publishing Company, 1971.

Roberts, Bruce, and Roberts, Nancy. *The Goodliest Land: North Carolina.* New York, NY: Doubleday, 1973.

Seabury, Samuel. *Two Hundred and Seventy-five Years of East Hampton, Long Island, New York: A Historical Sketch, Together with the Book of the Pageant Celebrating the Two Hundred and Seventy-Fifth Anniversary of the Founding of the Town Written by Miss Abigail Halsey.* East Hampton, NY: 1926.

Santelli, Robert. *The Jersey Shore: A Travel and Pleasure Guide.* Charlotte, NC: The East Woods Press, 1986.

Steiman, David B., and Nevill, John T. *Miracle Bridge At Mackinac.* Grand Rapids, MI: Wm. B. Erdmans Publishing, 1957.

Swan, James G. *Swan Among the Indians.* Portland, OR: Binfords & Mort, 1972.

Toole, K. Ross. *Montana: An Uncommon Land.* Norman, OK: University of Oklahoma Press, 1959.

Waller, George. *Saratoga: Saga of an Impious Era.* Gansevoort, NY: Friar Tuck Bookshop, 1966.

Westergaard, Barbara. *New Jersey: A Guide to the State.* New Brunswick, NJ: Rutgers University Press, 1987.

Wood, Edwin O. *Historic Mackinac.* Vols. I and II. New York, NY: MacMillan, 1918.

PERIODICALS

Buckley, Christopher. "A Designer's Cottage on the South Fork." *Architectural Digest,* June 1988, pp. 128–131, 215.

Kleveland, Tom. "Dwight Murphy Sells Historic San Marcos Ranch In Valley." *Santa Barbara News Press* (undated clipping).

New Jersey. A brochure from the New Jersey Department of Commerce and Economic Development, Division of Travel and Tourism. Trenton, NJ.

Peters, Mason. "The Carolina Coast; Unpainted Aristocracy." *The Virginian-Pilot and Ledger-Star,* July 3, 1988.

Scenic and Historic Tours of New Jersey: Crossroads of the Revolution. State Office of Tourism and Promotion, Trenton, NJ, 1976.

Spaulding, Selden. "Dwight Murphy." *Noticias,* Santa Barbara Historical Society, November, 1968.

Thompkins, Walter A. "Santa Barbara History Makers." *News-Press Library,* Murphy files (undated).

Thompson, Vivian. "Rancho San Marcos—Gateway to Santa Ynez Valley." *Santa Ynez Valley News,* January, 1979.

ONE GIANT LEAP

ONE GIANT LEAP

APOLLO 11 REMEMBERED

PIERS BIZONY

ZENITH PRESS

First published in North America in 2009 by Zenith Press, an imprint of MBI Publishing
Company, 400 First Avenue North, Suite 300, Minneapolis, MN 55401 USA

This edition published by arrangement with Aurum Press Ltd.

Zenith Press titles are also available at discounts in bulk quantity for industrial or
sales-promotional use. For details write to Special Sales Manager at MBI Publishing Company,
400 First Avenue North, Suite 300, Minneapolis, MN 55401 USA.

To find out more about our books, join us online at www.zenithpress.com.

On the cover: The most famous picture in space history: Buzz Aldrin on the moon.

On the back flap: What a rocket should look like: a test version of Saturn V on the launch pad.

Book design by Piers Bizony
Cover design by Simon Larkin

ISBN-13: 978-0-7603-3710-8

Printed in Singapore

CONTENTS

FOREWORD

WHAT IMAGE COMES to mind when we think of Apollo 11? We all know that famous picture of "the first man on the moon," don't we? There's a golden visor staring out at us, like the cold and passionless eye of some Cyclopean robot. The visor inside its bulky helmet caps a stiff-looking spacesuit. Fat white hoses snake in and out of blue and red valve connectors on the spaceman's chest, and the balloon-like arms of this clumsy creature are tipped by gray gloves with fingers like stubby sausages. The background is a flat expanse of gray, powdery soil and a pure black sky. There are no sepia tones to age the shot, no long-vanished clothing styles to help us date roughly when the picture might have been taken. The person in the spacesuit looks like any other person in a spacesuit, because you hardly ever see their faces inside those sunproof golden masks, and spacesuits still look pretty much the same today as they always have. The crisp, clean, high-quality color photo looks as if it might have been taken last year, last month, yesterday. The truth—that it was taken forty years ago—seems impossible. Stranger yet is the fact that no good photographs exist of the first man on the moon actually walking on it. What we see, in that eternally famous and almost perfectly composed picture of the first man on the moon, is the second man.

All the lunar astronauts deserve heroic status, and each Apollo mission was just as important as any other. All the flights were dangerous, ambitious, extraordinary. But we have a relentless fascination for people who do things for the very first time. The names of Neil Armstrong and Buzz Aldrin are memorable to us because they were the first men to land on the moon, and many people also recall Michael Collins, orbiting overhead in the command module, but only those space enthusiasts with a pedant's grasp of detail can recall exactly who commanded Apollo 14, or which astronaut stayed aboard Apollo 16's mothership while the other two went down to the lunar surface. History can be cruel, yet we cannot blame ourselves for concentrating on the highlights of events that, in many cases, happened while we were young, or even before we were born. Our minds are overloaded with what's happening today, never mind the details of events long past. This book is a celebration of Apollo 11, but it has to be considered as standing for the entire Apollo adventure, not just that one mission. That said, there is something unique about the photos taken during Apollo 11. Most of the astronauts who came afterwards had the luxury of spending more time on the lunar surface, and there were more opportunities for them to pause for a moment and take photos of each other. The bulk of the many fabulous images gathered together in countless Apollo retrospective books and exhibitions come from those later missions.

For the crewmen of that very first landing, taking photographs took second place to simply completing their mission without making mistakes that might kill them in their still relatively untested spacecraft. Even so, Armstrong and Aldrin had cameras strapped to their chests throughout their time on the surface: Hasselblads loaded with 70mm roll film. Orbiting overhead in the command module, Michael Collins was equipped with similar cameras. Nearly 600 frames were exposed during the mission. Yet in most books recounting this greatest of all space adventures, only a handful of the images tend to appear. Why is this?

Partly, it has to do with the fact that the Apollo 11 crew weren't always at the top of their game when it came to making beautiful photographic works of art. Many shots, and especially those taken inside the spacecraft, are blurry, under-exposed, or so random in the choice of subject matter that they can only have resulted from the shutter button being pressed by accident. For four decades, picture editors have looked at these apparently disappointing failures and set them aside. Now, looking at them with a fresh eye, we gain a vivid impression of men busy with urgent tasks; men unable, or unwilling, to concentrate for more than a few brief seconds at a time on taking photos; hurtling towards the moon at 25,000 miles per hour while checking that none of the ten dozen switch settings on their control panel hides the one incorrect flip that might kill them; men pressing strings of numbers into their computer, knowing that one wrong digit out of a hundred could spin them to their deaths in the wastes of space. The crew of Apollo 11 were trying to avoid potentially fatal errors among a thousandfold tasks during their eight-day voyage. Is it any wonder that their photos, snapped in very rare spare moments, were sometimes less than perfect?

If the task of getting to the moon occupied almost every waking second of the astronauts' time, then exploring its surface was just as demanding. In fact one of the great failures of this otherwise magnificent project was NASA's misplaced zeal for "professionalism" during every moment of the moon walk. Senior managers were worried that taxpayers would complain if the astronauts took time out from collecting rocks or digging for soil samples. Consequently the moon walkers' schedules were planned out in advance almost literally to the minute. There were various boxes of equipment to unwrap from the sides of the lunar module and a long list of scientific experiments to deploy in a certain order. Then there was "x" amount of terrain to cover and "y" pounds of rock samples to be gathered in a given time, and so on.

Those photos that were officially scheduled to be taken were of the moon itself: the texture of the soil, the locations of rocks and boulders, the geological (or, more properly, selenological) character of the immediate surroundings and far horizon. Of the two Hasselblad pictures that Aldrin took of Armstrong on the moon, one is almost comically incorrect, showing just a sliver of Armstrong's suit as he disappears out of the frame. Of course, some shots, and especially those of Aldrin taken by Armstrong, do work stunningly well, and it is these that have tended to dominate our cultural memories of Apollo 11 over the last four decades. Armstrong and Aldrin had to steal the odd moment or two from their schedules to look around and absorb the impact of what they were doing. No wonder they found it so hard to tell the rest of us about it afterwards—hard, perhaps, to tell themselves.

In some sense, the stars of these photos are the machines, not the men. Apollo really was a portent of the future: human flesh was concealed behind—or rather, inserted deep into—the convoluted tangle of Apollo's "man-machine interface." For historians and psychologists alike, the emphasis on shots of control panels, lunar lander legs, pieces of reflective foil, docking probes, and other pieces of equipment, and the relatively infrequent appearance of human faces, is telling. Man is here, in each and every picture, but represented by his fascination for the vehicles that he knows how to build and fly, rather than by Man himself.

The crew of Apollo 11 were professional, cordial, but not particularly intimate with each other, and sometimes it shows, although Buzz Aldrin's portrait of Neil Armstrong safely back in the lunar module after the moon walk is the very essence of generosity: an acknowledgement that the first man on the moon deserves to smile while the second sets his disappointment aside and takes his picture for posterity—perhaps aware, in retrospect, that he didn't really shoot enough of Armstrong while the two men were actually walking on the moon.

There was no special provision in Apollo 11's flight plan for taking good publicity photographs of "men on the moon," despite this mission supposedly being of such historic significance. The fact is that the global media machine of 1969 was not the instantaneous and all-consuming entity that it is today. Only at the last minute did NASA recognize the importance of those grainy television broadcasts of the moon walk—and the space agency almost entirely missed the importance, to people back on earth, of seeing photos of humans on the moon, not just rocks and soil, machines, and instruments.

Armstrong and Aldrin's familiarization with the TV cameras and Hasselblads was imperfect at best, a late and largely unwelcome addition to their training schedule. It was common for most astronauts to complain that photos and video footage got in the way of more urgent tasks. These men were test pilots trying to stay alive, not photographers or film directors trying to make art. Understanding all this, we can now look at a wide selection of Armstrong, Aldrin, and Collins's photographs with a fresh perspective, and see the hidden qualities of certain shots that might once have been regarded as "failures."

This book gathers together more images from Apollo 11 than any mass-market publication has attempted before. In gathering them, I called on many years of research, image cataloguing, and digital scanning conducted by Apollo historians, some of them working within NASA's History Office, but many more, it has to be said, dedicating private time and personal resources to help make the historical record of Apollo as complete as possible. I would like to thank: Paul Fjeld, Ed Hengeveld, Eric Jones, Mike Marcucci, Jack Pickering, and Kipp Teague, and from NASA, Steven Dick, Colin Fries, Mike Gentry, Connie Moore, and Margaret Persinger.

One view that we seldom see in the photos is of both Apollo craft docked together; and even when we do see the vehicles, the lighting conditions of deep space are such that the glare of reflected sunlight from one side of a ship dazzles the eye, while shadows obscure details on the other flank. I am grateful to an outstanding computer graphics artist, John Ortmann, for his digital artworks showing exactly what the spacecraft of Apollo 11 looked like, down to the last rivet and crinkled piece of foil. John Knoll, co-creator (with his brother Thomas) of Photoshop, has also made for this book a superb interior view of the lunar module's cabin. This is surely the closest that any of us will get to sharing the view out of Armstrong's window as he avoided a dangerous crater in the last few seconds before touchdown. David Mindell, Professor of the History of Engineering and Manufacturing at the Massachusetts Institute of Technology (MIT) has also been generous in giving me advice about Apollo's computer systems.

In the UK, I received valuable advice from Michelle Clarke at the Institution of Engineering and Technology (IET), and other support from her colleagues Dickon Ross and Vitali Vitaliev in the IET's publications division. Chris Riley, co-producer of the oustanding Apollo documentary film *In The Shadow Of The Moon*, was helpful with advice and encouragement. Thanks also to my old friend and constant advisor Doug Millard at the Science Museum in London, and to Michelle's husband Adrian, a true and generous Apollo fan. Finally—although I really mean first and foremost—I thank my wife, Fiona, and my family, for being the best "ground support" team that any space writer could have. Our two dogs and one cat, being incapable of reading, will simply have to accept my gratitude in the form of biscuits.

1 SETTING THE SCENE

1

A modern Soyuz rocket is almost indistinguishable from the hardware that launched Sputnik in 1957.

SETTING THE SCENE

THE STORY OF HOW AND WHY we sent men to the moon has been told many times. This book is a series of themed and illustrated essays about Apollo's cultural legacy viewed from the perspective of today, rather than a detailed history of events. Even so, it is probably worth reminding ourselves of the events leading up to that adventure:

In July 1969 an incredible machine thundered towards the moon. Apollo 11's Saturn V rocket highlighted the best and the worst of our desires. It satisfied our yearning to explore space in peace, but its design was inspired by wars on earth. Half a century ago, two brilliant engineers triggered a rocket competition between Russia and America. Each man had known the worst cruelties of his times. One narrowly avoided death in a labor camp, and the other may have been partially responsible for creating one. Both men designed and built rocket weapons of devastating destructive power, even as they propelled us into the cosmos.

In 1938, aircraft engineer Sergei Korolev was developing simple rockets at an army laboratory in St Petersburg when he fell victim to one of Stalin's terror purges. He was savagely beaten and tortured, then imprisoned in a freezing Siberian gulag. Three years later, on the brink of death, he was ordered to Moscow. The German army had invaded and Stalin suddenly needed engineers. In 1945 Korolev was sent into Germany to recover the remnants of rockets similar to those that he had dreamed of building. He found that a young German pioneer had already outstripped his wildest ambitions.

Wernher von Braun is probably the only "rocket scientist" whose name is familiar to everyone. Born into an aristocratic family, he was obsessed by space. When the Nazis came to power he persuaded Hitler that rockets would make effective weapons. He and his dedicated team developed the V-2 "Vengeance" rocket at Peenemünde, on the Baltic coast. During the war, a nightmarish underground factory was built at Nordhausen, where half-starved slave laborers

assembled the rockets under SS supervision. In the last months of the war, British, American, and Russian intelligence teams scoured the devastated German heartland for any remains of the V-2. This was, after all, the world's first guided missile, and its descendants would define the future balance of power. Competition among the teams was ruthless, even though they were supposed to be allies. Von Braun decided the Americans were his best hope, because they would probably employ him. The British couldn't afford him and the Russians might shoot him. He staged a brilliant escape for himself and his closest colleagues under the noses of SS squads, who were by now indiscriminately killing "disloyal" Germans.

There followed a decade of half-hearted V-2 tests in the White Sands desert of New Mexico. Von Braun was frustrated by the US government's lack of interest in him (he was rather an embarrassment, as well as a potential asset), so he became a public campaigner. In the late 1950s Walt Disney promoted him as a trustworthy crusader for space exploration. Korolev, meanwhile, created Raketa-7 (R-7), the first intercontinental ballistic missile, along with a vast and secret launch complex in the remotest reaches of Khazakstan. The R-7 was a weapon. Its purpose was to hurl heavy nuclear warheads across the Atlantic and onto America, but Korolev knew it could also carry lighter payloads all the way into space. On October 4 1957 he proved it by sending a satellite called Sputnik into orbit. A larger payload, Sputnik II, flew a

Almost like some sacrificial victim, Gordon Cooper is assisted into his capsule prior to flying a new and relatively untested rocket.

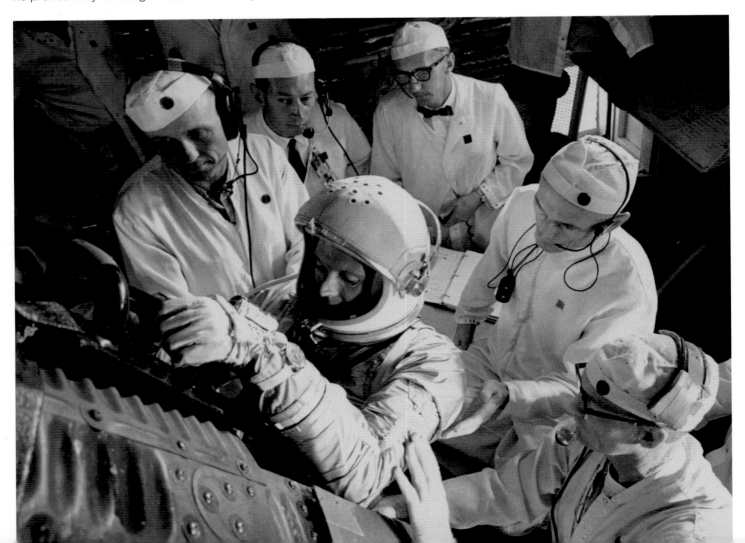

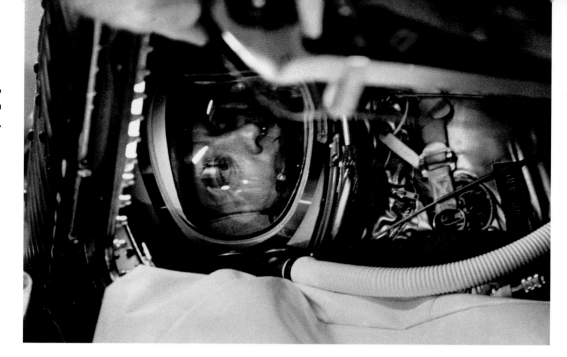

America's first man in space, Alan Shepard, prepares for launch in his tiny Mercury capsule.

similar trajectory on November 3, carrying a passenger, a dog called Laika. Korolev's intentions were clear enough. He wanted to launch a man. He now told the Red Army generals that he could build a satellite to spy on the West, but first he would have to enlist a pilot with excellent eyesight to look out of the satellite's window and check on what the spy cameras might see. The generals believed him, and in October 1959 a squad of "cosmonauts" was formed.

In America, President Dwight D. Eisenhower was reluctant to spend money on rockets. He feared the influence of what he called "the military–industrial complex". Only when a small-scale Navy satellite launcher called Vanguard blew up on the pad was von Braun summoned, at last, to rescue America's faltering space effort. The National Aeronautics and Space Administration, more usually known by its acronym NASA, was created in July 1958 and given just enough cash to develop a small manned space capsule, the Mercury. Eisenhower fervently hoped that what he dismissed as "all this Buck Rogers nonsense" would end soon.

THE RACE BEGINS

Von Braun and his colleagues, under the leadership of NASA's first chief administrator, Keith Glennan, and his hard-driving successor James Webb, were hard-pressed to catch up with their Russian rivals. On the evening of April 12 1961 America was extremely disturbed by yet another triumph for the R-7 missile. Yuri Gagarin flew into space aboard a spherical capsule called Vostok. A newly-elected president, John F. Kennedy, was desperate to respond. "If somebody can just tell me how to catch up. Let's find somebody. I don't care if it's the janitor over there, if he knows how." Three days later, a CIA-backed raiding party landed at the Bay of Pigs in Cuba, hoping to destroy Fidel Castro's regime. The invasion was a disaster, and Kennedy turned to space in a bid to restore America's international prestige.

On April 20 Kennedy asked his vice-president, Lyndon Johnson, an ardent advocate of US progress in rocketry, "Do we have a chance of beating the Soviets by putting a laboratory in space, or by a trip around the moon, or by a rocket to land on the moon? Is there any other space program which promises dramatic results in which we could win?"

**John Glenn became the first American to orbit the earth,
propelled into space by an Atlas missile (right).**

A final decision hinged on NASA literally getting their manned space program off the ground. On May 5 Alan Shepard was launched in a Mercury capsule, atop a small Redstone missile designed by von Braun. Shepard's flight was just a fifteen-minute ballistic hop, a mere fraction of an orbit, but it was enough to boost Kennedy's confidence. In a historic speech on May 25 1961, he told Congress, "I believe that this nation should commit itself to achieving the goal, before this decade is out, of landing a man on the moon." NASA's Apollo project, one of the greatest engineering achievements in history, was kicked off because America's first man in space was launched just twenty-three days after Russia's first man. Shepard should have flown in March 1961, but there had been last-minute problems with the Mercury. If it hadn't been for that slight delay, an American would have been first into space, and Kennedy might never have felt the need to send men to the moon.

With Soviet politicians eager to respond to Kennedy's dramatic move, Korolev was forced to adapt his Vostok to carry two cosmonauts in the same small capsule, and even three if they gave up their spacesuits. A veil of secrecy prevented the outside world from learning details of the hardware. Over the next five years, Russia appeared to stroll from one victory to the next: the first woman in space, the first multi-man crews, the first space walk, and even the first stab at an orbital rendezvous between two ships. These were real achievements, but they stretched the Vostok design to its limits. Korolev was exhausted. On January 14 1966 he died during what should have been a routine stomach operation. It turned out he was riddled with cancer, aggravated by old injuries from his time in the gulag. He had been planning the Soyuz, Russia's workhorse capsule which is still in use today. He had also embarked on a giant lunar booster, the N-1. Now his legacy was in the hands of less capable administrators. The N-1 was a disaster, and Russia never came close to landing a man on the moon, although there was some concern, by 1968, that it could, perhaps, send a single cosmonaut around the moon using an intermediate-sized rocket, the Proton, thereby stealing Apollo's thunder. NASA could not be sure about any of this at the time, because the Soviets were so secretive.

The Apollo project continued at breakneck pace, incurring its own terrible risks. In January 1967, three astronauts, Gus Grissom, Ed White, and Roger Chaffee, died in a launchpad fire while testing systems aboard the first Apollo capsule. After a tense two years of recrimination and redesign, NASA recovered its momentum. Apollo 8 carried Frank Borman, James Lovell, and William Anders around the moon during Christmas 1968. Seven months later, in July 1969, John F. Kennedy's pledge to land a man on the moon "before this decade is out" was fulfilled when Apollo 11's lunar module Eagle landed Neil Armstrong and Buzz Aldrin safely on the surface, while Michael Collins waited in orbit aboard the command module Columbia.

In 1975 President Richard Nixon called a halt to the space race. He sent the final Apollo craft to rendezvous in orbit with a Soviet Soyuz capsule, and today the fruits of that union can be seen in the International Space Station. An adventure born out of fear and rivalry now helps to maintain peaceful industrial and scientific cooperation between Russia, America, Japan, Canada, and the European Union.

2 ROCKETS & CATHEDRALS

The first unmanned prototype of the
Saturn V is prepared for a test
flight in September 1967.

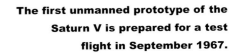

ROCKETS & CATHEDRALS

2

IT'S A CLICHÉ TO COMPARE the tall white spire of the Saturn V to a modern cathedral, but the thing about clichés is that they usually have some truth in them. The medieval castles were impressive statements of power and prestige, yet they were brutishly practical, and not nearly so much of a challenge to build—and, of course, not so joyously beautiful—as the extremely tall, very wide, and pointlessly ornate cathedrals, which were designed to show off what could be done with stone, wood, and glass when those materials were stretched to their limits. For all the practical reasons of Church and State that ensured their funding, the simple truth is that cathedrals rose up from the ground because communities wanted to express the utmost that they could achieve. But on a practical level, the communities who built them learned the art of managing large-scale construction projects, one of the foundations of modern civilization. Building cathedrals was—just as John F. Kennedy said of Apollo—"difficult and expensive to accomplish." Their scale and complexity required radically new techniques in architecture, mathematics, and structural engineering, and many other disciplines that were not apparently strictly needed for the everyday work of putting up houses and barns. No one can doubt the craft skills of medieval house-builders, nor the literally vital importance of the farmers' craft, but sometimes our ancestors wanted to do more than merely live.

Castles and forts exploited vast tonnages of stone and brick to deliver protective strength. They were rooted into the ground like vast boulders. In vivid contrast, cathedrals used as little stone as the masons felt they could get away with, in order to achieve an impression of lightness, taking to the air, ascending to the heavens. They may have been religious structures built by mortal men in honor of God, but they had a prideful, defiant character, too: a refusal to accept the apparent limits of Nature, and a desire to push a little further and see what the *real* limits might be. There was no stopping the push towards further extremes of height and scale, expressed with the strongest yet lightest materials. It was only a matter of time before some cathedral or other would stretch its spire indefinitely high into the sky.

The huge Vertical Assembly Building takes shape (left). Notice the three mobile launch towers. The technology of the gigantic Saturn V (above) was expected to have a long future.

The Saturn V launch vehicle for the Apollo project shared some of these qualities, especially in its expression of towering scale and strength derived from the lightest materials; and, just like the cathedrals, it was an expression of defiance against limitations. To take just one example: the people of Apollo took the most dangerous chemicals they could find and harnessed them, like sled drivers leashing a squad of snarling lions instead of tame huskies. Why? Partly because the unforgiving mathematics of the lunar flight demanded the use of lightweight hydrogen fuel, but also because they wanted to see if they could get away with it. The kerosene fuel used for the first stage was familiar to all aviation workers, but the super-cold liquid hydrogen in the upper stages was something new and terrible. It played havoc with the fabric of any structure that tried to contain it, and exploded with the power of a small atom bomb at the slightest spark. The tiniest variations in the thickness of welded seals in a metal tank were exaggerated into dangerous flaws by the thermal shock of liquid hydrogen pouring onto them. And this is the fuel that they chose for the Saturn: a substance that burns in the heart of the sun.

As if this wasn't enough of a challenge, hydrogen was only one of the dangerous chemicals that the Saturn had to contain. The rocket's combustion process also needed oxygen. To the inexact and non-technical imagination, liquid hydrogen stored at 300 degrees below zero seems pretty much "as cold as" liquid oxygen in an adjacent tank. In terms of the underlying physics, there's a 100-degree difference in temperature between them: as great as that which separates a pan of boiling water from a tray of ice cubes. Yet these fluids in their tanks had to share a common dome-shaped bulkhead, barely an inch thick, to make the most efficient use of all the space inside the stage. To cap it all, the structure as a whole had to be ridiculously, impossibly lightweight. According to NASA's brief, the metal skin, all the pipework, and the massive engines had to comprise no more than seven percent of an upper stage's entire

What a rocket should look like: a test version of Saturn V on the pad (right).

The monstrous first stage for a Saturn V takes shape.

weight when fuelled. At the same time, the thin shells of these metal cylinders had to withstand a thrust of six million pounds from below, while supporting the weight of yet another 130-ton third stage and lunar ship above.

Yes, this was a cathedral of sorts: a thunderous defiance against Nature, a prideful tower. But Saturn V was a prayer of humility too. It was something vastly greater than anything that one man or woman working alone could have created. So long as human civilization persists, the Saturn V will be remembered, long after the names of all the thousands of people who built it have been forgotten. The space visionary Arthur C. Clarke couldn't have put it better when, in 1972, he wrote, "An age may come when Apollo is the only thing by which people remember the United States, or even the world of their ancestors, the distant planet Earth."

THE HEAVENS AND THE EARTH

A kind of spiritual urge played a role for both sides in the Cold War space race. The genuine joy that Russians felt about putting Sputnik and Gagarin into orbit was tied to a sense of what those achievements promised: that the Communist dream might actually be possible, despite the dreadful hardships that this colossal social experiment had yielded so far. Soviet planners dreamed of taming Nature in the service of Man. Sputnik suggested that even the stars themselves might be tamed. If the Russian people's long-held religious faith had been denied by the earthly politics of Marx, Lenin, and Stalin, now it was free to express itself in a more materialist kind of language. What were rockets but new cathedrals? What was the Sputnik if not a polished metal prayer? The cosmos was an analog of heaven that ordinary Russians were allowed to dream of reaching. There was even a new kind of god to worship. The Kremlin insisted that the identity of Sergei Korolev, the architect of Russia's early space triumphs, should remain a secret for fear that American spies would assassinate him. Perhaps by accident, but surely to the Kremlin's satisfaction, this measure created an anonymous, faceless deity, "The Chief Designer," who inspired love and awe among Russians and an eerie sense of dread in America. Lethal tensions that had existed between the Soviet State and the Russian Orthodox Church briefly found some respite among the rockets.

> "An age may come when Apollo is the only thing by which people remember the United States, or the world of their ancestors, the distant planet Earth."
>
> **Arthur C. Clarke, 1972**

Meanwhile, NASA hitched its wagon to America's favorite dream. On the new space frontier, astronauts were the latest bunch of cool-hand cowboys heading off in a thunder of hooves and a cloud of dust towards some new horizon. In the classic pioneering myth, a small fleet of ships sets sail across an uncharted ocean to discover new territory; a settlement is established at the point of landing; a settlement becomes a town. In time, other ships arrive with families of settlers to populate the new territories. Inspired by Wernher von Braun, NASA's champions talked of "colonizing the space frontier." Always, their plans were worked out with the most exact attention to fuel weights, rocket thrusts, orbital heights and speeds. As Arthur C. Clarke has pointed out, "No achievement in human affairs was ever so well documented before the fact as space travel."

An eerie machine for a surreal project: a lunar landing simulator suspended from a gantry on wire cables.

The flaw in the plan was simple. Where was the trade? Ships could be sent into orbit or to the moon, but what could they be expected to bring back as a return on the investment required to build them? What gold or silver could the space cowboys stash in their saddle bags to pay their way over the next horizon? This fundamental economic problem could not be wished away by any amount of romantic language. Even in the 1950s NASA's engineers had proved, on paper, that a flight to the moon was possible, and that there were many good scientific and spiritual reasons for attempting one; but there was no obvious way to justify spending the vast sums of money required to build the rockets.

Cathedral-building sent us moonwards. In the wake of Sputnik, the economic arguments against rocket adventures became strangely inverted, so that the drawbacks became, instead, the justifications. By accepting the huge expense of these abstract adventures without any prospect of a sensible financial return, both Russia and America set out to show what their rival societies might be capable of on earth: how much *more* they could do than merely running their domestic economies or equipping their armies. They built rocket–cathedrals because there was only so much pride that two global superpowers could take in the unpleasant business of war, or the dull, unremarkable process of simply keeping their people alive. They aspired to more—and so did a great many of their citizens.

It is essential for us to realize that neither of the Cold War superpowers would have reached for space—let alone the moon—if that prize hadn't meant something to the millions of ordinary people they were trying to impress. The moon sat at the top of the tallest spire that anyone could think of building. So they built it. And it didn't fall down. All that happened in later years was simply that people stopped going to that particular church.

THE HERETICS

Of course, not everyone was sold on the Apollo dream. In the late 1960s the counterculture was in full swing, and for the hippy generation NASA represented something devilish: The Man, that figurehead of the White Anglo-Saxon Protestant (WASP) capitalist élite, crushing human instinct in service of the profit motive, subverting Nature to his will and creating a global army of robot zombies. Norman Mailer, the famed writer and self-appointed spokesman for a rebellious generation, covered Apollo 11 for a book project, and found himself stirred and alarmed in equal measure. On the one hand he found the thunderous Saturn V immensely moving. "I had a poor moment of vertigo at the thought that man now had something with which to speak to God. A ship of flames was on its way to the moon."

Mailer even wondered if the tirelessly energetic WASPs were right in their ambitions for progress, and the hippies, feckless, lazy, and doomed? At the same time, he was depressed and frustrated by the Space Age's bland public face:

Everybody in NASA was courteous, and proud of their ability to serve interchangeably for one another, as if the real secret of their discipline and their strength and sense of morale was that they had depersonalized themselves. I had never before encountered as many people whose modest purr of efficiency apparently derived from being cogs in a machine. They spoke in a language not fit for a computer of events that might yet dislocate eternity.

Mailer had the good grace to question his assumptions, but to some people Apollo seemed a cold and clinical achievement, a stark warning about the perils of a technological society. To them NASA was the chilly realm of white middle-aged men in uniform white shirts and dark suits; men made of flesh and blood, yet incapable of expressing emotion, rendered soulless by mechanistic conformity. The irony is that Apollo was almost entirely a product of emotion and instinct. Logic was far down the list of reasons for doing it. The machinery made possible the performance of certain tasks. It still remained up to humans to determine *what* those tasks should be. Let us stress, yet again, that America did not choose, single-handedly, to go the moon. There would have been no international prestige at stake unless, at some level at least, most of humanity shared the same dream. Rationalism handled the "how." Human emotions were always in charge of the "why."

John F. Kennedy attends a NASA briefing in 1962. NASA chief James Webb and Vice-President Lyndon Johnson are on the far left of the group.

THINKING BIG

Historians still debate the role played by President John F. Kennedy in shaping NASA's fortunes, but rather less attention is given to the man who actually led the agency while it prepared Apollo for the moon. It wasn't Wernher von Braun, despite his great celebrity and his skilled leadership of the Saturn V's development. The man in overall charge of America's space program was an unlikely figure, a burly, talkative bureaucrat with little knowledge of space or rockets. What *he* understood was politics, and how it intersected with business.

When President Kennedy took office in 1961 NASA was still a relatively minor arm of the federal government. The White House advisors made contact with at least seventeen distinguished scientists and business leaders, asking if they might like to head the agency, but at that time NASA didn't seem such a tempting prospect. In January 1961 it had sent a chimpanzee called "Ham" to the edge of space, riding on top of a slender rocket hastily adapted from a medium-range Army missile. Ham's mission, a preliminary towards launching astronauts on similar suborbital hops, lasted sixteen minutes and carried him a mere 420 miles from his original launch site on the east coast of Florida. There were some malfunctions during Ham's short ride. When he was plucked from the Atlantic after splashdown, frightened and wet, but safe, the new man in the White House, John F. Kennedy, wasn't that much impressed by the whole thing. His science advisor Jerome Weisner warned him, "A failure in our first attempt to place a man into space would create serious national embarrassment. We should stop advertising this as our major objective." No wonder no one wanted the NASA job. In some desperation Vice-President Lyndon Johnson strong-armed an unlikely candidate, a lawyer from North Carolina, into accepting the post.

James Webb: headstrong and ambitious, he was the right man at the right time.

James Edwin Webb was born in October 1906, in the small town of Tally Ho, North Carolina. As a young man, his first jobs were classic small-town means of helping his family to get along: working on farms, helping out in nickel-and-dime stores, and truck driving on construction sites. His father was the superintendent of schools in Granville County, and his mother was equally concerned about education and social progress. The highly intelligent young man cut his teeth as an education bureaucrat in the 1930s, and signed up to be a part of President Roosevelt's New Deal, a bold attempt to get America moving again after the Depression years, using vast sums of tax money to pay for infrastructure developments and social projects. Webb was hooked on this idealistic environment. He also turned out to be a smart political operator and a successful businessman. In 1938, by now happily married, he joined a Washington law firm, then became an executive at the Sperry Corporation in New York as it geared up for the coming war, before leaving in 1944 for a tour of duty with the Marine Corps.

> ### "*Somebody* in the government has got to tie it all together!"
>
> **James Webb, 1961**

After the war, Webb returned to public service, rising to the rank of Director of the Bureau of the Budget, a position he held until 1949. President Truman then asked him to serve as Under Secretary of State. But when the Truman administration ended in 1953, Webb didn't like the

idea of working for the new and staunchly Republican president, Dwight D. Eisenhower. He left Washington for a senior position at Kerr-McGee, the giant oil and nuclear power company in Oklahoma City. And there his contribution to the greater sweep of history might have come to an end. He could have finished his career as a talented and successful businessman just like many others, albeit with some flair for charitable works and public service: the embers from his youthful New Deal fires not yet burned out. Today, we might not have had cause to remember him in any broader context. But history wasn't finished with Jim Webb.

On January 17 1961, just as President Eisenhower prepared to hand over to a new leader with ideas very different from his own, he gave an extraordinary address to the nation, in which he reminded American citizens that a gigantic armaments industry had been created since the Second World War, where none had existed previously. In his opinion, it threatened to change all of society for the worse:

In the councils of government, we must guard against the acquisition of influence, whether sought or unsought, by the military–industrial complex. The potential for the disastrous rise of misplaced power exists and will persist. We must never let this endanger our liberties or our democratic processes.

It took just eight years for NASA to progress from the tiny Redstone rocket (below) to the immense Saturn V (left).

Eisenhower also warned that "public policy could become the captive of a scientific-technological élite." He would have been dismayed if he'd known that the newly-formed NASA would soon be under the control of a man who believed that, rather than being any threat to America's future, "a scientific–technological élite" could be the solution to all its ills. Webb believed that industry wasn't meeting the challenge posed by Soviet strength. He also felt that the colleges and universities were not creating a sufficient number of graduates properly equipped for the technological world that lay ahead. "You see, you've got the physicists here, the astronomers here, and the chemists over there—*somebody* in the government has got to tie it all together!" Webb said. And he was determined to be that somebody.

If President Kennedy had known how important space was about to become, he would undoubtedly have appointed someone more to his liking as chief of NASA. The political writer Charles Murray observes:

Stocky and voluble, Webb was of an older generation than most of the others in this new administration, and he came from a different world. Instead of Harvard and wire-rimmed glasses, clipped accents, and dry wit, he was University of North Carolina, all rumpled collars and down-home homilies: a good ol' boy with a law degree.

But he was the right man at the right time. While many NASA insiders thought that the great new lunar adventure announced by Kennedy in 1961 must surely continue for generations to come, Webb understood that this was a fragile, fleeting moment in history, a rare window of opportunity that would slam shut as suddenly as it had opened. Moving with a speed and decisiveness that seems hard to imagine today for any government bureaucrat, he swiftly consolidated NASA's influence across a vast crescent-shaped swathe of states: California, Texas, Mississippi, Louisiana, Alabama, Florida, Virginia, Maryland, and Ohio, the one inland state. Webb spent most of his time at NASA headquarters in Washington, from where he could keep an eye on the politicians.

A sensible way of running a rocket facility might be to put the launch pads, control centers, and construction hangars all in one location, and no one doubted Webb's reasons for expanding a small Air Force missile testing station at Cape Canaveral, on the Florida coast, into a giant moonport. But why build the mission control center so far away, in Houston, Texas of all places? And why build the Apollo capsules in California, booster components in Alabama and Louisiana, and yet more huge chunks of equipment in Long Island? His wide dispersal of NASA operations and private industrial contracts angered many people, not least the Congressional representatives of states where the NASA contracts were not so thick on the ground. They saw the distributions as politically motivated, perhaps even unethical. But Webb was almost impossible to intimidate. "I made up my mind early in the game that I couldn't let anybody dictate decisions that were at a technical level, whether it was the President, the Vice-President, or the scientists," he said in later years.

> "In the councils of government, we must guard against the acquisition of unwarranted influence by the military–industrial complex."
>
> **President Eisenhower, 1960**

SPREADING THE BENEFITS

He was playing a clever game. He wanted to ensure that as few Congressional representatives as possible would wish to block NASA's funding, for fear of losing space-related jobs in their particular home states. Hence, the spreading of NASA activities across the country. Second, as an old-style Democrat he believed passionately that one of the proper purposes of any large government undertaking should be to distribute jobs and education opportunities as widely as possible across the nation. While NASA's workforce grew to 30,000 people in the mid-1960s, private contractor staff amounted to ten times that number. It could never last, but for a few years at least, Webb's large-scale manipulations delivered jobs and a sense of self-worth and idealism to half a million space workers, from rocket scientists and computer experts to metal benders, building contractors, secretaries, and caterers. NASA's expansion triggered real-estate booms in Florida, California, Texas, Alabama, Virginia, and other states besides, as the various "field centers" grew from modest laboratories into complexes the size of small cities, and with suburbs to match.

Webb also fought behind the scenes to ensure that the Apollo project would not define NASA to the exclusion of everything else. The less glamorous robot probes and science projects were just as important, he believed. We take this multi-faceted character of space exploration for granted, but in the feverish atmosphere of the 1960s moon race, it had to be defended. President Kennedy made many eloquent speeches about the benefits of Apollo, and always steadfastly supported NASA in public, but privately he told Webb that the estimated costs of reaching the moon appalled him. "I'm not that interested in space," he admitted bluntly at a White House meeting in November 1962. "We're ready to spend reasonable amounts of money, but we're talking about these fantastic expenditures, which wreck our budget on all these other domestic programs, and the only justification for it, in my opinion, is because we hope to beat the Russians!"

Kennedy wanted an assurance: did Webb think that Apollo was NASA's number-one priority? "No sir, I do not," Webb replied. "I think it is *one* of the priorities." He argued that America would best benefit from a broader range of activities in space. Onlookers were amazed as a nasty shouting match threatened to brew between the two men, but Kennedy was apparently swayed and Webb's view prevailed. Throughout his tenure at NASA he fought to protect and promote the unmanned scientific and astronomy programs that we now celebrate as among the agency's most valuable achievements: probes to Venus, Mars, Jupiter, and worlds beyond, and the first steps towards funding an orbiting space telescope.

These are just the uppermost assemblies for the Saturn V's huge F-1 rocket engines.

Roosevelt had championed technocratic "Big Thinking" to salvage an ailing nation in the 1930s; wartime mobilization made it mandatory; Eisenhower had grave doubts in an era of 1950s post-war complacency but continued to sanction it; Kennedy took it pretty much for granted

boast the most successful management of complex engineering and manufacturing projects that the world had ever known. Even so, NASA's enemies feared that it was overstepping its bounds by a country mile. In 1963, an alarmed senator, William Proxmire, told Congress, "The space program is probably the most centralized government spending program in the United States. It concentrates, into the hands of a single agency, authority over an important sector of our economy. It could well be described as corporate socialism."

And Proxmire was a Democrat. Maybe he had a point. A very strange relationship had emerged between NASA and the private aerospace sector. It wasn't an expression of pure free-market economics, because the space agency intervened in the fortunes of private companies by placing substantial contracts at the taxpayers' expense, while those companies, in their turn, became dependent on the agency's patronage; and the relationship wasn't exactly socialist either, because the companies remained privately owned, and were therefore permitted to keep their profits. Yet it was a mirror image of Soviet Russia's command economy. Politicians set the agenda, determined budgets and decided what space vehicles they wished to see manufactured (albeit advised by NASA) and what new technologies they wished to encourage. The tens of thousands of employees in the NASA-funded aerospace factories were, by any sensible definition, workers for the state. If only three percent of a typical rocket company's trade was conducted in the private free market, how could it be otherwise?

The patchy illusion of free enterprise was preserved by the rules of competition. Companies vied for federal contracts by exhibiting cost efficiencies, technical prowess, and other fine virtues in their sales presentations. But it wasn't just the prospect of cash that drove leading aerospace manufacturers to compete, with rare and strident fury, for that greatest prize of all: the chance to build a ship to go to the moon. One renowned aviation designer, Harrison Storms, had made his name building well-armed fighter planes. Apollo, he said, offered him a chance, at last, to make a "wonderful flying machine that doesn't have a gun on it."

And in the end, the sums of money involved were not so terrifying as Proxmire made out. A simple comparison between the population census figures and NASA's expenditure during the 1960s tells us that it reached the moon for less than two dollars a month from each American citizen. Per day, it was the price of a stick of gum.

3 SPACESHIPS OF THE MIND

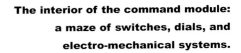

The interior of the command module: a maze of switches, dials, and electro-mechanical systems.

The interior of the command module: a maze of switches, dials, and electro-mechanical systems.

SPACESHIPS OF THE MIND

3

ONE MYTH WE CAN DISPENSE WITH is that the technology of Apollo is now so old-fashioned it can safely be consigned to the shelves of museums. On the contrary, a good deal of it still hasn't been matched. For instance, in late 2007 a team of NASA engineers designing new hardware for a new moonshot, planned for the coming decade, removed a panel from an old Apollo capsule on display in Washington DC's Air and Space Museum, and took a look inside the maze of wiring and pipework. They wanted the answer to a problem that had beaten the best minds in modern space engineering.

At the end of a mission, and just prior to re-entry into the earth's atmosphere, a crew capsule must separate cleanly from the equipment module that has contained most of its air, water, electrical power supplies, and rocket fuel. How is this to be done reliably, and in a fraction of a second? Dozens of power wires, data cables, and fluid conduits have to be disconnected in an instant, not to mention the three or four heavy attachment bolts that have held the capsule snug against the equipment module during the mission. The NASA team discovered inside the Apollo a tiny set of explosive guillotines, through which all the cables and lines snaked in a neat bundle. When the time came for the capsule to drop away, the guillotines sliced through metal and plastic as though they were butter. A backup set of guillotines, powered by a different electrical circuit, insured against failure—and all in a box the size of a car battery. Forty years later, Apollo still had lessons to teach.

In popular culture, spaceships are supposed to look sleek and futuristic, but even today the real-life hardware sometimes lacks a certain stylishness, and there is a subtle reason for this. Take a look, for instance, at how commercial airliners are built. The production runs are large enough to justify the initial costs of purpose-built factory tooling and templates. The cabins have moulded interior fittings that tuck neatly into the corners and meet seamlessly with the windows; the foldaway tables look like they belong on the back of the seats, and so on. There'll

The Apollo 11 command module on display at the National Air and Space Museum in Washington DC (right). The glossy exterior finish burned away during re-entry.

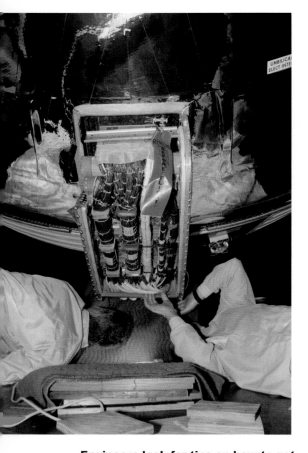

Engineers look for tips on how to get back to the moon (above) using rare unflown backup Apollo hardware (right) at NASA's Kennedy Space Center.

be some decorative flourishes, probably featuring the airline's logo, adding consistency to the various pieces. Inside and out, everything fits together into a more or less coherent whole. The same cannot be said of a typical spacecraft. These are hand-made machines, with populist styling absolutely not on anyone's priority list. It makes very little business sense for aerospace companies to create production lines for machines that are only going to be built a few times. Consequently there is a nuts-and-bolts feel to most spacecraft that causes some unprepared observers to think of them as disappointingly crude, almost wilfully antique.

The cultural reference point for what spaceships are supposed to look like is almost certainly Stanley Kubrick's 1968 science-fiction film *2001: A Space Odyssey*, itself a product of the Age of Apollo. Kubrick's prop designers first sat down at their drawing boards in 1964, at the start of what would turn out to be a long and complex production. The ships they invented still look futuristic. It is fascinating that the new space tourism companies, such as Virgin Galactic, have created interiors for their suborbital spacecraft that satisfy our expectations of how things *should* be, with digital control panels, soft padding on the cabin walls, and space meals you can suck through a straw, just like in *2001*. This is all an illusion, a marketing ploy. In real life, the interiors of space shuttles or Soyuz capsules look quite similar to the Apollo cabins, at least in their detailing of bolts, screws, and switches.

> "As a teenager, I thought that everything that happened before I was born was just ancient history. I didn't think I needed to know all about it. So I can't be too critical of this generation."
>
> **Neil Armstrong, 2001**

Visitors to aerospace museums sometimes expect gleaming science-fiction props. The real spacecraft that they encounter can leave them unmoved. People peer through the hatch of an Apollo capsule and see a dimly lit interior encrusted with ancient clockwork. There are no touch-sensitive screens or plasma displays. The instrument panels are a mechanical maze of switches and dials, and the thousand-fold electrical energies that once powered them are no longer in evidence to lend them some life. People are struck by how clunky, or even downright primitive, everything looks; and in countless historical reappraisals of Apollo, we are told repeatedly—aren't we?—that a child's little hand-held electronic game is more advanced than the computers used for Apollo.

Perhaps life changes so fast now that our culture has lost the ability to conceive of any world older than last year's. If we want to gain an impression of how futuristic Apollo seemed four decades ago, we need to make a couple of time-travel journeys of the imagination. Picture Louis Blériot in 1909 making what seemed at the time an epic journey, crossing the English Channel by air in a monoplane of such fragile design it seems unthinkable, today, that anyone could have entrusted their life to it. Look also at Lindbergh's plane, the *Spirit of St Louis*. Would you expect that machine, with its home-made finish, to have carried a man safely across the Atlantic Ocean? Yet when these two famous vehicles flew their missions, they were heralded as portents of a new world. They were *futuristic*.

John Knoll's digital recreation of the view from Armstrong's window as the lunar module approached close to a dangerous crater.

To the generation who witnessed it, Apollo was futuristic and then some. Imagine the command module brand new, completely covered in mirror-smooth silver foil insulation so that it looks like a single piece of polished metal. (The foil burns off during re-entry, leaving the capsule a drab brown color. It's best to think of it in its launch-day finery.) Now visualize the interior of the spacecraft, surgically clean and brightly lit so that the astronauts can see what they are doing. There is not a single scuff mark in the paintwork. The air-conditioning units are humming, and the control panel is a shimmer of lights and trembling dials. Apollo seems almost alive. By the standards of the 1960s this was the most advanced machine in history.

A CHILD'S TOY

The same applies to Apollo's on-board computer. True, the working memory inside it was only 256 kilobytes—and, yes, that capacity is easily outstripped by the cheapest modern toy. The computer on which this book was written pushes gigabyte files through microchips the size of stamps in less than the blink of an eye; but *this* computer is plugged into just a couple of fairly simple and low-powered interfaces with the outside world: a printer, a backup disc drive, and a telephone socket. By contrast, the input and output wiring of the Apollo computer connected it with a bewildering array of heavy-duty devices, from radio and radar systems to gyroscopic compasses and optical star trackers, and, ultimately, to the gas thrusters and powerful rocket engines that actually drove the ship through space. The computer responded to what the spacecraft was telling it, and told the craft what to do next. When the astronauts punched instructions into the computer's keypad, or nudged their pistol-grip thrust controllers to alter the spacecraft's orientation, these inputs were simply another of the myriad factors that the computer had to deal with and respond to, delivering its output in the form of tangible action, expressed as movements of the spacecraft itself.

"Our autopilot was taking us into a very large crater about the size of a football stadium, with steep slopes, covered with very large rocks. That was not the kind of place I wanted to try and make the first landing."

Neil Armstrong, 2005

A vast effort of design went into making sure that the computer could recover from crashes in less than half a second. Even when Apollo 12 was struck by lightning soon after launch, and the whole interior of the Apollo capsule blacked out for a moment, the computer survived. It was a reliable piece of equipment because it *had* to be. Astronauts' lives depended on it not failing. Forty years later, PC manufacturers and software writers have simply not delivered to us that same robustness. Our computers are vulnerable to the smallest upsets. Until one sits on your desk that can work on many complex calculations for a fortnight without seizing up, no one can talk again of the primitive nature of Apollo's computer.

Contrary to any number of accounts, not least those of some of the astronauts themselves, there was not one moment during any lunar mission (apart from Apollo 13) when humans had to "take over" from wayward electronics and fly the vehicles themselves for fear that some misfiring circuit was steering them to their doom. A famous Apollo 11 incident is worth retelling, because—contrary to the way that it has been interpreted in some popular accounts—it is a story of men and machines working in harmony, rather than against each other, in what's now commonly known as a "fly-by-wire" system:

Just as the lunar module (LM) was plunging towards the lunar surface in final approach, the computer display in the cabin suddenly started flashing. "Program alarm," said Armstrong. Alongside him, Buzz Aldrin punched a key on the display board. "1201," he reported.

At Mission Control, 26-year-old Steve Bales was sitting at the guidance console, monitoring the LM's computer system. Senior flight controller Gene Kranz came on the microphone loop and demanded to know, "What's a 1201?" Bales was suddenly in the spotlight. The LM was rushing towards the moon and the computer was saying that something was wrong. He needed a few seconds to think. "Stand by," he replied, trying to buy time. But Aldrin wanted an answer right away. "Give us the reading on the 1202 alarm," he said. In astronaut-speak, he was asking if Armstrong and he should abort the landing. Bales had no time left. The LM was plunging into what NASA insiders privately called the "Dead Man's Zone."

After undocking from the orbiting command module to begin its separate voyage, the LM's crew module (ascent stage) could punch away from the lower descent stage at more or less any time if anything went wrong. The ascent stage's engine could power the astronauts back into orbit to rejoin the command module. But the Dead Man's Zone was a brief period of uncertainty that nobody could do anything about. Within the last three minutes of the landing approach, there was a ten-second phase when the LM was hurtling downwards so fast that if the ascent stage's engine fired in an emergency abort, the entire fuel reserve would be wasted counteracting the downward momentum. The ascent stage wouldn't be able to climb back up to join the mothership. Instead it would crash on the moon.

As the computer alarms sounded, the Dead Man's Zone was coming up in twenty seconds. If Bales was going to recommend an abort, he had to do it right now. Making the bravest and possibly the most reckless decision of his life, he spoke into his headset for Kranz and all the other controllers to hear. On the tapes that survive to this day, his voice is shaky, fearful. For this moment at least, the entire Apollo program rests on his young shoulders, not to mention the lives of two men out in space. "We're 'Go' on that alarm," he said. This was a signal for the astronauts to ignore the alarm and carry on.

> "The lunar module may have seemed terrifyingly fragile, but we had faith in the people who built it. We entrusted our lives to it."
>
> **Buzz Aldrin, 1997**

Kranz was surprised, but he trusted all his controllers completely. He let the decision ride, and the LM plunged down into the Dead Man's Zone. Strictly speaking, Bales should have called off the landing, but he didn't quite believe the 1201 code. Even as the computer was flashing warning signals, it was still feeding the proper information to the astronauts' control panels, and the descent was going pretty much according to plan. The only solid evidence that Bales had was his memory of similar alarms cropping up during training sessions. Forty years later, and Bales still isn't sure about the decision he made in that terrifying moment. "Nobody really knew what was causing the problem, and I couldn't be a hundred percent sure that the judgement I was making was okay. It was based more on instinct than hard facts." Bales decided that so

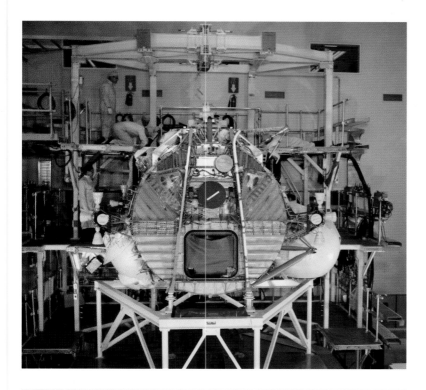

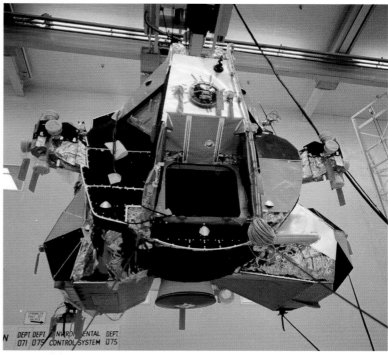

Assembly of the lunar module at the Grumman factory
in Bethpage, New York, and (overleaf) John Ortmann's
digital recreation of the two Apollo spacecraft.

COLUMBIA

EAGLE

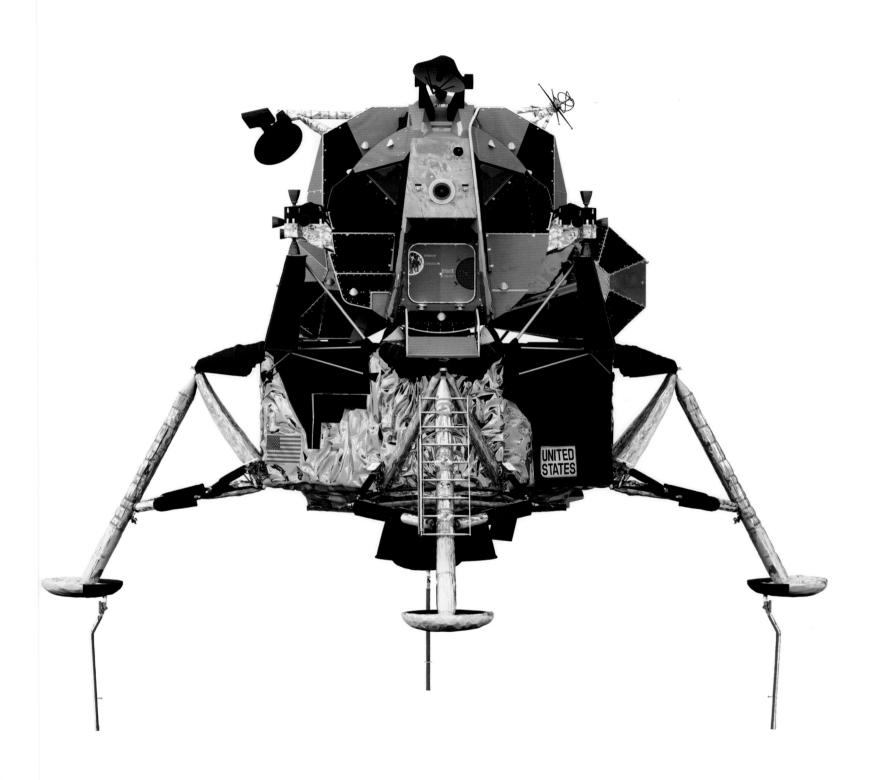

The command module is prepared for mating with the Saturn V (above). Blue plastic sheeting protects the brand-new capsule from damage.

John Ortmann's artwork (left) shows something we never see in the mission photos: both spacecraft docked.

long as the computer was still working, it was working, and that was that. Just as he was recovering from the computer scare, CapCom Charlie Duke was radioing a warning up to the Apollo crew: "Sixty seconds." Listening to the original NASA dialogue tapes, it's impossible to tell that anything was wrong, but in technical shorthand, Duke was really saying to Armstrong, "Your engine only has sixty seconds-worth of fuel left in its tank."

Duke called out another warning. "Thirty seconds." Chief astronaut Deke Slayton, standing behind Duke, said softly to him, "Shut up Charlie, and let 'em land." Any moment now, and the LM's engine was going to sputter and die. The instant it did so, the ascent stage would automatically separate and begin an emergency return to lunar orbit. Firing the ascent stage under these chaotic circumstances was no guarantee of safety, even out of the Dead Man's Zone, but it was better than simply crashing the LM onto the moon.

Kranz and his team then saw something amazing on their telemetry screens. With less than a hundred feet remaining before touchdown, it seemed that the LM was pitching forward and skimming over the lunar terrain at thirty miles per hour. Had the two best pilots in NASA suddenly lost control of their ship? Another ten seconds crawled by. At last, Aldrin radioed, "Contact light. Mode control to 'Auto.' Engine Arm off." Those were, in fact, the first words ever spoken by a human being on the surface of another world. Armstrong chipped in a moment later with phrases more easily understandable to the general public. "Tranquility Base here. The Eagle has landed."

Mission Control erupted into applause, and Duke's radioed response, "We're breathing again. You've got a bunch of guys about to turn blue. Thanks a lot," was almost lost among the whoops and hollers of delight. Amstrong sounded apologetic when he radioed to explain what had happened in the last minute of descent. "Houston, that may have seemed like a very long final phase, but the [guidance system] was taking us right into a crater with a large number of boulders and rocks." He had needed a few precious extra seconds to hover a few meters above the surface and nudge the ship forward until he could find a safe place to land. Later, the newspaper and television reporters talked of Armstrong heroically "switching off the computer" and "seizing manual control" to steer the little craft away from danger. In fact there was never any conflict with the computer, because the astronauts were always supposed to be able to choose the exact patch of ground they wanted to land on. That's why the LM had windows for them to look out of.

Apollo 11's landing site on the Sea of Tranquility had been chosen on the basis of the most scrupulous orbital scans and telescope observations, but matters were very different when the LM was hovering just a few tens of feet from touchdown. At that point, dangerous rocks, boulders, and craters, too small to be observed from orbit, made themselves apparent. Armstrong quite properly took evasive action to avoid hazards, working in tandem with the computer—not against it—to bring the little craft down safely. Like an upright pencil teetering on a fingertip, the LM was balanced on a plume of engine thrust from a single nozzle, and it was only with constant help from the computer that any human could maneuver the craft. As for the apparently urgent alarms flashing on the display panel: they did not foretell impending failure. They were just warnings that several computational tasks were baying for attention all at once and, given the urgency of the landing, the computer was sending non-essential jobs to the back of the line. A late decision had been made, prior to the mission, that it might be sensible to have one of the LM's radars keeping tabs on the orbiting mothership, while the other dish pointed down to the lunar surface. The computer decided that the mothership data had to wait. But it did *not* misfunction. No wonder its young designers at the Massachusetts Institute of Technology (MIT) felt that their achievements had been somewhat misrepresented by the media. And in their old age, how weary they must have become of hearing that you could navigate to the moon today with a child's toy.

Apollo 11 command module pilot Michael Collins strikes a heroic poise inside the training simulator.

Kubrick's 1968 film *2001: A Space Odyssey* told us what the spaceships of the future were supposed to be like.

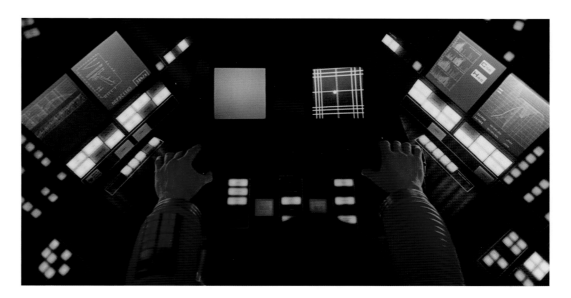

THE LANGUAGE OF APOLLO

The endless repetition by the media, parrot-style, of the NASA jargon soon bored the public, for this was not a language in which ordinary people would expect to speak about such epic events. Soon the events themselves seemed less momentous: just an inevitable product of a Lunar Orbit Insertion and an Extra-Vehicular Activity followed at the Time-Nominal moment by a Trans-Earth Injection Burn. Many journalists and TV reporters were diverted from the true drama by this barrier of language, occasionally steeping themselves in it like "wannabe" space travellers, but more often feeling dislocated by it. As Norman Mailer confessed:

In fact I was bored. Sitting in the Manned Spacecraft Center movie theatre, I noticed the press reporters were also bored. We all knew the engine burns would succeed and Apollo 11 would go into the proper orbit. There seemed no question of failure. I could not forgive the astronauts their resolute avoidance of an heroic posture.

It is only now, some forty years later, that we are gradually learning to appreciate just what a "heroic posture" the men of Apollo actually adopted, each and every time they climbed into those capsules.

NASA's acronyms are like medical terms, precise, exactly defined, specialized, and devoid of emotional loading. A potentially terrifying fuel leak on the pad is an "anomalous discharge." A cataclysmic explosion on a shuttle is "a major malfunction." No one dies or is killed. Rather, a crew "fails to respond." Charlie Duke didn't radio to Armstrong, "According to my readouts down here in Mission Control, you have maybe a minute or so of fuel left. Is that right? Is that what it says on your panel, too? Anyway, you be careful not to crash, you hear?" He simply said, "Sixty seconds." Space people share with the military an instinct that distressing situations can only be handled by keeping some sense of emotional distance. Keeping calm is important for men and women operating dangerous machinery. Astronauts cannot afford the ambiguities of poetry. Their lives often depend on knowing, in a split second, exactly what some particular word or phrase means.

Hundreds of thousands of people are still fascinated by space exploration today, and millions more take at least a passing interest, but those multitudes may not be sufficient to ensure a long-term continuation of the human space flight at a major national level. The drama of human rocket flight is as great now as it ever was, but astronauts do not seem to captivate us as they once could, and rockets have lost some of their ability to inspire awe. There is a problem in the language of space if young people no longer find as much excitement in the adventure as their parents did fifty years ago, when they, in their turn, were young. The cockpit chatter of space professionals will always remain terse and business-like, but perhaps NASA needs to speak to the rest of us in a more honest way that engages our emotions as well as our minds.

Armstrong in the lunar module simulator: a machine even more complicated than the real thing, because of the many exterior computers, photo projectors, and other systems that made it work.

"Machines are getting better all the time, but there's still a place for us—some reason for us, *Homo Sapiens*, to carry on existing."

Neil Armstrong, 2001

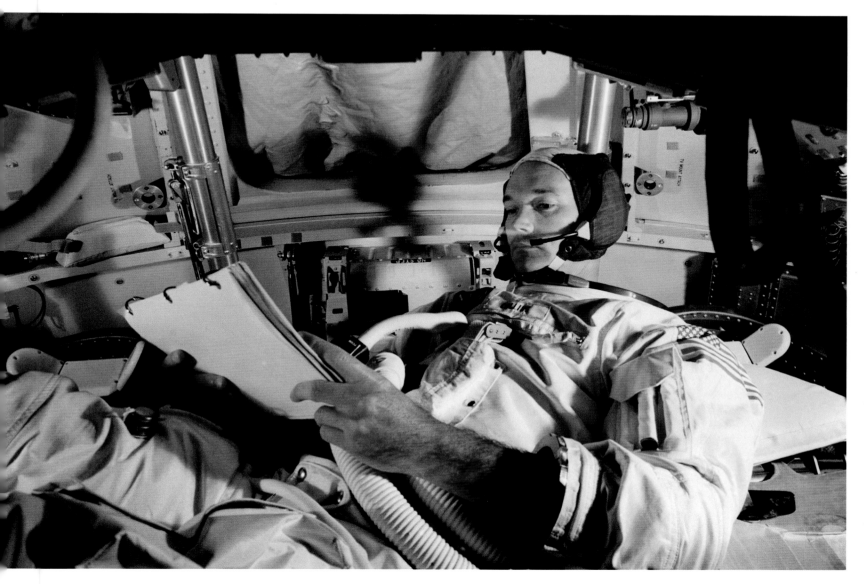

Collins in the command module simulator. Some sessions would last for several days on end, in order to acclimatize the astronauts to long periods inside the capsule.

We also need to send more people into space with more of a gift for telling us about what they see up there. By all means, let cool-headed minds prevail over the cockpit controls, but give the dreamers a chance, now and again, to stare out of the windows and ponder. Apollo 11's Michael Collins recognized this when he said, "I think a future flight should include a poet, a priest, and a philosopher. Then we might get a much better idea of what we saw."

THE ART OF SPACE

Artworks other than photography should also play a role in space flight. In 1962 Hereward Cooke of the National Gallery of Art in Washington DC wrote a letter of invitation to a number of prominent artists, inviting them to tour NASA and create works based on their impressions. He was eloquent about the need for both art and science in any space endeavor. "When a major rocket launch takes place, more than two hundred cameras record every split second of the activity," he wrote:

Every nut, bolt, and miniaturized electronic device is photographed from every angle. But the camera sees everything and understands nothing. It is the emotional impact, the interpretation and hidden significance of these events that lie within the scope of the artist's vision.

Cooke assured the selected artists that they would be given access to NASA facilities, and would be subjected to no editorial pressures. The only stipulation was that "the materials used must be of proven permanence. I do not want fading pictures in a government archive."

Paul Calle, famous for his scenes of life in the Old West, took up the challenge, making superb pencil drawings of astronauts and their capsules. Robert Rauschenberg's abstract silk-screen prints seemed both celebratory and mildly sarcastic at the same time; Lamarr Dodd captured an impressionistic morass of wires, switches, and dials, with silver-clad humans embedded into the machinery of their ships. James Wyeth's watercolors showed the forlorn scrublands surrounding NASA's launch complex. Rockets had to keep their distance from the ordinary human realm of towns and streets and family backyards. The drab safety-zone territories around the pads were a sort of endless "nowhere." A more inward landscape was explored by Mitchell Jamieson: the psychological drama behind the space age's political rhetoric. It needed only the lightest sweep of an artist's brush to expose the religious and mystical desires implicit in cosmic exploration. Jamieson's geometrically fragmented astronaut in his spacesuit brings to mind the saintly figures in a cathedral's stained-glass window.

Astronauts in training have a forlorn and vulnerable look to them. They are so out of place on the earth.

Aldrin, in the red jacket, gets to grips with a Hasselblad camera while Armstrong looks on.

The resulting art collection, a major body of work, is now under the guardianship of the Air and Space Museum in Washington DC. However, times have changed. In 2004 the singer and performance artist Laurie Anderson accepted a year-long commission as artist-in-residence for NASA. With her penchant for dreamlike electronic experimentation and her restless curiosity about modern technological culture, she was the perfect artist to take a quirky, sideways look at the space business. Sadly, by then Congress had forgotten the importance of art. When it got wind of Anderson's modest honorarium of $20,000 for a year's work, there were calls to halt her project, and unfortunately they were succcessful. One Congressional representative said that "NASA should not be spending taxpayer dollars on a performance artist."

That narrow-minded kind of thinking could cost America its future in space. Just think: if those medieval cathedral-builders had tried to save a few scraps of money by cutting back on the painted altarpieces, or the filigree stone carvings on the parapets, then so many of the intricate and expressive details that have helped those cathedrals to speak to future generations would have been lost to us, and we might not be so keen to preserve them, even at some expense. In much the same way, NASA should be allowed to communicate through art as well as rocket engineering, so as to reach as wide a spectrum of society as possible.

4 AN ELEMENT OF RISK

AN ELEMENT OF RISK

4

THE UNAVOIDABLE GULF between astronaut-speak and the way that rest of the world talks remains a problem today, for people are still surprised when missions occasionally go wrong. This generation is not accustomed to danger, either personal or global. No language has yet been invented that can persuade the public to fund rocket adventures in which, at some point, people are bound to die. They expect that NASA should be able to predict all risks, and that space vehicles fuelled with the energy equivalent of small thermonuclear bombs should be made as safe to fly as ordinary aircraft; at least, they should be if the government is paying for them with tax dollars. Surely all that dry, technical babble means that NASA must understand what it's doing by now, and that failures must therefore be the result of incompetence?

But rockets can be lethal, and space will always be an environment hostile to life. People make errors of judgement, and they can be very serious ones that lead to disaster; and sometimes people's animal instincts save a mission even when all the dials and read-outs are indicating trouble. Apollo 11's little lander could so easily have crashed on the moon, plunging America into a fantastic international humiliation that would have echoed to this day. The doomed space shuttle Columbia could so easily *not* have been struck by fuel tank debris in January 2003.

To date, fewer than six hundred people have flown into space. Three were killed before their craft ever left the earth, another crashed to the ground, three were suffocated during re-entry, seven were blown apart soon after launch, and seven died in an atmospheric disintegration of their ship. This is a fatality rate of one space traveller in twenty-eight. A dangerous profession indeed. Yet somehow, the illusion persists that journeys into space should be routine, and that accidents are blameworthy. As a consequence, it is harder, today, to build a ship for the moon than it was forty years ago. No matter how much money NASA spends, and how many checks it makes, it can never satisfy the modern craving for perfect safety. Astronauts in the Apollo era accepted the risks because the prize on offer seemed worthwhile to them: the chance to push

Armstrong's official portrait prior to Apollo 11, and (below) his younger self in the early 1960s, not long after he had joined NASA.

Neil Armstrong as he is today: shy, unwilling to promote himself, and refusing to adopt "a heroic posture."

at the frontiers of human experience and gain at least some degree of public glory for flying higher, faster, further away than anyone else in history. If the public understands that something new is being accomplished with a space mission, it tends to be more understanding about the potential hazards.

Part of the mystery of Apollo is that our generation is not so used to taking risks. When the bid for the moon was announced in 1961, almost all American leaders or managers in the prime of their professional adult lives—say, 40 to 50 years old—had fresh memories of the Second World War, and for them the Cold War was business as usual but with bigger and scarier bombs. The idea of risking the necks of a handful of astronauts in the service of their country didn't seem all that unusual. Apollo was accepted as a dangerous adventure. Indeed, that was part of its appeal. NASA's astronauts, and their rivals in the Soviet system, accepted huge personal risks in the struggle to reach the moon. In January 1967 three of them, Gus Grissom, Ed White, and Roger Chaffee, died in the most horrific circumstances imaginable, sealed inside a cramped capsule, a prototype for the Apollo, while it exploded into flame.

Some of the blame for the fire was laid at the door of North American Aviation, the California-based company responsible for building the capsule. Faulty wiring caused a tiny short-circuit spark. Ordinarily that should not have been a disaster, but NASA had chosen to pump pure oxygen into the Apollo's cabin for the astronauts to breathe. At the time of the fire, the oxygen supply was pressurized at higher than normal levels so that the capsule would not be contaminated by dust and moisture creeping in from the Floridian air. Oxygen is highly flammable under pressure, and somehow NASA missed this danger.

DOUBLE STANDARDS?

Congress expressed its dismay and blamed the fire on serious incompetence within NASA. Investigators concluded that many fire risks had been ignored or overlooked, such was the mood of confidence at that time after the brilliant successes of all the earlier flights. NASA had completed sixteen manned missions in two different kinds of spacecraft (Mercury and Gemini) without losing any crewmen. Just three months later, a Russian pilot, Vladimir Komarov, died when his parachutes failed and his Soyuz thudded into the Russian steppes like an unrestrained meteorite. The early years of space flight delivered what we would call a "steep learning curve."

In 1967 no one commented on the high standards expected of NASA in the same year that 56,000 American soldiers were wounded in action and 9,400 killed, during a campaign whose management was uncertain, whose purpose was undefined, and whose execution, even by the most charitable judgement,

Michael Collins (above) showed flair as a writer. This helped him come to terms with the stresses of Apollo 11. His crewmate Buzz Aldrin (right) was a man driven to succeed, sometimes at the cost of his happiness.

was flawed. The soldiers in Vietnam had little or no choice about their exposure to risks. The war could never have withstood the scrutiny that was applied to Apollo, but NASA's crewmen knew they were in a dangerous adventure and climbed willingly into their capsules. Some of them even expressed the view that they had it easy in comparison to their many aviator friends who were still in active military service. In April 1970, Jim Lovell, Fred Haise, and Jack Swigert, the crew of Apollo 13, nearly lost their lives when an oxygen tank exploded on the outward trip to the moon. There were many people in the space business who were rather relieved when the lunar landing missions were brought to an end in 1972 before a crew was actually lost out there. Senior Apollo manager George Mueller resented the fact that NASA had been under pressure to make unrealistic promises about safety:

How do you explain to the public at large that there's a certain danger in space flight, and you've got to accept that risk? We haven't been able to do that in our society. People are quite willing to accept risk for race drivers, for example, and clearly that's a hazardous operation. But when one of them gets killed, you don't have a Congressional investigation or a Presidential commission looking at it.

"Space is not just about having fun.
It's also the pursuit of achievement,
of service, of challenge."

Buzz Aldrin, 1999

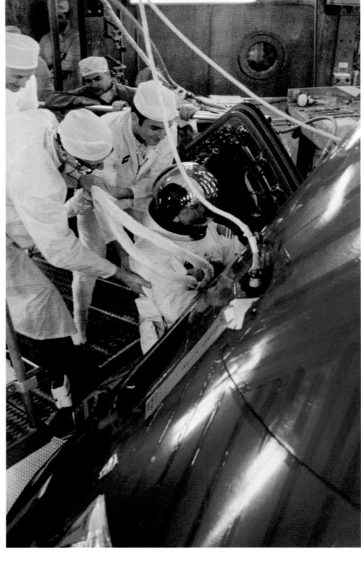

On November 9 1967, the world's largest and most powerful rocket, the Saturn V, lifted off for the first time, in an unmanned test mission known as Apollo 4. NASA announced that Apollo was back on track after the fire, at least as far as the launch vehicle was concerned. Unfortunately, the Saturn still had some nasty surprises up its sleeve. On April 4 the next year, another unmanned Saturn took off, designated Apollo 6. (The earlier Apollo 5 flight of January 22 was an unmanned capsule test using a much smaller rocket.) From the press stands five miles distant from the pad, everything looked wonderful. The five thunderous F-1 engines lit up and the Saturn rose into the sky on a gigantic column of fire. As it turned out, few newspapers or TV stations were concerned to report the launch, because a tragedy of global significance had turned their attention elsewhere. Civil rights leader Martin Luther King was shot and killed that same day. If the press pack hadn't been distracted by the assassination, they might have asked a few questions about that second Saturn flight.

For a start, two of the five F-1 main engines had failed shortly after lift-off, leaving the rocket unstable. Mission controllers kept their fingers hovering over their abort buttons, because at one point—too high in the trajectory for ground observers to notice—the rocket keeled over and headed nose-down towards earth before levelling out again. Somehow, the rocket's guidance computers compensated for the missing engines, and the upper stage, with its unmanned Apollo

"It would have been impossible for them to realize that the day might come when Americans would say, 'Oh yes—now, which one was he?'"

Tom Wolfe, 1979

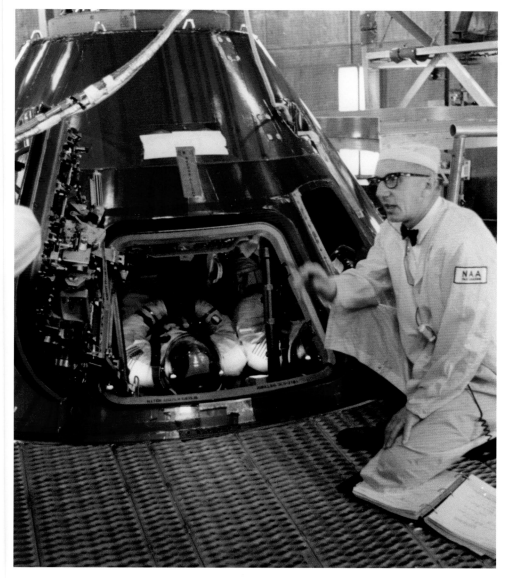

Would you choose to spend a day, let alone a week or more, sealed into one of these capsules? Here, an Apollo crew tests the capsule in a vacuum chamber that creates conditions similar to those in space.

capsule, just about limped to orbit. It wasn't exactly dignified. After careening like a drunken elephant, the Saturn's upper stage ended up flying backward around the earth. The Apollo capsule suffered heavy vibrations during the terrible launch, and many of its control systems failed. Also, the conical section of rocket skin beneath the capsule, designed to house the spider-like lunar landing craft in future missions, had lost one of its four panels, leaving the Apollo, still perched on the Saturn's upper stage, structurally weak. The next task in the mission was to relight the upper stage's engine and see if it could boost the shaken Apollo in the moon's general direction. The engine wouldn't even start.

The mission was a catastrophe. If there had been astronauts aboard, they would probably have lost their lives. At best, they would have had to fire the small escape rockets on their capsule and make a dangerous bid for an emergency splashdown. The Saturn V wasn't safe to fly. In the light of all this bad news, a senior Apollo manager, George Low, made an incredible decision. Next time the Saturn lifted off, it would carry a full crew—and it would take them all the way to the moon. When NASA chief James Webb heard about Low's plan, he exploded in fury. "Are you out of your mind? You're putting our agency and the whole Apollo project at risk!"

THE RACE ACCELERATES

Webb had good sense on his side, but data from the Pentagon's spy networks soon persuaded him that Low's plan was worth the risk after all. There were only twenty months left before John F. Kennedy's "before this decade is out" deadline for a lunar landing ran out, but NASA wasn't just racing to redeem a pledge of honor made by a dead president. Soviet Russia was also heading for the moon. The intelligence agencies knew that the Russians' massive N-1 lunar landing booster was years behind schedule, and no great threat to the Apollo timetable, but a smaller Russian rocket presented more of a challenge. The Proton, still in use today, was at an advanced level of development by 1968. And so was the new multi-crew space capsule, Soyuz, which would become the sturdy Russian workhorse.

There was a reasonable chance that the Proton could send a "stretched-limo" version of Soyuz around the moon by the end of 1968, even if it had to be so crammed with fuel and oxygen that only one cosmonaut could fit inside. If this mission succeeded, then it would be another Communist triumph: first satellite in space, first animal, first man, first spacewalker, first woman, and now, the prospect of being first to the moon. If Russia did manage this makeshift trip in a Soyuz–Proton combination, then Apollo would be shamed into second place. Of course NASA would eventually make an actual landing on the lunar surface, but the world would perceive America to have lost in space yet again. There could be no further delays in Apollo. There was no choice but to launch the Saturn V on a lunar mission as soon as possible. The lunar module landing craft (LM) wasn't yet ready to make a flight, and the only short-term option available was to send Apollo 8's crew to the moon without their lander. First, however, someone had to find out why the Saturn V wasn't working, and fix it.

Thousands of engineers worked on fixing the Saturn. Analyzing the failures was tricky because there was no wreckage from the last launch to examine (unless you counted the expended first and second stages lying at the bottom of the Atlantic, beyond salvage). The only evidence was radio telemetry data describing the flight in numbers and symbols on computer print-outs. From this slender evidence, an incredible detective effort resolved the problem. Kerosene and oxygen fuel thrumming at high speed through the pipework of the five main engines had set up a resonance that shattered the fuel lines. It's a bit like the effect you get in a tiled bathroom when you whistle at a certain pitch and the whole room suddenly hums. Make the tiles out of several different materials at random, and you can eliminate the humming. With a similar theory in mind, the pipework for the F-1 engines was redesigned with a new mix of materials, and all the vibrations in the fuel lines were eliminated. It was a brilliant effort: probably one of the cleverest and least-known engineering achievements in history.

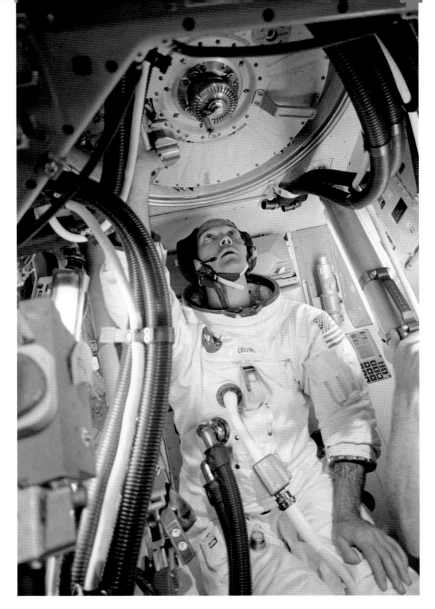

Collins looks warily at the complicated hatch mechanism in the nose of the command module.

Ground tests confirmed that the fix had worked, but it was still a huge risk to launch the next Saturn V with men aboard. However, it seemed necessary at the time. On September 14 1968, Russia finally succeeded in swinging an unmanned capsule around the moon and returning it to earth. In response, NASA sent Apollo 8 around the moon during the Christmas of 1968. That was what you call taking a chance. Men had ventured to the moon in urgent circumstances, flying new and hazardous machines, but somehow the true significance of that fact was not reflected by NASA's dry presentation. The dangers of the mission—precisely those dangers that might have excited and moved the general public into understanding just how incredible this achievement really was—were somehow lost in translation. This was why Tom Wolfe was able to write such prescient words about the astronauts in his 1979 book *The Right Stuff*:

The mantle of Cold Warrior of the heavens had been placed on their shoulders without their asking for it; and now it would be taken away again without their knowing that either. It would have been impossible for them to realize that the day might come when Americans would hear their names and say, "Oh yes—now, which one was he?"

THEY REALLY DID LAND

But even Wolfe, with his taste for a sarcastic aside, wouldn't have imagined that the day might come when the Apollo astronauts were accused of *faking* their missions. Many thousands of people around the world believe that we never landed men on the moon. They claim that the ghosty TV pictures of Neil Armstrong stepping onto the lunar surface in July 1969 were set up in a giant studio as part of one of the biggest conspiracies of all time. The simplest argument that the conspiracy theorists use is that there should only be one very concentrated source of light in the Apollo lunar photos—the sun—but many of the shots look as if they were snapped using some kind of much broader and softer illumination. The harsh sunlight on the moon should create deep black shadows, with no subtle shading in between; yet in most of the shots the astronauts seem suprisingly softly lit, like male models flaunting the latest craze in clumsy clothing. The shadows look as if they've been filled in by lights other than the sun.

The explanation is simple. The astronauts and their lunar module are standing on a gigantic gray-white photographic reflector. The moon's surface is a bright gray-white, as any pair of lovers will notice when they look up and see how brightly the moon bounces sunlight back into space. Photographers and movie makers are familiar with using large reflector panels to "fill in" the shadow areas of their subjects, particularly when counterbalancing very bright directional sunlight. On the moon, the surface terrain works a treat, and the astronauts are lit almost as perfectly as the NASA publicists could have hoped for.

Not to be confused with the real thing: Armstrong and Aldrin train for the moon walk in front of a mock-up lunar module.

The other argument from the conspiracy addicts is that countless stars should be visible in the black and airless lunar sky, yet there is not so much as a single speck of starlight visible on any of the 600 film frames snapped by Apollo 11's astronauts. This is a mystery that almost any photographer can solve after a moment's thought. An astronaut in a white spacesuit in bright sunlight needs an exposure of only a few fractions of a second, but stars are too distant and dim to register on photographic film unless exposure times of several seconds are used. This also explains why modern space shuttles and space stations photographed in orbit invariably appear against the same pure black sky. Time and again, space travellers tell of the vast panoply of stars they can see, yet those stars never appear on their photos.

Collins in a dummy command module cockpit, awaiting a centrifuge session.

A HISTORICAL ANOMALY

These are just the technical arguments against an ungenerous accusation of fakery. On a wider level though, the conspiracy stories probably reflect unease about Apollo's place in the history of machines. In 1886 Karl Benz patented the first automobile. Forty years later, the American car industry was manufacturing four million of them a year. The Wright Brothers flew the first human-carrying powered aircraft in 1903. Forty years later, commercial air travel and its darker cousin, aerial combat, were routine, and some people even had their own private planes. In the 1950s, a few large companies and institutions were using computers to do their payroll or solve complex equations. Forty years later, we all had one to play games on. And so it goes, and so it goes. The lunar adventure nourished countless areas of the economy in subtle yet important ways, speeding up developments in software, metallurgy, precision welding, and other profitable but unglamorous skills, such as personnel recruitment and management, risk analysis and information flow. But these benefits, although many and varied, haven't been so easy for most of us to identify. The more obvious impact that we might have expected, judged according to previous historical trends in machinery, are absent. We don't all have rockets in our garages and we can't all travel to the moon. This bucks the trend of just about any other branch of technology that has ever been invented.

Strangest of all, NASA and the US government tell us that it's almost as hard, and nearly as expensive, to build a lunar spacecraft now as it was forty years ago. And they're promising to do it in a dozen years or so, when last time it took less than a decade. Naturally, some people mutter that if we could accomplish Apollo using 1960s technology, then we should be able to

Three ordinary men. Collins once remarked that the main qualification for flying to the moon was to have been born at the right time—in 1930, give or take two or three years.

Armstrong narrowly avoided getting killed in this machine, a jet-powered training vehicle designed to mimic the behavior of the lunar module during its final descent to touchdown.

do it all again today, and at less cost, what with all the modern microchips and materials at our disposal, not to mention the vast backlog of knowledge and experience already accumulated in NASA's brain bank. The fact that we can't suggests that Apollo must have been some kind of a miracle the first time around. In a sense, that's just what it was. An accidental series of alignments in history made Apollo possible, bringing it to the forefront somewhat ahead of time. In the 1960s we weren't quite ready for lunar travel, yet a moonship appeared.

By the end of the Apollo era there was a wide sense of public distrust towards large-scale technological enterprises, but the counter-culture campaigners and peace-promoting liberals who so much hated the Vietnam war, and who feared the technocracy represented by Apollo, were *not* the people who assumed the greater measure of power in America after 1968. The true pull back of NASA-style Big Thinking wasn't just a liberal backlash against technology. It was the Republicans' response to what they perceived as the over-reaching intrusion of the government into the nation's affairs. Even as Apollo 8 was prepared for its circumlunar mission, James Webb stepped down as NASA's chief, exhausted and out of step with the changing mood, both in Congress and at the White House.

> "We didn't devote a great deal of our time to investigating the scariest aspects of our flight. Sometimes there is a morbid human curiosity about death-producing events."
>
> **Buzz Aldrin, 1998**

In 1969 Webb's successor, Tom Paine, found that President Nixon was, at best, lukewarm towards space, and Paine wasn't ready to accept that NASA had to change. He thought that the lunar landing missions had set a precedent for further large-scale space projects, but he was wrong. Apollo had been the exception, not the rule. It was Paine who was actually forced to call a halt to the moon program, cancelling missions 18, 19, and 20, and trying to save money and appease the new president. However, he did successfully salvage a working Saturn V for use in the last vestige of the Apollo program, the Skylab orbital workshop of 1973, America's first space station. Unfortunately, Paine was no match for Nixon's advisors, and he resigned after a tenure of less than two years. "I finally left because I did not think that I could deliver the kind of relationship with the President that the head of NASA really ought to deliver."

A SENATOR'S JUDGEMENT

On July 19 1979, a decade after the Apollo 11 lunar landing, the highly respected Democrat senator Margaret Chase Smith wrote an impassioned letter to be lodged with the Library of Congress. It stands as a fine testimony to Apollo. It is also a rebuke, on permanent record, for a nation whose gigantic achievements in space exploration were too carelessly cast aside:

I am saddened by, and disappointed with, three matters. The first is the public's apathy about the space program. Once we had a man on the moon, the American public lost interest. My second disappointment was the inevitable consequence of public apathy. It was the decline of the Senate Space Committee. When the public lost interest, its elected representatives in Congress found the space program less productive in terms of providing votes for reelection. After 1973 the Senate struggled to get someone to chair the Committee, because none of the sitting members were particularly interested. My third disappointment has been the lack of recognition for the person who put a man on the moon: James Webb, NASA's Administrator during its most crucial years. He had to take the heat and fire of partisan political attacks from headline-hungry politicians. I saw this first-hand in my work on the Space Committee! What recognition or material benefits did Jim Webb, and the thousands of people behind the scenes that he typified, receive? Minimal, if any—and today, they are forgotten people of a forgotten program. What we need today on the energy crisis is another Jim Webb.

The "energy crisis" Smith was referring to was the oil price escalation of the early 1970s, which sent many western economies into a tailspin. Four decades later that issue remains one of our most pressing concerns. Who, then, will manage the necessary solutions? Who will take charge? Leadership can be a terrifying threat to the freedoms of ordinary people excluded from the chain of command, or it can be the knife which cuts through confusion and seeks out the common good. Webb's case is fascinating, for his career as NASA chief exemplified the unnerving power of large-scale governmental manipulation, even as it showed the wonders that could be achieved when so many people worked towards solving a particular challenge.

Of course, when we tell stories about the past, we have a tendency to focus on just a few key individuals, such as Webb and von Braun or their brave Russian rival Sergei Korolev. History books are replete with kings whose biographies are an easily digestible shorthand for how their entire kingdoms behaved. We read about the tactics of generals who led grand armies, because we cannot sensibly absorb the stories of every soldier and every last skirmish on the battlefield. Likewise, all tales of the space age must be subject to these limitations, for by the mid-1960s, during a brief few years at least, more than half a million people were working somewhere in or around the Apollo project, and all of them were essential.

NASA's administrators spent most of their time handling the politics and the broader daily management challenges of space, and relied on many other colleagues to deal with the finer engineering details. A valid argument can be made that Webb's immediate deputy, Robert Seamans, ran NASA at a day-to-day level; and until illness called him away, Hugh Dryden was NASA's wise elder counsel and co-administrator. Other engineer-managers in the vast Apollo team became familiar to the public in the 1960s, for a few years at least, such as Robert Gilruth, George Mueller, Sam Phillips, Joe Shea, Gene Kranz, Rocco Petrone, and Max Faget. Neil Armstrong, Buzz Aldrin, and Michael Collins were just the tip of a colossal pyramid of human endeavor and dedication. The significant legacy of Apollo is not technological but moral. NASA's staffers were unafraid to accept responsibility for their appointed tasks, whether they resulted in luminous success or horrific failure. Part of the reason for their fearlessness is that they were trusted to do their jobs, and trust tends to bring out the best in people. This lesson, above all, needs to be retained from the lunar adventure. As we send Apollo's machines to the museum, we should keep alive the memory of its people.

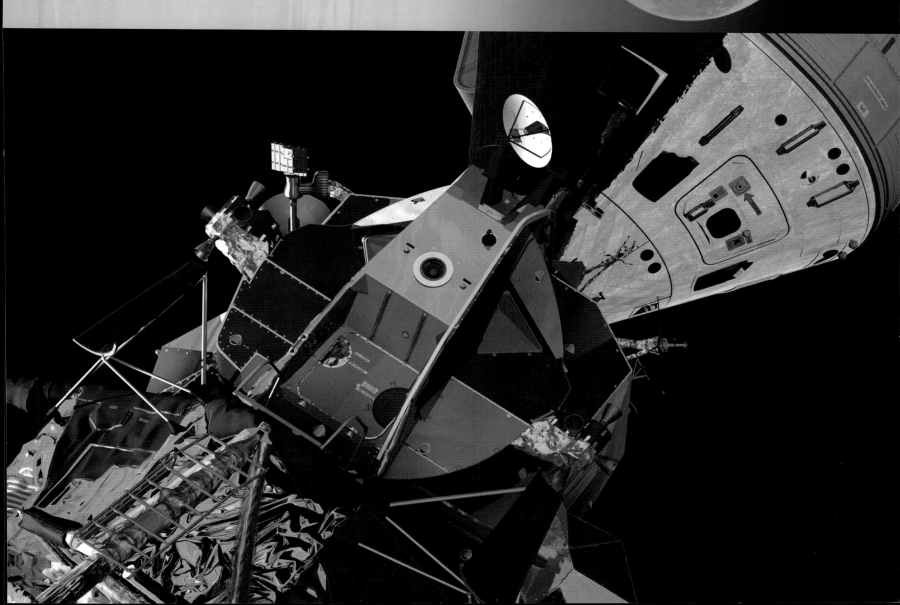

5 RETURNING TO THE MOON

RETURNING TO THE MOON

5

IF NASA WANTS TO REVISIT THE MOON by the year 2020, as it has recently promised, then it must hope to find staffers of similar drive and determination, then relearn how they did things in the 1960s and do likewise again. But times have changed, and it is no longer obvious that government agencies are best equipped to create the technology for space adventures. Half a century ago, keen-eyed politicians could identify useful areas for national research, such as aviation, computing, rocketry, and nuclear energy. Today it's all anyone can do to just keep in touch with the bewildering pace of developments in medicine, genetics, electronic consumer goods, personal computing, and global communications. Politicians find it difficult enough to respond to the social and environmental impact of the myriad technologies that are already on the loose, let alone urge the invention of new ones.

In the 1960s, NASA was at the vanguard of a new technology. Today it may be the custodian of an old one. Rockets are no longer one of the defining machines of our times. The ballistic missiles that heralded the space age have lost their edge in an era of "asymmetrical warfare." A few fanatics with ten cent craft knives can change the world in a day, while the expensive nuclear megatons in their underground silos are all but impotent now that our dread of nuclear weapons has been overtaken by our fear of terrorism. But none of these pessimistic thoughts can take away the glory from Apollo. It reached the moon in the fulfilment of a dream that had enticed humankind for many generations; and the scale and ambition of NASA in those years was an expression of political idealism from an America rather different to the one we know today: a nation that hoped for a better future rather than simply trying to protect itself from the present. Some people would like to revive that spirit, at least in space affairs.

NASA has some rebuilding of trust to do. On January 28 1986 space shuttle Challenger lifted off into a freezing winter sky, and seventy-three seconds into the flight it blew apart. All seven crew members were killed: Commander Dick Scobee and his co-pilot Mike Smith; mission

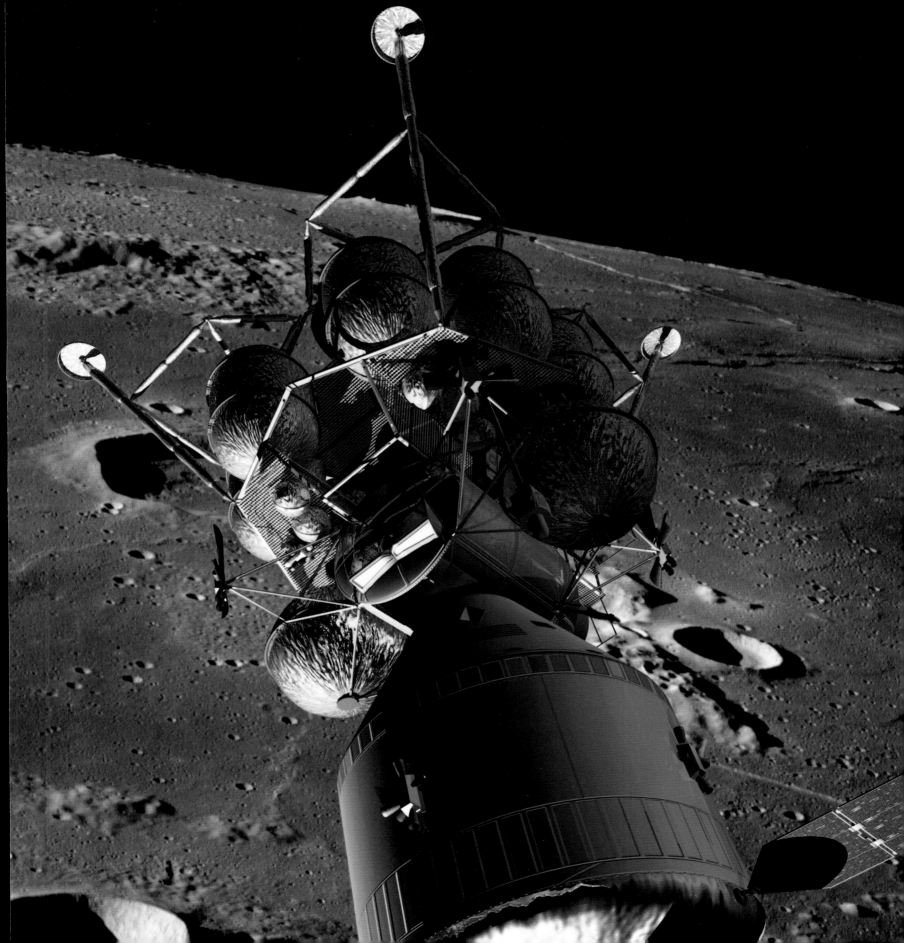

specialists Judy Resnick, Ellison Onizuka, Ron McNair, and Greg Jarvis; and a young teacher launched as part of a schools' education project, Christa McAuliffe. Today we can compare and contrast the 1967 Apollo accident with the Challenger's loss. The people of Apollo were caught off-guard by something that they had never encountered before, a dramatic fire in a spacecraft sitting quietly on the ground. The shuttle disaster was flagged by earlier failures, and in particular, repeated instances of partially burned rubber seals in boosters: exactly the problem that doomed the Challenger. Taxpayers are, perhaps, willing to forgive such disasters, but only if NASA can be said to have acted in good faith to try and prevent them.

A MAVERICK INVESTIGATOR

After the Challenger accident, the renowned physicist Richard Feynman was asked to join the board of inquiry, known as the Rogers Commission. Frustrated by the dull and pointless verbiage of due process, he staged an unauthorized little drama for the TV cameras that forced the pace. He dipped a piece of rubber into a glass of iced water and showed how it hardened when it got cold. "Do you think this might have some relevance?" he asked, knowing very well that it did. He'd created a memorably vivid demonstration of the notorious "O" ring leak that had destroyed the shuttle during a freezing winter launch. Feynman wanted to probe further: "If NASA was slipshod about the leaking rubber seals on the solid rockets, what would we find if we looked at the liquid-fuelled engines and all the other parts that make up a shuttle?" He was told the inquiry wasn't briefed to look at those, because no problems had been reported; so he made unauthorized trips to several NASA field centers and did some digging. As a very charming and sympathetic physicist, he had little difficulty winning the trust of staffers at ground level. "I had the impression that senior managers were allowing errors that the shuttle wasn't designed to cope with, while junior engineers were screaming for help and being ignored."

A shuttle-derived solid rocket booster sends the Orion capsule into orbit.

Finally, he turned to the complex relationships between the space agency's many departments and their suppliers: "NASA's propulsion office in Huntsville designs the engines, Rocketdyne in California builds them, Lockheed writes the instructions, and NASA's launch center in Florida installs them. It may be a genius system of organization, but it seems a complete muddle to me." In the last days of the inquiry, he made a plea for realism. "For a successful technology, reality must take precedence over public relations, because Nature cannot be fooled."

Other commentators identified a malaise within NASA, where a bureaucracy that was created to get a specific job done—going to the moon—had become, instead, an organization whose only purpose is to ensure its own survival. That crisis stemmed from a lack of strong, committed leadership in the setting of goals, both from within NASA and the White House. If the people in an organization have a goal to believe in, they will work cooperatively. If that goal is lacking, then people start worrying about simply keeping hold of their jobs. They will then compete with each other, internally, and the organization will fail.

On February 1 2003, a second space shuttle, Columbia, was destroyed when it disintegrated during re-entry. The entire crew of seven astronauts died. An investigation over the ensuing months concluded that a suitcase-sized chunk of foam insulation from the huge external fuel tank had peeled off during launch. It slammed into the front of the shuttle's left wing, making a small but ultimately lethal hole in the heat-resistant panels. This disaster, horribly echoing the Challenger disaster of 1986, forced America to reconsider its entire space effort.

The Columbia Accident Investigation Board (CAIB) concluded that it is inappropriate to carry astronauts in the same part of a spacecraft that contains the rocket engines, because of the risk of explosions, collisions, or aerodynamic break-up of the structure. The Board noted that Apollo's tough and compact crew compartment could always be instantly separated from other modules or booster rockets. When a section of the Apollo 13 spacecraft exploded on the way to the moon in April 1970, the rear service module with the rocket engine was torn open, but the crew capsule itself was unharmed, and it returned safely to the earth. The shuttle has no such self-contained module capable of separating its crew from the rest of the machinery

A full-scale dummy version of the new Orion capsule arrives at a NASA center.

in the event of a problem during flight. The CAIB also recommended that future crew modules for any spacecraft should be carried on the uppermost tips of their carrier rockets, so that no launch debris can fall onto them from any hardware above, as had happened in the Columbia disaster (and, to a less destructive yet still alarming degree, during many other shuttle missions too). The CAIB also urged that NASA's remaining shuttles, Atlantis, Endeavor, and Discovery, should be retired from service by 2010. But what should replace them?

A heavy-lift launch vehicle, aided by solid rocket boosters inherited from the space shuttle system, hauls the new lunar landing craft into earth orbit.

NEW PLANS FOR THE MOON

After deliberating with his advisors for many months, President George W. Bush made a televised speech in January 2004 during a special visit to NASA headquarters in Washington. "Today I announce a new plan to explore space and extend a human presence across our Solar System." The first goal, he said, was to return the shuttles to flight status, so that they could participate in the long-delayed completion of the International Space Station.

No surprises there. But as his speech continued, radical new ideas emerged: "Our second goal is to develop and test a new spacecraft, the Crew Exploration Vehicle, by 2008, and to conduct the first manned mission no later than 2014. Our third goal is to return to the moon. Using the Crew Exploration Vehicle, we will undertake extended human missions to the moon

Launched separately on a smaller rocket, the Orion crew capsule docks with the lunar lander, attached to its heavy-lift rocket. The upper stage of that larger rocket then fires again to carry the combined spacecraft towards the moon.

as early as 2015, with the goal of living and working there. With the experience and knowledge gained on the moon, we will then be ready to take the next steps of space exploration: new human missions to Mars and to worlds beyond." He summed up by saying:

In the past thirty years, no human being has set foot on another world, or ventured farther into space than 386 miles, roughly the distance from Washington, DC to Boston, Massachusetts. America has not developed a new vehicle to advance human exploration in space in nearly a quarter-century. It is time for America to take the next steps.

The Crew Exploration Vehicle (CEV) otherwise known as Orion, is a reversal of much that NASA has worked towards over the past three decades. The dream of an all-purpose shuttle, flying cheaply and regularly like a commercial cargo plane, never came to fruition. Every time that a shuttle puts a satellite or a space station module into orbit, the costs are exaggerated because astronauts always come along for the ride. The launch weight given up to life support and crew cabins limits the amount of useful payload a shuttle can carry in its cargo bay. It would be more efficient, say Orion's designers, to haul cargo in uncrewed rockets, and then launch the astronauts separately in a small module that carries people and nothing else. There's no need for the shuttle's huge wings and cargo bay doors. All that's left to worry about is the crew cabin at the front. Replace that with a capsule that fits on the end of a conventional rocket, and it can serve as an escape pod if anything goes wrong. It all looks very familiar. Robert Seamans, NASA's Deputy Administrator in the Apollo era, was one of a dozen ageing veterans called upon to advise Orion's designers:

I served on what they called the "Graybeard Committee," all these old hands who knew how we'd reached the moon the first time around. Astronaut John Young was there, and he'd flown in Gemini, plus two Apollo missions, and he'd commanded the first shuttle flight. We didn't fool around. What we came up with is very similar to what we did with the Apollo capsule.

After more than three decades, it is impossible to recreate Apollo's giant Saturn rockets and launch gantries. All the factory tooling was scrapped, and even the original drawings have been lost. Instead, the Orion capsule will be launched on top of a solid rocket booster, as currently employed by the shuttle. A lunar landing craft, the Altair, will be carried into orbit, unmanned, aboard a heavy-lift rocket. The Orion and its crew will locate it in orbit, make a docking, and head to the moon. On completion of the outward journey, Altair will detach and drop down to the surface. At the end of its mission, the lower part of the craft will stay behind, while the crew module blasts back into lunar orbit and makes a rendezvous with Orion, which then heads back to Earth for an Apollo-style parachute landing.

> "Don't tell me that man doesn't belong out there. Man belongs wherever he wants to go—and he'll do plenty when he gets there."
>
> **Wernher von Braun, 1958**

Is this progress, or a leap back in time? Aerospace engineer and writer Robert Zubrin has worked tirelessly over the past decade to promote a human Mars mission. (His lobbying group, the Mars Society, has some 8000 members.) The wayward logic of space planners sometimes exasperates him. "In the 1970s, when President Nixon killed the Apollo program and ended lunar exploration, NASA said we would do all that again one day, after we had developed cheaper transportation to orbit using a winged shuttle. We've spent thirty years trying that, but the shuttle has cost us more to fly than the Saturn boosters that we had for the lunar flights. Now the shuttle is going to be replaced with a little capsule just like the Apollo."

A NEW SPACE RACE?

Perhaps that's not such a terrible thing. A modern replay of Apollo might seem like a brand new adventure to the very many people on this earth who were not even born when Armstrong and Aldrin touched down on the Sea of Tranquility. But can we be sure that America will be in charge this time around? There is a politically sensitive gap between the year 2010, when the shuttle is retired, and 2015, when the Orion makes its debut. Other countries will not miss an opportunity to try and fill the gap, both technically and in terms of global prestige.

The "back to the future" technology for Orion is shaping up fast, but there is no guarantee that it won't be cancelled before it reaches the moon. NASA marks its many astonishing achievements over the last half-century with budgetary doubts clouding its future. John Logsdon, the influential head of the Space Policy Institute in Washington DC, has warned that everything could change at a moment's notice, subject to the whims of Congress. "If the proposals for

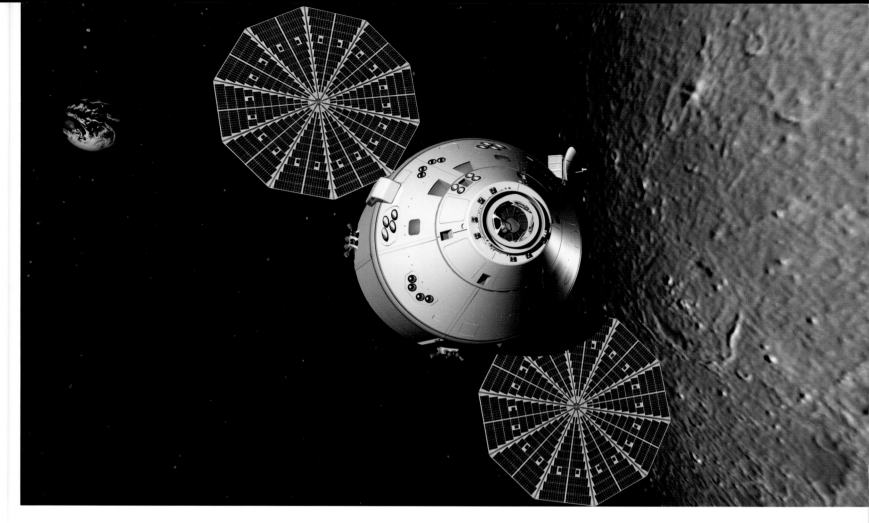

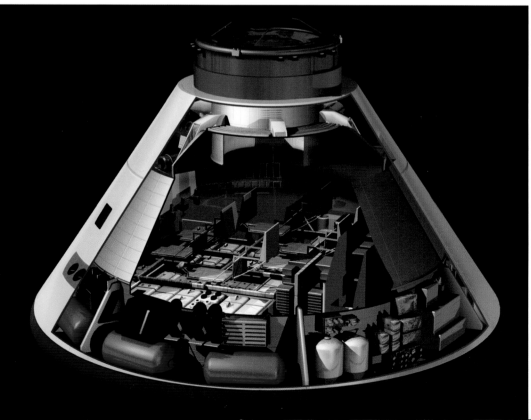

The Orion capsule for a return to the moon (above and right) has been described by some NASA insiders as "Apollo on Steroids."

human space exploration fail politically, then major initiatives that depend on government spending could lose momentum. It's far from certain that we're going back to the moon, let alone on to Mars. I think we are still struggling to answer the most basic question: why is the government in the business of sending people into space?" Maybe Logsdon's pessimism is well-founded, but history tells us that if the White House senses anyone else bidding for the moon, NASA may be called on to deliver another stunning victory.

China has begun its own human spaceflight program, launching missions at the rate of one every two years: a cautious rate which, the Beijing authorities say, will accelerate over the next decade. In all likelihood, political tensions will prevent China from playing any role aboard the International Space Station. The same cannot be said of Russia, Japan, or the European Space Agency ESA. Together they are developing the Crew Space Transportation System (CSTS). It should be capable of reaching lunar space by the end of the next decade. CSTS will exploit technology from a ship that ESA has already built and flown. The Automated Transfer Vehicle (ATV) delivers eight tons of supplies and equipment to the Space Station. Launched to orbit by ESA's Ariane V rocket, but carrying its own independent propulsion and guidance systems, the ATV has a pressurized cargo module designed for crew access over a period of several months during its attachment to the station. It therefore already satisfies most of the criteria for human spaceflight. The Russian contribution to the CSTS will be their many years' experience of bringing crews back to earth by the use of re-entry capsules. Meanwhile, private companies, such as Constellation Services and Space Adventures, want to revive Russia's 1960s project to send cosmonauts around the moon without landing on it. Upgraded Soyuz machinery could accomplish this, so long as investors are prepared to put up $100 million. Such companies are, perhaps, about to transform a wide range of space activites, both in earth orbit and on or around the moon—and one day, perhaps far beyond.

Certainly these companies—and the potential international alliances between different space agencies—have a great deal to contribute in terms of hardware and new devices, just so long as NASA and its political overseers in Congress allow this to happen. The next generation of crewed lunar landing craft will be larger and tougher than the Apollo modules from the 1960s. Astronauts will live aboard them for several weeks at a time, and inflatable modules could be attached to the airlocks after touchdown, adding even more room. Permanent living quarters may eventually be constructed under protective blankets of lunar topsoil. Pressurized wheeled rovers, the ultimate "off-road" vehicles, will allow astronauts to travel great distances in search of scientific data. The rovers, living modules, and other lunar hardware will be designed so that the technology for a Mars mission can be derived from them in the future. In this new scenario, no ideological clash exists between human and computer-controlled exploration. An extended family of robotic tools will support astronauts rather than competing with them: long-range scout rovers, mapping orbiters, communications relays, cargo ferries, energy supply systems, and astronomical instruments.

Since future astronauts will stay on the moon for many weeks or even months at a time, rather than just a few days, the question arises: where on the moon should they live? In full daylight the lunar surface can reach blistering temperatures of 100°C, while at night it plunges to -180°C. This environment will place great stresses on a habitable base. The long nights (two terrestrial weeks) would also play havoc with solar power supplies. Luckily, there is at least one location that remains permanently in daylight, while benefiting from a relatively benign temperature all year round of -50°C: not much worse than the temperatures we encounter in the Antarctic, and perfect for a base designed for long-term habitation. One magic spot is on the

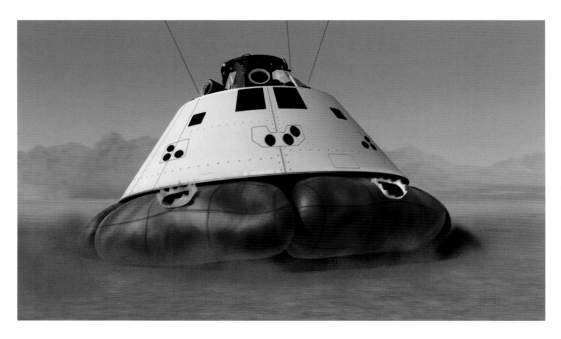

The crew capsule will touch down on land, with the help of airbags, or at sea.

"Looking back, we were really very privileged to live in that thin slice of history where we changed how we look at ourselves, and what we might become, and where we might go. So I'm very thankful that we got to be a part of that."

Neil Armstrong, 2001

6 APOLLO 11 MISSION IMAGES

The crew of Apollo 11 are assisted into their spacesuits, then leave for the launch pad.

The crew enter the base of the pad, then take a lift up to the capsule.

The crew are inserted
into the command module (left).

Launch controllers (below) watch
the Saturn V's ascent (right) from
the firing room at the Kennedy
Space Center, while Lyndon Johnson
(overleaf) watches from the VIP
observation stands.

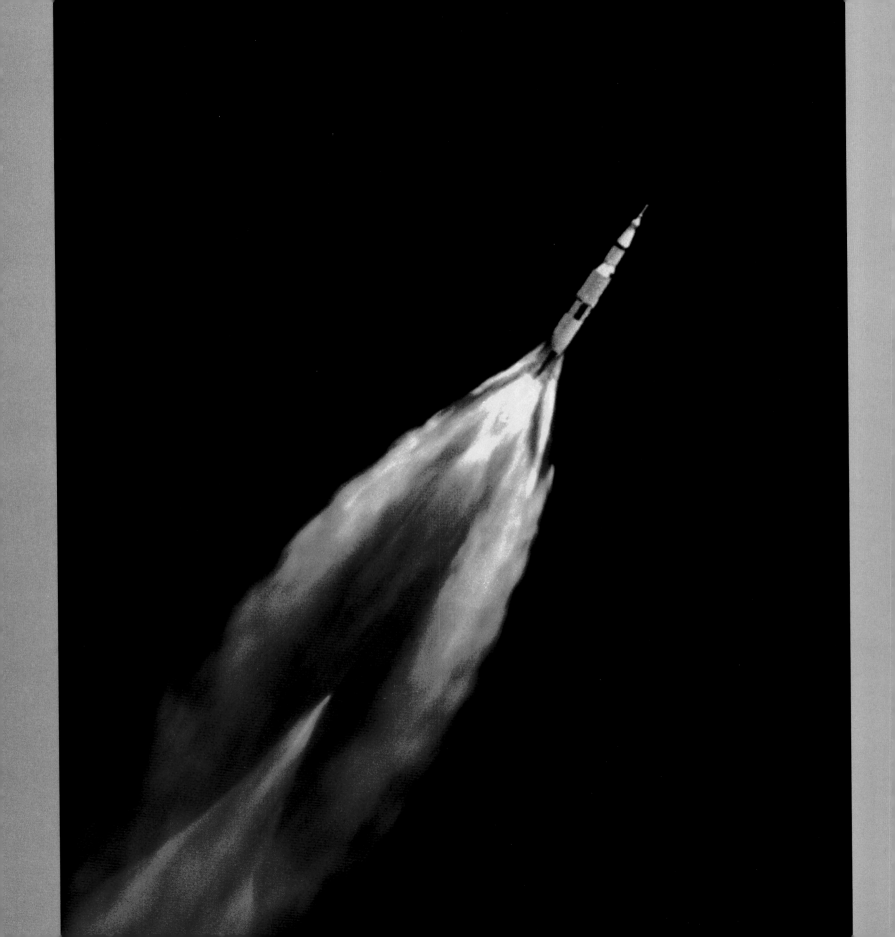

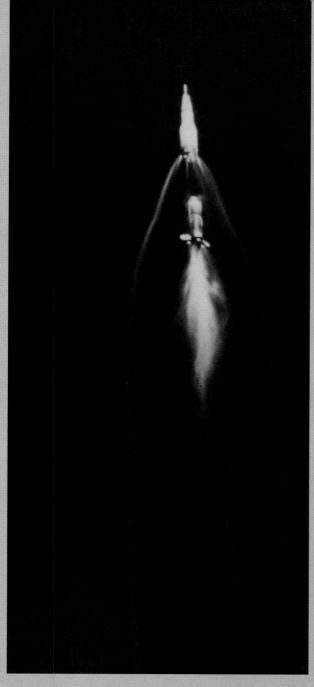

**The Saturn V ascends on a plume of flame,
then drops its spent first stage.
From the moment of lift-off, the entire
ascent to earth orbit takes just
nine minutes and thirty seconds.**

"We shall send to the moon, 240,000 miles away from the control station in Houston, a giant rocket more than 300 feet tall, made of new metal alloys, some of which have not yet been invented, capable of standing heat and stresses several times more than have ever been experienced, fitted together with a precision better than the finest watch, carrying all the equipment needed for propulsion, guidance, control, communications, food, and survival, on an untried mission, to an unknown celestial body, and then return it safely to earth, re-entering the atmosphere at speeds of over 25,000 miles per hour, causing heat about half that of the temperature of the sun."

John F. Kennedy, 1962

Apollo 11 enters earth orbit.

Neil Armstrong during the flight.

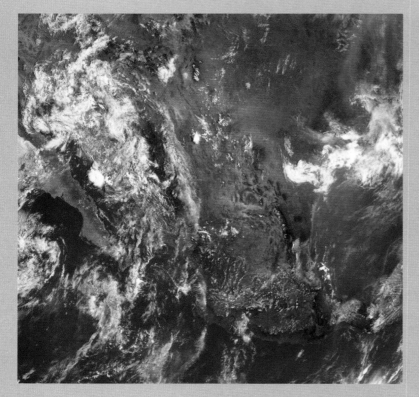

"This was a project in which everybody involved was, one, dedicated, and, two, fascinated by the job they were doing."

Neil Armstrong, 2001

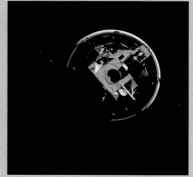

As earth recedes, the command module swivels around to connect with the lunar module.

The lunar module's fragile outer skin is evident in this view.

The earth dwindles to a disc so small that the astronauts can hide it behind a thumb.

Testing out a television camera inside the docking tunnel linking the two ships.

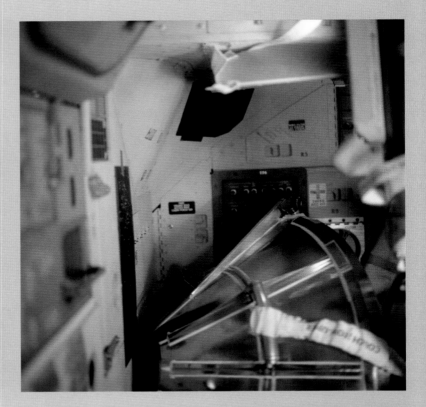

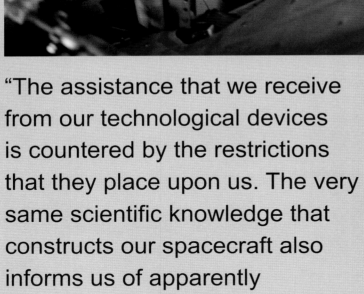

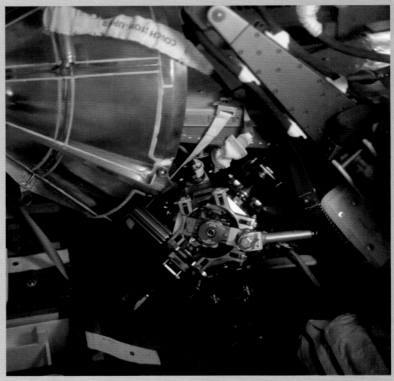

"The assistance that we receive from our technological devices is countered by the restrictions that they place upon us. The very same scientific knowledge that constructs our spacecraft also informs us of apparently insurmountable physical limits."

Charles Lindbergh, 1974

Cramped mechanisms: the disassembled docking probe, and (top left) the maze of switches in the capsule.

Another shot of Armstrong mid-flight. The white streak is random glare from the interior lighting.

A confident-looking Aldrin, photographed by Armstrong.

"I had been to the moon. What could I possibly do next? I suffered from what the poets have described as 'The melancholy of all things done.' Without some new goal, I was aimless."

Buzz Aldrin, 1973

Aldrin's work station on the right-hand side of the lunar module's cabin.

The moon approaches.

The moon can be a hostile place to visit—yet we persist in wanting to go there.

"I can remember at the time thinking, 'There's got to be a better way of saying this.' If you're going to tell three human beings that they can leave the gravitational field of earth, what are you going to say? You'll invoke Christopher Columbus, or a primordial reptile coming up out of the swamps onto dry land for the first time, or you'll go back through the sweep of history and say something meaningful. Instead, all we had was our technical jargon."

Michael Collins, 1997

"The earth looks so small. You see an ocean and gaseous layer, just a tiny bit of atmosphere around it, and compared with all the other celestial objects, which in many cases are much more massive, more terrifying, it just looks like it couldn't put up a very good defense against a celestial onslaught."

Neil Armstrong 2001

As Apollo 11 completes its first orbit of the moon, the blue earth rises over the horizon.

"I think a future flight should include a poet,
a priest, and a philosopher.
We might get a much better idea
of what we saw."

Michael Collins, 1974

The lunar module undocks in preparation for the landing descent.

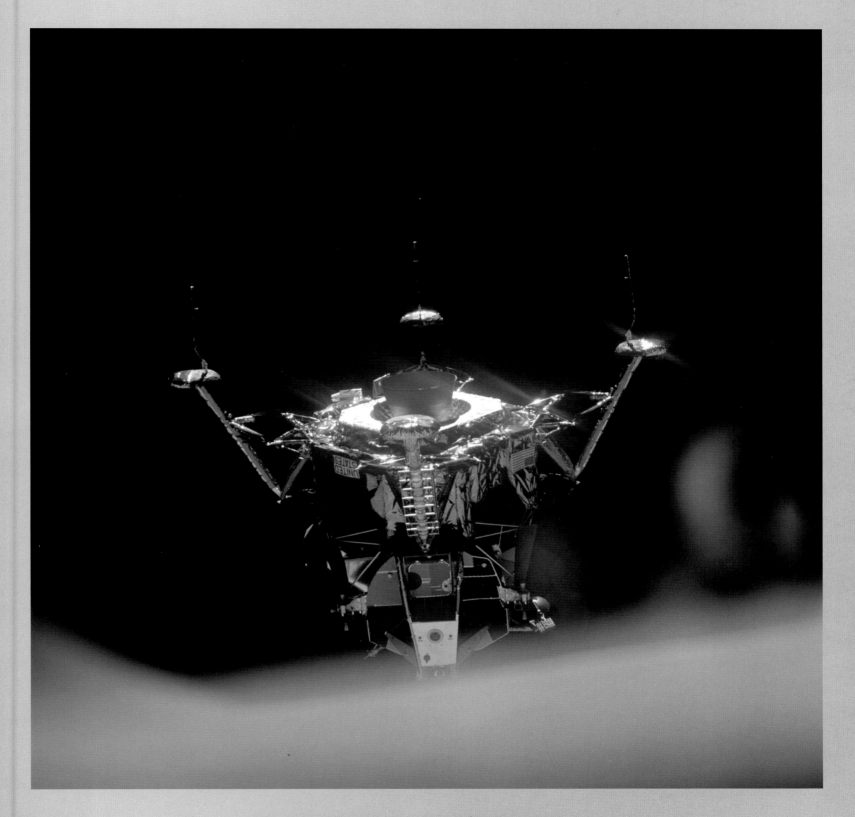

The notion of "upside-down" doesn't mean much in space.

Everything is in the detail: small rocks, craters, and other hazards await.

Touchdown on the Sea of Tranquillity.

Bootprints and the flag.

Aldrin is the second man on the moon, but the first to be photographed there.

Aldrin is safely down—without tripping: a fear for all the lunar astronauts.

The commemorative plaque on the lunar module's front landing leg.

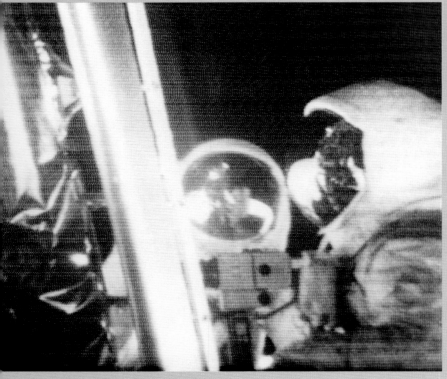

"I just don't deserve the attention for being the first man on the moon. Luck and circumstance put me in that particular role. That wasn't planned by anyone."

Neil Armstrong, 2005

Ghostly TV pictures of the moon walk, relayed around the world via NASA's mission control.

Aldrin salutes the American flag.

"I expected the unexpected, and I went with an open mind. I think that the visual scene was best described by my words on first landing: 'magnificent desolation.' It was magnificent because of the achievement of being there, and desolate for the eons of lifelessness."

Buzz Aldrin, 1998

These two photographs are the only ones to show Neil Armstrong on the lunar surface.

The most famous picture in space history: Buzz Aldrin on the moon.

Aldrin deploys a foil sheet to collect subatomic particles streaming from the sun.

These bootprints are still on the lunar surface today, undisturbed by wind or rain.

"The tools of the Apollo project were not developed for people to live on the moon on a long-term basis. Therefore, economically and politically, they could not be sustained and supported once all the original missions had been completed."

Buzz Aldrin, 1998

Shots of the lunar module, showing its hand-made construction.

One of the footpads sitting in the very shallow soil.

Portrait of an extraordinary machine, unlike anything that we normally experience.

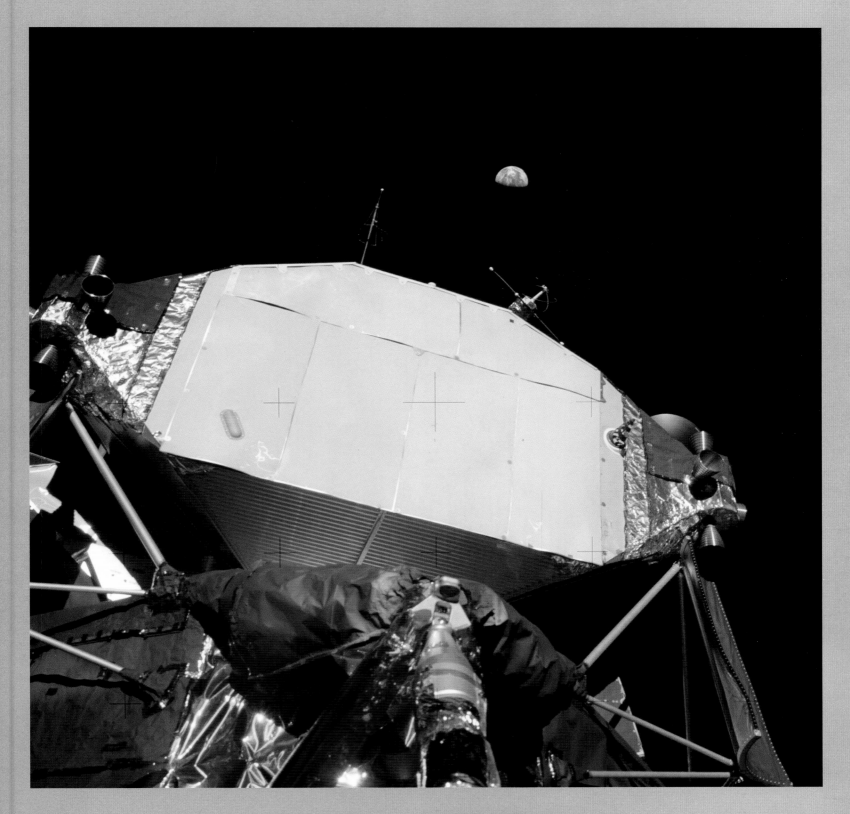

The earth seen above the rear of the lunar module.

Collecting equipment from the flanks of the lander.

Aldrin walks into the distance to deploy scientific instruments.

Aldrin deploys a seismometer to measure moon quakes.

"In those days, I did get tired of being asked the same things over and over and over and over and over and over and over again. 'What was it like?' You can see it in their eyes, 'What kind of a person is this? He's just come back from the moon, and he's not even excited about it.' It isn't the fact that I'm not excited. It's the fact that I've been asked that same question ten million times."

Michael Collins, 1979

"Magnificent desolation."

A happy Neil Armstrong, photographed by Aldrin after the successful moon walk.

"I was aware that this was a culmination of the work
of 300,000 or 400,000 people over a decade, and that
the nation's hopes and outward appearance to the rest
of the world largely rested on how the results came out.
With those pressures, it seemed the most important thing
to do was focus on our job as best we were able to,
and try to allow nothing to distract us from
doing the very best job that we could."

Neil Armstrong, 2001

Against the immensity of the moon, Apollo 11's command module can just be seen.

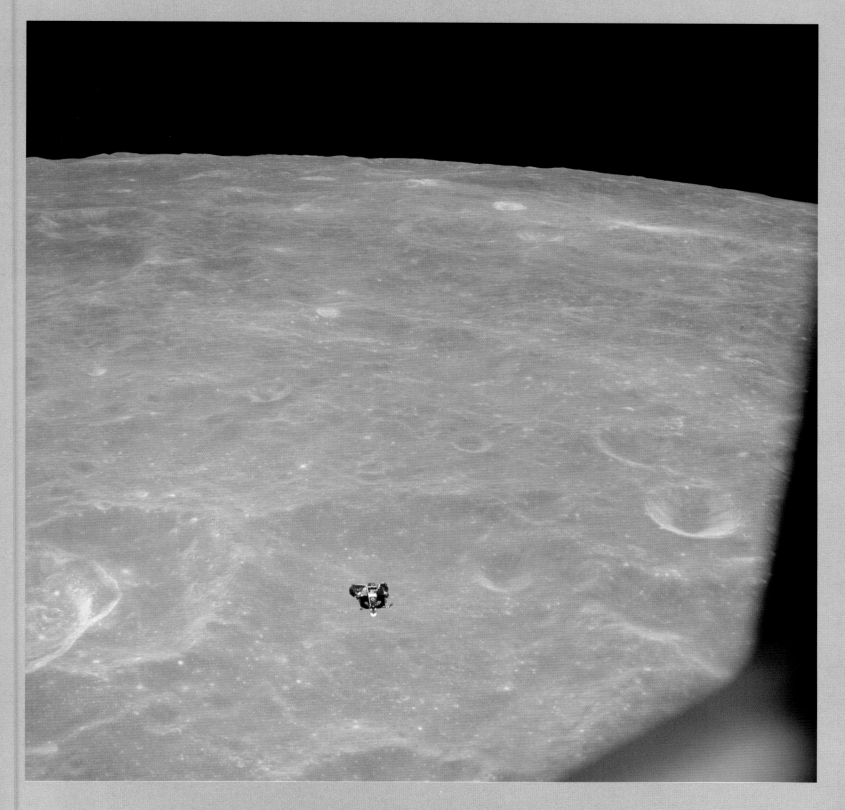

The ascent stage of the lunar module climbs back to rejoin the mothership.

Michael Collins steers the command module towards the second and final docking.

The ascent stage of the lunar module closes in for final approach.

Daedalus Crater seen from orbit.

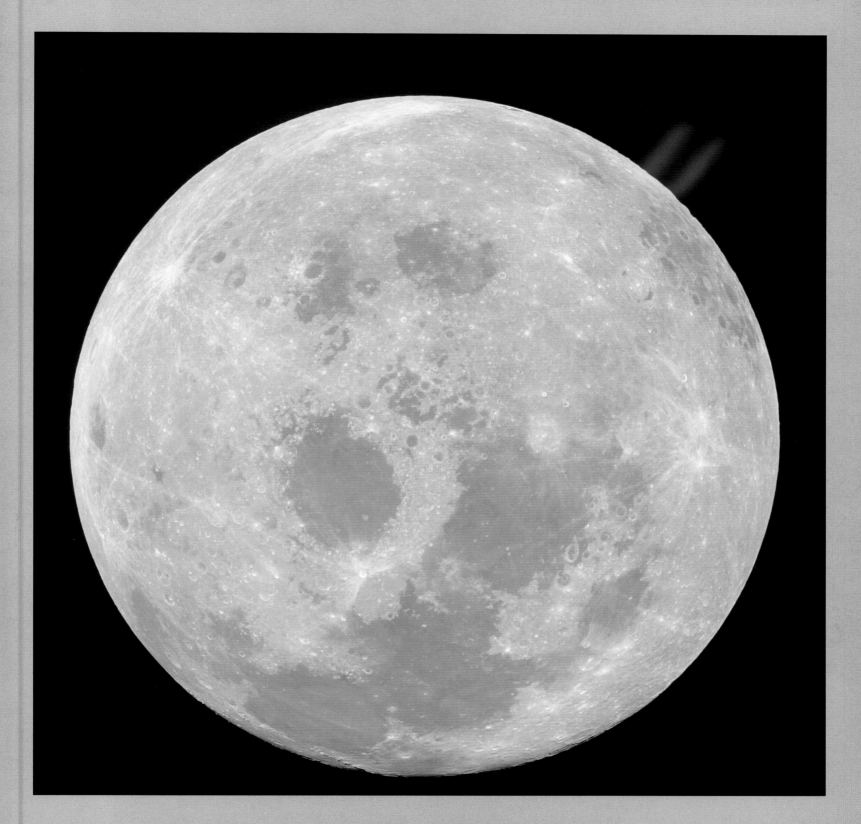

The moon recedes as Apollo heads home.

The crew of Apollo 11 in the quarantine facility.

"Space flight is a spiritual quest in the broadest sense—one promising a revitalization of humanity and a rebirth of hope."

Buzz Aldrin, 1999

"We set sail on this new sea because there is new knowledge
to be gained, and new rights to be won, and they must be won
and used for the progress of all people. For space science,
like nuclear science and all technology, has no conscience of its own.
Whether it will become a force for good or ill depends on man.

"Space can be explored and mastered without feeding
the fires of war, without repeating the mistakes that man
has made in extending his writ around this globe of ours.

"We choose to go to the moon in this decade, and do the other things,
not because they are easy, but because they are hard—because
that goal will serve to organize and measure the best of our energies
and skills—because that challenge is one that we are willing to accept,
one we are unwilling to postpone, and one which we intend to win.

"Space is there, and we're going to climb it, and the moon and
the planets are there, and new hopes for knowledge and peace
are there. And, therefore, as we set sail, we ask God's blessing
on the most hazardous and dangerous and greatest adventure
on which man has ever embarked."

John F. Kennedy, 1962

APOLLO 12: Pete Conrad, Alan Bean, Dick Gordon.

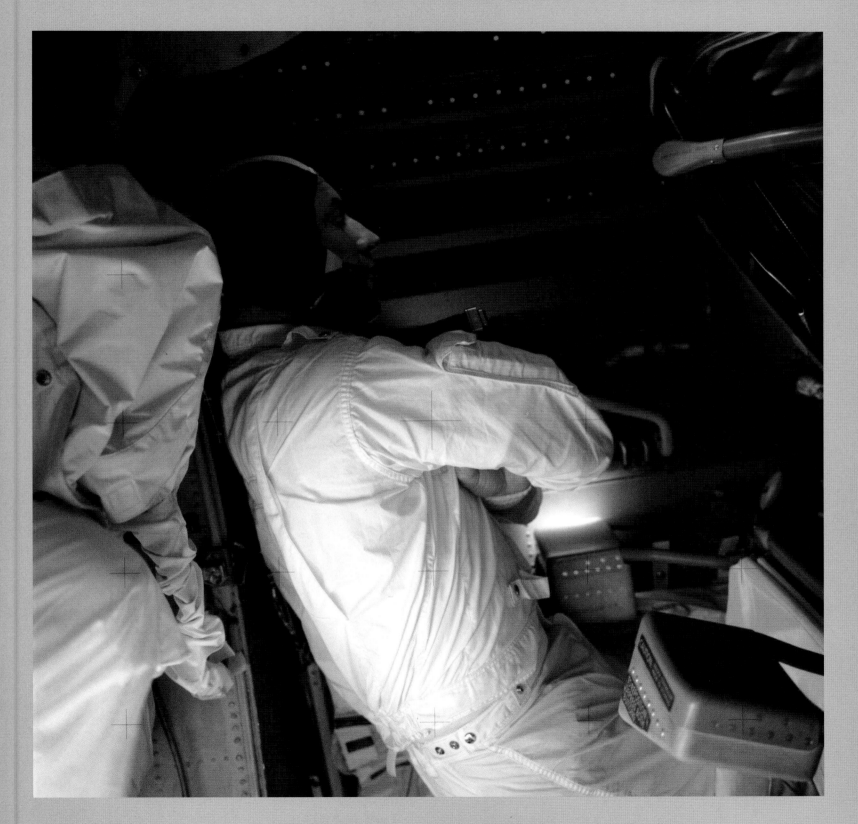

APOLLO 13: Jim Lovell, Fred Haise, Jack Swigert.

APOLLO 14: Alan Shepard, Ed Mitchell, Stuart Roosa.

APOLLO 15: Dave Scott, Jim Irwin, Al Worden.

APOLLO 16: John Young, Charlie Duke, Ken Mattingly.

APOLLO 17: Gene Cernan, Harrison Schmitt, Ron Evans.

Gene Cernan, commander of Apollo 17: the last man on the moon . . . so far.

NASA launch controllers and other staffers turn out in force to say goodbye to the Apollo
era, as the last mission heads off to the moon in 1972 . . . and overleaf, a reminder
of what we *won't* find out in space—the richness of life on earth.

"I trained hard for many years to fly around the moon and take a close look at it, because I thought that's what the mission was. When we got home, we realized we had discovered something much more precious out there: the earth. I believe the environmental movement was tremendously inspired by those missions. That alone is worth the relatively few billions of dollars that we spent on Apollo."

Apollo 8 astronaut Bill Anders, 1998

BIBLIOGRAPHY

Cadbury, Deborah
Space Race
Fourth Estate, 2005

Chaikin, Andrew
A Man on the Moon
Michael Joseph, 1994

Cooke, Hereward Lester, & Dean, James D.
Eyewitness to Space
Harry N. Abrams Inc., 1970

Harford, James
Korolev
John Wiley & Sons, 1997

Lambright, Henry W.
Powering Apollo: James E. Webb of NASA
Johns Hopkins University Press, 1995

Launius, Roger
*NASA: A History of the US
Civil Space Program*
Krieger, 1994

Mailer, Norman
A Fire on the Moon
Weidenfeld & Nichsolson, 1970

McDougall, Walter A.
*The Heavens and the Earth: A Political
History of the Space Age*
Basic Books, 1985

Murray, Charles and Bly Cox, Catherine
Apollo: The Race to the Moon
Secker & Warburg, 1989

Wolfe, Tom
The Right Stuff
Farrar, Straus and Giroux, 1979

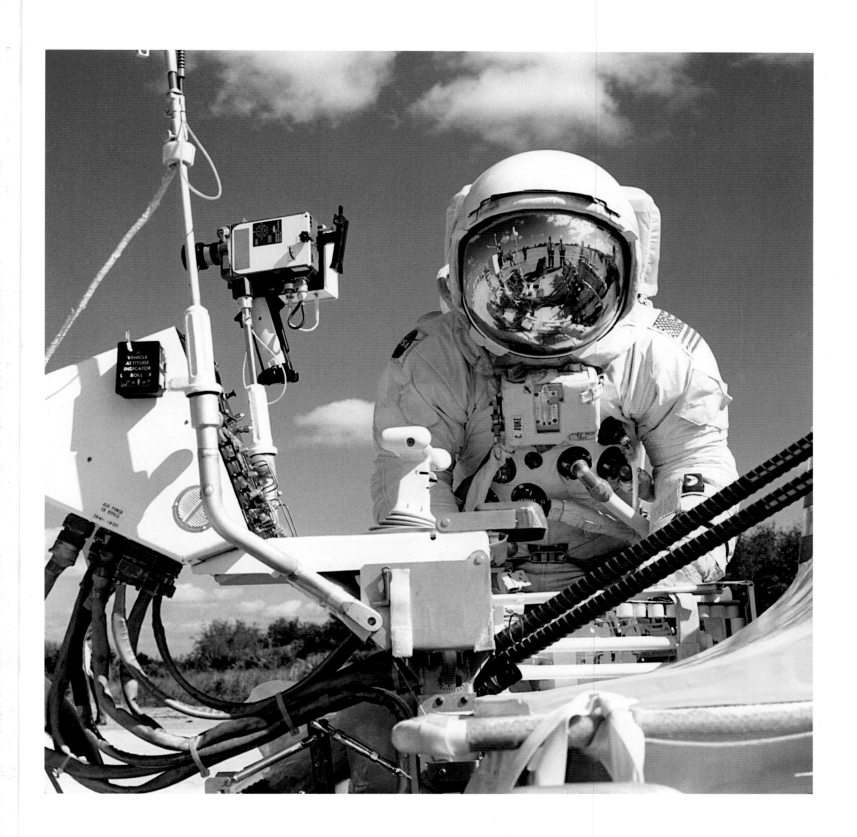

All pictures are courtesy of NASA, with the exception of:

Page 41 & 42 (top): Smithsonian Institution/Eric Long

Page 44: John Knoll

Pages 48–50, and chapter headers: John Ortmann

Page 53: Warner Brothers/Ronald Grant Archive

Page 158: Alma Haser

Additional image research and processing:

Paul Fjeld, Mike Gentry, Ed Hengeveld, Eric Jones,

Mike Marcucci, Jack Pickering, and Kipp Teague